Educational Reform
for a
Changing Society

Educational Reform
for a
Changing Society

ANTICIPATING TOMORROW'S SCHOOLS

Research for Better Schools, Inc.

edited by

Louis Rubin

Allyn and Bacon, Inc.
Boston • London • Sydney

Library of Congress Cataloging in Publication Data

Research for Better Schools, Inc.
  Educational reform for a changing society.

  Includes index.
  1. Educational innovations—Addresses, essays,
lectures. 2. Educational planning—Addresses,
essays, lectures. 3. Educational sociology—
Addresses, essays, lectures. I. Rubin, Louis J.
II. Title.
LB1027. R445 1977   370.1   77-23813
ISBN 0-205-05827-2

Contents

Foreword   vii

1. Urie Bronfenbrenner   **1**   *Children in America:*
                                        The Roots of Alienation

Commentary   **49**
Issues   **55**

2. Elise Boulding   **57** *Learning to Make New*
                                        Futures

Commentary   **75**
Issues   **81**

3. Shirley Chisholm   **83** *Rescue the Children*

Commentary   **90**
Issues   **95**

4. Robert G. Scanlon   **97** *Administering for Reform*

Commentary   **107**
Issues   **112**

5. R. Buckminster Fuller   **113** *Humans in Universe*

Commentary   **119**
Issues   **125**

6. **Jonas Salk**   127   *Anticipating Tomorrow's*
                                       Schools

    Commentary **151**
    Issues   **157**

7. **Richard S. Schweiker**   159   *Preparing Students*
                                       for a Working Future

    Commentary **169**
    Issues   **174**

8. **Ralph W. Tyler**   177   *Education:*
                                       Past, Present and Future

    Commentary **188**
    Issues   **192**

9. **Louis Rubin**   195   *The Reformation*
                                       of Schooling

Index   211

Foreword

This book represents the belief of Research for Better Schools that schools of the future should be influenced by planning in the present. Research for Better Schools, a nonprofit corporation, is dedicated to the development and implementation of educational programs, from early childhood through adult life.

The essays in this book emphasize the trends now shaping society that will have a profound effect on schools in the decades to come. Following each essay, Louis Rubin, of the University of Illinois, highlights the inherent implications for education and extracts significant research and development issues.

Historically, schools have tended to respond to social change somewhat tardily. The results have been both too little and too late. We believe, however, that if educators begin now to consider alternatives for reform, they can, at least to some extent, influence their own destiny. Thus, by carefully examining future trends, despite their predictive uncertainty, we can seek solutions that avoid early obsolescence and decay. We must confront our obstacles directly and forthrightly, seeking stability amidst change, and attack the needed reforms with confidence.

In the current decade we are faced with decreasing school enrollments and increasing educational costs. Confrontations and disputes between educators and taxpayers are therefore inevitable. Yet, through sound planning and sensible fiscal management, systematic techniques can be found to overcome the crisis.

Of greatest importance is the continuing need to plan ahead, to formulate alternatives, and to choose wisely among the options. Through the efforts of Research for Better Schools, we hope the work of educators and researchers alike can be invigorated by an increased awareness of societal needs. Schools can only keep pace with an evolving social system through a conscious effort to anticipate, project, and reform as exigencies demand. It is my hope that the reader will agree that the provocative ideas set forth in this volume are a significant contribution to necessary planning efforts. The future of education, like that of society, will not arrive on a particular day; it will unfold slowly as the interplay of events produces new needs, new aims, and new adaptations.

Jo Ann Weinberger
Assistant to the Executive Director
Research for Better Schools

Notes on the Writers

Urie Bronfenbrenner is a professor of Human Development, Family Studies and Psychology at Cornell University. He is a leader in the field of child development who initially specialized in cross-cultural studies. His studies of comparative childrearing practices in the U.S.S.R. and the United States have formed the basis for his book, *Two Worlds of Childhood*. As a result of his recent investigations of Chinese families, the film "Three Worlds of Childhood: U.S.-U.S.S.R.-China" has evolved. Out of his concern for the development of our young people, he argues that children are the largest single alienated group in our society. He feels the root of the problem and the remedy lie in the social institutions that produce alienation, and in the failure of these institutions to be responsive to the most basic human needs and values of a democratic society. In particular, he feels that the schools, as they are presently organized, contribute to this alienation. Bronfenbrenner has recently completed a study of the effectiveness of early intervention programs, and has reached the conclusion that current preschool programs contribute to the alienation of the young.

Elise Boulding is a professor of Sociology and the project director of the Institute of Behavioral Science at the University of Colorado. A sociologist with a global view, she has undertaken numerous cross-national, transnational, and international research studies on conflict resolution, war and peace, family life, and women in society. She is nearing completion of a major historical study of women's changing social, economic, and political roles over four millenia entitled, *The Underside of History*. No latecomer to the field of women's studies, her early publications reflect her great concern for the role of women in industrialized societies. A prodigious writer, editor, and lecturer, she is also an advocate for social change and an activist in peace movements, serving as international chairperson of the Women's International League for Peace and Freedom from 1968 to 1970. Her work in the area of futures studies dated from 1961 when she translated Fred Polak's classic work, *Image of the Future*, from the Dutch: her publications indicate her continued focus on women, children, and the family unit as agents for nonviolent social change and global friendship.

Shirley Chisholm, Congresswoman from the Twelfth Congressional District of New York, and a specialist in early childhood education and child welfare, entered politics more or less by public demand in 1964 when she successfully ran for the New York State Assembly. Since then, she has risen to national prominence in the U.S. House of Representatives but still retains her close identity and contact with her community. An articulate champion of the rights of the downtrodden, she has sought House Committee assignments that she felt had relevance to the needs and problems of her impoverished congressional district. She now serves on the House Education and Labor Committee and with the Select Education, General Education, and Agricultural Labor Subcommittees. On January 25, 1972 Chisholm declared herself a candidate for the presidency of the United States in order to give the disenfranchised people of the country a voice in presidential politics. Her efforts (recounted in her book, *The Good Fight*) resulted in 152 delegate votes at the Democratic Convention and a new place for women in American politics.

Robert G. Scanlon is executive director of Research for Better Schools, Philadelphia, Pennsylvania. Prior to his present affiliation, he earned national distinction as the administrator of the Oakleaf Elementary School in Pittsburgh, Pennsylvania, a highly lauded experimental school that pioneered in the individualization of instruction. He also served as director of elementary education in the Middletown (New York) schools. Dr. Scanlon is the current chairperson of the Council for Educational Development and Research and has also served as a special consultant to UNESCO and the United States Naval Command. A member of the Society for Applied Learning Technology, he has written about a variety of problems relating to educational research and development, computer-assisted instruction, and school administration. In addition to his administrative responsibilities at Research for Better Schools, Scanlon is interested in the politics of public education.

R. Buckminster Fuller is a professor at Southern Illinois University and a World Fellow in Residence at a consortium of eastern colleges. A unique humanist of the twentieth century, his central concern revolves around man's relation to nature and the earth. Fuller is perhaps best known for his invention of the geodesic dome, 100,000 of which now appear in half the countries of the world. His innovative intellect has not been limited to architecture, but spans all areas of human endeavor from engineering to poetry producing an outpouring of creative thought. In 1962, he published *Education Automation* in which he stated that technology would revolutionize education. During the last several years, he has addressed the problems of world resource management from the prospective of one who sees our planet and its people as one large, interconnected, total system—a spaceship Earth—whose continued existence lies in cooperative effort.

Jonas Salk is director and resident fellow of the Salk Institute for Biological Studies in San Diego, California. In two of his books, *Man Unfolding* and *The Survival of the Wisest,* Salk speaks from the viewpoint of a biologist about the prospects and alternatives for the future of man. As a biologist he concentrates on studies of the immune mechanism. During his stay at the University of Michigan and the University of Pittsburgh, he conducted studies that ultimately led to the first successful vaccine against paralytic polio. In 1963 he founded the Salk Institute for Biological Studies, a unique research institution where outstanding scientists and scholars pursue the great problems of modern biology amidst an atmosphere of shared concern for the implications of their work for man and for society. Current studies center around major diseases such as cancer, multiple sclerosis and diabetes. Another ongoing program at the Institute is the study of the biological foundation of language acquisition and learning.

Richard S. Schweiker, United States Senator from Pennsylvania, has sought to serve his fellowman through an active life in the political arena: having been elected to the 87th Congress in 1960 from the Thirteenth Congressional District (Montgomery County, Pennsylvania), he served until 1968 in the U.S. House of Representatives where he co-authored a widely publicized plan for mutual de-escalation of the Vietnam War. During this time he also coauthored the book, *How to End the Draft,* which spelled out the formula that has been used to establish the All-Volunteer Army. Elected in 1968 as a Senator he serves on the Senate Appropriations, Labor and Public Welfare, and Joint Economic Committees as well as on the Select Committee on Nutrition and Human Needs and the Technology Assessment Board. Through his service on the Labor–HEW Subcommittee of the Appropriations Committee and the Education and Labor Subcommittees of the Labor and Public Welfare Committee, he gains his interest and specialization in educational problems.

Ralph W. Tyler is director emeritus of the Center for Advanced Study in the Behavioral Sciences. He has taught at the University of

Chicago, Ohio State University, the University of Nebraska, and the University of North Carolina. From 1948 until 1953 he was dean of the Division of Social Sciences at the University of Chicago, and prior to that, chairman of the university's Department of Education. His distinguished work as director of evaluation for the Eight–Year Study has been internationally recognized. A former president to the National Academy of Education, Tyler has also served as chairman of the National Commission on Resources for Youth, the National Commission for Cooperative Education, and vice-chairman of the National Science Board. He has written widely on the social forces influencing American education, educational evaluation, and curriculum. His *Basic Principles of Curriculum and Instruction,* published by the University of Chicago Press, is now in its thirty-first printing. At present, among his other diversified activities, he serves as senior consultant for Science Research Associates.

Louis Rubin is affiliated with the Department of Elementary and Early Childhood Education, at the University of Illinois. He is an inveterate speaker who is constantly lecturing on a variety of educational concerns to practitioners across the nation helping them keep abreast of the latest educational issues. He views his informative role very seriously since he believes that all too many educators have not kept themselves aware of the changes in their field. Despite the variety of topics covered, a definite pattern to his interests is evident. His preoccupation with schools of the future is an outgrowth of an early involvement in educational change, an early recognition of institutional resistance to innovation and the bonds between teacher retraining and school improvement. These notions are shaped by a deep familiarity with the educational environment: Rubin has taught in public schools, served as a university dean, authored or edited several books, and headed a Washington-based agency designing programs for educating the public about education. Throughout his lectures and articles, he remains strikingly optimistic about the future of our schools and society.

urie bronfenbrenner
cornell university

CHILDREN IN AMERICA:
THE ROOTS OF ALIENATION

This chapter presents empirical data and theoretical argument for the importance of research on the *ecology of human development* and of the reciprocal relations such research entails between issues of science and public policy. In support of the thesis, evidence is adduced to document profound changes over the past quarter century, in the institution bearing primary responsibility for the care and development of the Nation's children—the American family. The general trend reveals progressive fragmentation and isolation of the family in its child rearing role. As many more mothers have gone to work (now over half of those with school-

*An adaptation of this chapter was published by the American Philosophical Society in 1975. I wish to express appreciation to the Foundation for Child Development for support in the development of the work presented in this paper and of the program of research grants in which the research recommendations are now being implemented. I am especially indebted to the following colleagues for their creative assistance in this endeavor: the members of the Foundation staff particularly Orville Brim, Heidi Sigal, Jane Dustan, and their predecessors Robert Slater and Barbara Jacquette; the devoted consultants to the FCD Program, Sarane Boocock, Michael Cole, Glen Elder, William Kessen, Melvin Kohn, Eleanor Maccoby, and Sheldon White; and my hard working administrative aide and research assistants, Joyce Brainard, Susan Turner, Lynn Mandelbaum, and Carol Williams. I am also grateful to many colleagues and students whose suggestions and criticisms have been a major stimulus to my own thinking and some whose ideas I have probably assimilated as my own. Among them are the following: David Goslin, Kurt Luscher, Edward Devereux, Maureen Mahoney, James Garbarino, Eduardo Almeida, David Olds, Moncrieff Cochran, Julius Richmond, John Condry, John Hill, Harold Watts, Mary Keyserling, and David Knapp. Thanks are due as well to cooperative colleagues in the Bureau of the Census and the National Center for Health Statistics, in particular Howard Hayghe, Robert Heuser, Arthur Norton, and Alexander Plateris.

1

age children, one-third with children under six, and 30 percent with infants under three, two-thirds of all those mothers are working full-time), the number of adults left in the home who might care for the child has been decreasing to a national average of two. Chief among the departing adults has been one of the parents, usually the father, so that today one out of every six children under eighteen is living in a single-parent family. This is often not a temporary state, since, on a national scale, the remarriage rate, especially for women, is substantially lower than the rate of divorce in families involving children, and this differential has been increasing over time. A significant component in the growth of single-parent families has been a sharp rise in the number of unwed mothers; more young women are postponing the age of marriage, but some of them are having children nevertheless.

All of these changes are occurring more rapidly among younger families with younger children, and increasing with the degree of economic deprivation and urbanization, reaching their maximum among low income families living in the central core of our largest cities. But the general trend applies to all strata of the society. Middle class families, in cities, suburbia, and nonurban areas, are changing in similar ways. Specifically, in terms of such characteristics as the proportion of working mothers, number of adults in the home, single-parent families, or children born out of wedlock, the middle class family of today increasingly resembles the low income family of the early 1960s.

Although levels of labor force participation, single-parent-hood, and other related variables are substantially higher for blacks than for whites, those families residing in similar economic and social settings show similar rates of change. The critical factor, therefore, is not race, but the conditions under which the family lives.

Concomitant and consistent with changes in structure and position of the family are changes in indices reflecting the well-being and development of children. Youngsters growing up in low income families are at an especially high risk of damage physically, intellectually, emotionally, and socially. Evidence is also cited for disturbing secular trends indicated by declining levels of academic performance and rising rates of child homicide, suicide, drug use and juvenile delinquency.

While cross-sectional differences in the well-being of families and children are strongly linked with economic status, the longitudinal trends appear to be a function of more complex social changes associated with increasing urbanization. It is suggested that the destructive effect of these changes derives from the progressive segregation by age in American society, resulting in the isolation of children and those responsible for their care. The key to corrective policy and practice is seen in the development of *support systems* for families, not only economically, but also socially, through the involvement of all segments of society in mutually rewarding activities for and, especially, *with* children and those primarily responsible for their well-being and development.

In the sphere of developmental research, social change focuses attention on the scientific importance of studying development *in context*. It is argued that the strategy of choice for such research is not descriptive analysis of the *status quo*, as exemplified in this paper, but what may be called *experimental human ecology*, an approach involving systematic efforts to alter existing environments in controlled experimental situations. Examples of such research problems and designs, both existing and potential, are presented as illustrations of work currently being planned and conducted in the Program on the Ecology of Human Development sponsored by the Foundation for Child Development.

My concern here is with research in human development, the real world, and what constitutes a rational interconnection between the two. The last is no easy task, for much of the research in my field is carried out not in reality, but in artificial settings believed to be more conducive to scientific investigation. And even when we do conduct studies in the actual environments in which children live and grow, we focus far more attention on the developing organism than on its surroundings. In particular, we have little conception or knowledge of how environments change, and the implications of this change for the human beings who live and grow in these environments. In short, we know little about the *ecology of human development*.

Especially in recent years, the term *ecology* has been applied to a wide variety of phenomena. It does, however, have a core meaning that is especially appropriate for our concern and is reflected in its etymology. Ecology comes from the Greek root "oikos" meaning "home." With reference to human growth, an ecological perspective focuses attention on development as a function of interaction *between the developing organism and the enduring environments or contexts in which it lives out its life.*

The term *enduring* in the foregoing formulation has special significance. There is no implication, of course, that short-lived settings cannot be consequential for development. Indeed, the immediate situation can be critical. For the fish out of water, it is a matter of survival. The example brings out an important principle. Ecology implies a fit between the organism and its environment. If the organism is not only to survive but to develop, the fit must be even closer. Moreover, *development* connotes progressive structural and functional change *over time* as Fuller and Salk indicate (Chapters 5 and 6), in the relation between the organism and its environment. This, in turn, implies *continuity* both in the organism and its surround. In sum, development can take place only where the environment has some stability through time. Hence the emphasis, in our formulation, on contexts that are *enduring*. But even the most stable settings also change; that is, environments also undergo development, and thus may affect, and be affected by the organisms that inhabit them.

All this is somewhat abstract. I now propose to make it concrete by documenting the changes over time that have been taking place in one enduring context that is critical for human development—the family.

A closer look at these changes will perhaps dramatize other social forces that impinge upon the family, diminishing its childrearing capacities.

Finally, from a consideration of this interplay of ecological systems, we shall derive perspectives for public policy and for research in human development that are somewhat different from those that prevail in our field today.

THE CHANGING AMERICAN FAMILY

The American family has been undergoing rapid and radical change. In 1975, it was significantly different from what it was only a quarter of a century ago. In documenting the evidence, I shall begin with aspects that are already familiar, and then proceed to other developments that are less well known. I will then show how these various trends combine and converge in an overall pattern that is far more consequential than any of its components.

Since my aim is to identify trends for American society as a whole, the primary sources of almost all the data I shall be presenting are government statistics, principally the *Current Population Reports* published by the Bureau of the Census, the *Special Labor Force Reports* issued by the Department of Labor, and the *Vital and Health Statistics Reports* prepared by the National Center of Health Statistics. These data are typically provided on an annual basis. What I have done is to collate and graph them in order to illuminate the secular trends.

1. More Working Mothers.   Our first and most familiar trend is the increase in working mothers (Figure 1-1). There are several points to be made about these data.

1. Once their children are old enough to go to school,
    the majority of American mothers now enter the
    labor force. As of March 1974, 51 percent of
    married women with children from six to seventeen
    were engaged in or seeking work; in 1948, the rate
    was about half as high, 26 percent.

2. Since the early 1950s, mothers of school age
    children have been more likely to work than
    married women without children.

3. The most recent and most rapid increase has been
    occurring for mothers of young children. One-third
    of all married women with children under six were
    in the labor force in 1974, three times as high as in
    1948. Mothers of infants were not far behind; three
    out of ten married women with children under three
    were in the work force last year.

4. Whether their children were infants or teen-agers,
    the great majority (two-thirds) of the mothers who
    had jobs were working full time.

5. These figures apply only to families in which the
    husband was present. As we shall see, for the
    rapidly growing numbers of single-parent families,
    the proportions in the labor force are much higher.

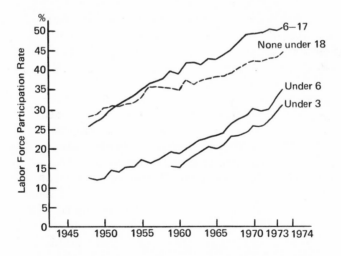

Figure 1-1. Labor force participation rates for married
women by presence and age of children. 1948–1973. Data
through 1955 from *Current Population Reports* 1955, P-
50, No. 62, Table A; from 1956, *Special Labor Force Reports* 1969, No. 7, Table 1 and 1974, No. 164, Table 3.

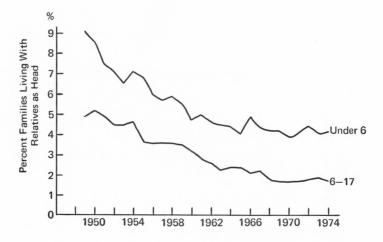

Figure 1-2.   Parent families living with a relative as family head as a percentage of all families with children under 6 and 6 through 17 years of age. 1948–1974.

2. Fewer Adults in the Home.   As more mothers have gone to work, the number of adults in the home who could care for the child has decreased. Whereas the number of children per family is now about the same today is it was twenty to thirty years ago, the number of adults in the household has dropped steadily to a 1974 average of two. This figure of course includes some households without children. Unfortunately, the Bureau of the Census does not publish a breakdown of the number of adults present in households containing children. A conservative approximation is obtainable, however, from the proportion of parents living with a relative as family head, usually a grandparent.[1]

As shown in Figure 1-2, over the past quarter century the percentage of such "extended" families has decreased appreciably. Although parents with children under six are more likely to be living with a relative than parents with older children (six to seventeen), the decline over the years has been greatest for families with young children.

1.   This proportion represents a minimum estimate since it does not include adult relatives present besides parents, when the parent rather than the relative is the family head. For example, a family with a mother-in-law living in would not be counted unless she was regarded as the family head, paid the rent, etc. The percentage was calculated from two sets of figures reported annually in the *Current Population Reports* (Series P-20) of the U.S. Census: (a) the number of families (defined as two or more related persons, including children living together) and (b) the number of subfamilies (a married couple or single parent with one or more children living with a relative who is the head of the family). Since 1968, information has been provided as to whether or not the relative was a grandparent. This was the case in a little over 80 percent of all instances.

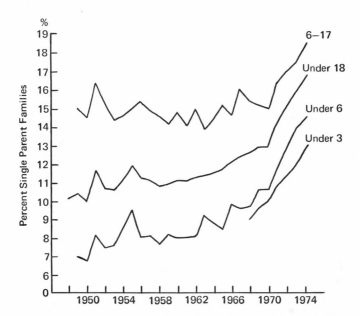

Figure 1-3.   Single parent families as a percentage of all
families with children under 18, under 6, and 6 through 17
years of age. *Current Population Reports,* Series P-20.
1948–1973.

3.   More Single–Parent Families.   The adult relatives who have
been disappearing from families include the parents themselves. As
shown in Figure 1-3, over a twenty-five year period, there has been
a marked rise in the proportion of families with only one parent
present, with the sharpest increase occurring during the past
decade. According to the latest figures available, in 1974, *one out of
every six children under eighteen years of age was living in a single-
parent family.*[2] This rate is almost double that for a quarter of a century ago.

With respect to change over time, the increase has been most
rapid among families with children under six years of age. This percentage has doubled from 7 percent in 1948 to 15 percent in 1974.
The proportions are almost as high for very young children; in 1974,
one out of every eight infants under three (13 percent), was living in
a single-parent family.

Further evidence of the progressive fragmentation of the
American family appears when we apply our index of "extended
families" to single-parent homes. The index shows a marked decline
from 1948 to 1974, with the sharpest drop occurring for families

2.   This figure includes a small proportion of single-parent families headed by
fathers. This figure has remained relatively constant, around 1 percent since 1960.

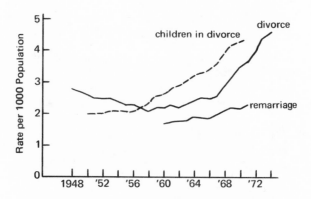

Figure 1-4. Rates of divorce, number of children in divorce, and remarriage.

with preschoolers. Today, almost 90 percent of all children with only one parent are living in independent families in which the single mother or father is also the family head.

The majority of such parents are also working, 67 percent of mothers with school age children, 54 percent with youngsters under six. And, across the board, over 80 percent of those employed are working full time. Even among single-parent mothers with children under three, 45 percent are in the labor force, of whom 86 percent are working full time.

The comment is frequently made that such figures about one parent families are misleading, since single parenthood is usually a transitional state soon terminated through remarriage. While this may be true for some selected populations, it does not appear to obtain to the nation as a whole. Figure 1-4 depicts the relevant data. The solid line in the middle shows the divorce rate for all marriages, the cross-hatched curve indexes divorces involving children, and the broken line describes the remarriage rate. To permit comparability, all three rates were computed with the total population for the given year as a base. It is clear that the remarriage rate, while rising, lags far behind the divorce rate, especially where children are involved.

Moreover, there is good reason to believe that the remarriage rate shown on the graph is substantially higher than that which applies for divorced, widowed, or other persons who are single parents. The overwhelming majority of single parents, about 95 percent, are women. In 1971, the latest year for which the data are available, the female remarriage rate per 1000 divorced or widowed wives, was 37.3; the corresponding figure for men was 130.6, four times as high. Given this fact, it becomes obvious that the rate of remarriage for single-parent families involving children is consider-

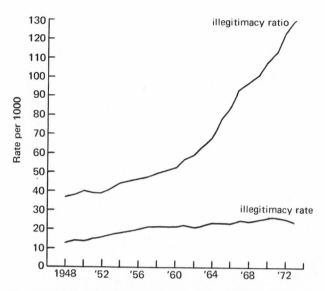

Figure 1-5. **Illegitimate births per 1000 live births (ratio) and per 1000 unmarried women (rate). 1948–1973.**

ably lower than the remarriage rate for both sexes, which is the statistic shown in the graph.

4. More Children of Unwed Mothers. After divorce, the most rapidly growing category of single-parenthood, especially since 1970, involves unmarried mothers. In the vital statistics of the United States, illegitimate births are indexed by two measures: the *illegitimacy ratio*, computed as the ratio of illegitimate births per 1000 live babies born; and the *illegitimacy rate*, which is the number of illegitimate births per 1000 unmarried women aged fifteen to forty-four years. As revealed in Figure 1-5, the ratio has consistently been higher and risen far more rapidly than the rate. This pattern indicates not only that a growing proportion of unmarried women are having children, but that the percentage of single women among those of childbearing age is becoming even larger. Consistent with this conclusion, recent U.S. census figures reveal an increasing trend for women to postpone the age of marriage. The rise in percent single is particularly strong for the age group under twenty-five; and over 80 percent of all illegitimate children are being born to women in this age bracket.

These findings suggest that the trends generally characteristic of the nation as a whole may be occurring at a faster rate in some parts of American society, and more slowly, or perhaps not at all, in others. What implications, then, can be derived from these circumstances?

WHICH FAMILIES ARE CHANGING?

Which Mothers Work? Upon analyzing available data for an answer to this question, we discover the following:

1. With age of child constant, it is the younger mother, particularly one under twenty-five years of age, who is most likely to enter the labor force. This trend has been increasing in recent years particularly for families with very young children (i.e., infants under three).

2. One reason why younger mothers are more likely to enter the labor force is to supplement the relatively low earnings of a husband just beginning his career. In general, it is in families in which the husbands have incomes below $5000 (which is now close to the poverty line for a family of four) that the wives are most likely to be working. And for families in this bottom income bracket, almost half the mothers are under twenty-five. All of these mothers, including the youngest ones with the youngest children, are working because they have to.

3. But not all the mothers whose families need the added income are working. The limiting factor is amount of schooling. It is only mothers with at least a high school education who are more likely to work when the husband has a low income. Since, below the poverty line, the overwhelming majority (68 percent) of family heads have not completed high school, this means that the families who need it most are least able to obtain the added income that a working mother can contribute.

4. In terms of change over time, the most rapid increase in labor force participation has occurred for mothers in middle and high income families. To state the trend in somewhat provocative terms, mothers from middle income families are now entering the work force at a higher rate than married women from low income families did in the early 1960s.

But the highest labor force participation rates of all are to be found not among mothers from intact families, on whom we have concentrated so far, but as we have already noted, among mothers who are single parents. Who are these single-parent families, and where are they most likely to be found?

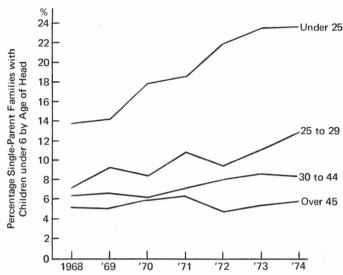

Figure 1-6. Percentage of single parent family heads
with children under 6 by age of head. 1968–1974.

Who and Where are Single-Parent Families? As in the case of
working mothers, single parenthood is most common and is growing
most rapidly among the younger generation. Figure 1-6 shows the
increase, over the past six years, in the proportion of one-parent
families with children under six classified by age of head. By last
year, almost one out of four parents under twenty-five heading a
family was without a spouse.

The association with income is even more marked. Figure 1-7
shows the rise, between 1968 and 1974, in female-headed families for
seven successive income brackets ranging from under $4000 per
year to $15,000 or over. As we can see from the diagram, single-
parent families are much more likely to occur and increase over time
in the lower income brackets. Among families with incomes under
$4000, the overwhelming majority, 67 percent, now contain only
one parent. This figure represents a marked increase from 42
percent only six years before. In sharp contrast, among families
with incomes over $15,000, the proportion has remained consis-
tently below 2 percent. Further analysis reveals that single-parent-
hood is especially common for young families in the low income
brackets. For example, among family heads under twenty-five with
earnings under $4000, the proportion of single parents was 71 per-
cent for those with all children under six, and 86 percent with all
children of school age. The more rapid increases over the past few
years, however, tended to occur among older low income families,
who are beginning to catch up. It would appear that the disruptive

processes first struck the younger families among the poor, and are now affecting the older generation as well.

But a word of caution is in order. It is important to recognize what might be called a pseudo-artifact, pseudo because there is nothing spurious in what appears in the diagram, but the pattern is susceptible to more than one possible interpretation. For example, though the percentage for the highest income group is very low, it would be a mistake to conclude that a well-to-do intact family is at low risk of disruption, for there is more than one explanation for the falling fencepost we see in Figure 1-7. The interpretation that most readily comes to mind is that families with children are more likely to split up when they are under financial strain. But the causal chain could also run the other way. The break up of the family could result in a lower income for the new, single-parent head, who, in the overwhelming majority of cases, is, of course, the mother.

Evidence on this issue is provided by the average income for separated and nonseparated family heads. For example, in 1973, the median income for all families headed by a male with wife present and at least one child under six was $12,000. The corresponding figure for a single-parent female-headed family was $3600, less than 30 percent of the income for an intact family, and far below the poverty line. It is important to bear in mind that these are nationwide statistics.

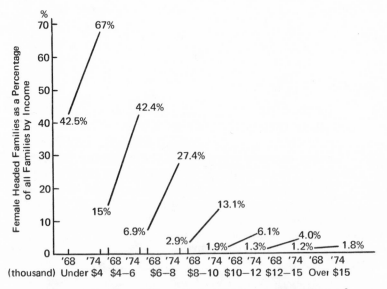

Figure 1-7.   Female-headed families as a percentage of all family heads under 65 with children under 18 by income in previous year. 1968-1974.

The nature and extent of this inequity is further underscored when we take note that the average income for the small proportion of father-headed single-parent families with preschool children was $9500. In other words, it is only the *single-parent mother* who finds herself in severely strained financial circumstances. Economic deprivation is even more extreme for single-parent mothers under the age of twenty-five. Such a mother, when all her children are small (i.e., under six), must make do with a median income of only $2800. Yet there are more than a million and a half mothers in this age group, and they constitute one-third of all female-headed families with children under six.

We can now understand why the frequency and rate of increase of single parents are so low among families in the highest income brackets. There are simply few single parents who have incomes as high as $10,000. Once separation occurs, family income drops substantially, transferring the family into lower income brackets in the left-hand portion of Figure 1-7.

Does this mean that the low income is primarily a consequence rather than a cause of single-parent status? To answer this question directly we would need to know the income of the family before the split. Unfortunately this information was not obtained in the census interview. We do have data, however, that are highly correlated with the family's socio-economic status and generally precede the event of separation; namely, the mother's level of schooling. Is it the well-educated or poorly educated woman who is most likely to become a single parent?

The answer to this question appears in Figure 1-8. In general, the less schooling she has experienced, the more likely is the mother to be left without a husband. There is only one exception to the general trend. The proportion tends to be highest, and has risen most rapidly, not for mothers receiving only an elementary education, but for those who attended high school but failed to graduate. It seems likely that many of these are unwed mothers who left school because of this circumstance. Consistent with this interpretation, further analysis reveals that the foregoing pattern occurs only for women in the younger age groups, and is most marked for mothers of children from birth to three years of age. In 1974, among mothers of infants in this age group, 14 percent, or one out of every seven, was a high school dropout.

This diagram is misleading in one respect. It leaves the impression that there has been little increase recently in the percent of single-parent families among college graduates. A somewhat different picture emerges, however, when the data are broken down simultaneously by age of mother or child. When this is done, it becomes apparent that college graduates are more likely to defer

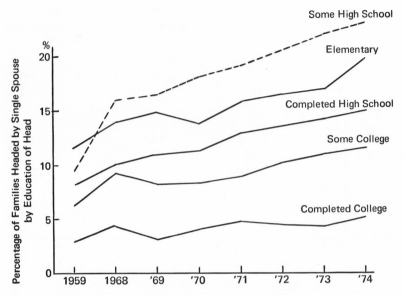

Figure 1-8. Families headed by a single spouse as a percentage of all family heads with children under eighteen. 1959–1974.

family breakup until children are older. Once they can be entered into school, or even preschool, the rates of parental separation go up from year to year, especially among the younger generation of college educated parents.

In the case of split families, we are in a position to examine not only who is likely to become an only parent, but also where, in terms of place of residence. Figure 1–9 shows the rise over the last six years in the percentage of single-parent families with children under six living in nonurban and suburban areas, and in American cities increasing in size from 50,000 to over 3,000,000. The graph illustrates at least three important trends. First, the percentage of single-parent families increases markedly with city size, reaching a maximum in American metropolises with a population of over 3 million. Second, the growing tendency for younger families to break up more frequently than older ones is greatest in the large urban centers and lowest in nonurban and suburban areas. Thus the proportion of single parents reaches its maximum among families with heads under thirty-five who live in cities with more than 3,000,000 persons. Here one out of three to four households has a single parent as the head. Finally, the most rapid change over time is occurring not in the larger cities, but in those of medium size. This pattern suggests that the high levels of family fragmentation that, six years ago, were found only in major metropolitan centers, are now occurring in smaller urban areas as well.

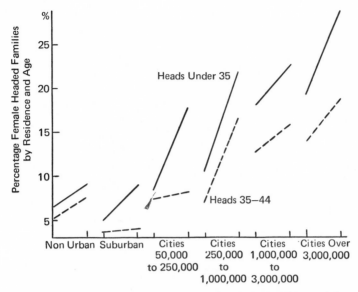

Figure 1-9. Percentage female-headed families with
children under 6, by place of residence and age of family
head. 1968-1974.

The Ecology of a Race Difference.   The question may well arise
why, with all the breakdowns we have made—by age, income, education, and place of residence—we have not presented any data
separately by race. We have deferred this separation for a reason
that is apparent in Figure 1-10. It shows the rise, between 1960 and
1970, in the percentage of single-parent families by income of head
within three types of residence areas: urban, suburban, and nonurban, separately for black and white families. Unfortunately, no
breakdown was available within the urban category by city size so
that, as a result, the effects of this variable are considerably
attenuated. Nevertheless, it is clear that both income and place of
residence make an independent contribution to the level and size of
broken families.

Turning to the issue of race, note that in the graph, the rising
lines for blacks and whites are almost parallel. In other words, within each setting and income level, the percentage of single parents is
increasing about as fast for whites as it is for blacks. To put it in
more general terms, *families that live in similar circumstances,
whatever their color, are affected in much the same ways.* To be
sure, at the end of the decade, the blacks within each setting and
income bracket experience a higher percentage of single-parent
families than do the whites. But they entered the decade in the same
relative positions. This suggests that some different experiences
prior to 1960 must have contributed to the disparity we now

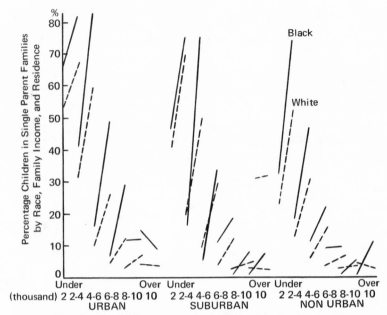

Figure 1-10. Percentage of children in single-parent families by race, family income in previous year, and residence. Each line segment shows change from 1960 to 1970.

observe between black and white families living in similar conditions. One does not have to seek long in the historical records, especially those written by blacks, to discover what some of these experiences may have been. Indeed, the observations by Congresswoman Chisholm, in Chapter 3, provide a ready illustration.

But, of course, in reality the overwhelming majority of blacks and whites do not live in similar circumstances. It is only in our artificially selected comparison groups, especially in the context that is most homogeneous, namely suburbia, that data for the two races begin to look alike. Without statistical control for income and urbanization, the curves for the two races are rather different; they are much farther apart, and the curve for blacks rises at a substantially faster rate. Specifically, between 1960 and 1970, the percentage of single-parent families among blacks increased at a rate five times that for whites, and at the end of that period the percentage was over four times as high, 35 percent versus 8 percent. In the last four years, both figures have risen and the gap has widened. In 1974, the percentage of single-parent families with children under eighteen was 13 percent for whites and 44 percent for blacks.

This dramatic disparity becomes more comprehensible, however, when we apply what we have learned about the relation of urbanization and income to family disruption. Upon inquiry, we discover that in 1974 about 6 percent of all white families with children under eighteen were living in cities with a population of 3 million or more, compared to 21 percent for blacks, over three and one-half times as high; this ratio has been rising steadily in recent years.

Turning to family income, in 1973, the latest year for which the data are available, the median income for an intact family with children under six was $12,300 when the family was white, $6700 when it was black. Ironically, single-parenthood reduced the race difference by forcing both averages down below the poverty level—$3700 for whites, $3400 for blacks. Consistent with these facts, the percentage of black families who fall below the poverty line is much higher than that for whites. In 1973, 33 percent, or one-third, of all black families with children under eighteen, were classified in the low income bracket, compared to 8 percent for whites, a ratio of over four to one. Moreover, the advantage of whites over blacks in family income, which decreased during the 1960s, reversed itself at the turn of the decade and has been increasing since 1969. In the language of the latest census report:

> The 1973 median income for black families was 58 percent of the white median income and this continued a downward trend in this ratio from 61 percent, which occurred in both 1960 and 1970. In contrast to the 1970's, the ratio of black to white median family income had increased during the 1960's.[3]

We can now understand why nonwhite mothers have gone to work in increasing numbers and at rates substantially higher than their white counterparts. In 1974, almost one-third of white married women with husbands present and children under six were in the labor force; the corresponding fraction for nonwhite families was over half (52 percent.) Fifteen years ago, the gap between the racial groups was smaller, 18 percent versus 28 percent, and it is of course the nonwhites who have increased at the faster rate.

But the more vulnerable position of black families in American society becomes clearer when we examine the comparative exposure of both ethnic groups to the combined effects of low income and urbanization. Unfortunately, once again the data are not broken down by city size, but we can compare the distribution of black and white families with children under eighteen living in so-called "poverty areas" in urban, suburban, and rural settings, further sub-

3.   U.S. Bureau of the Census, "Money Income in 1973 of Families and Persons in the United States," *Current Population Reports*, Series P–60, No. 97, (Washington, D.C.: U.S. Government Printing Office, 1975), p. 5.

classified by family income. A poverty area is a census tract in which 20 percent or more of the population was below the low income level in 1969. As might be expected, more white families with children (44 percent of them) reside in suburbia than in central cities or rural areas, and the overwhelming majority (70 percent) live outside of poverty areas and have incomes above the poverty line. In contrast, the corresponding percentages for black families are much smaller, 17 percent and 32 percent respectively; well over half of black families (58 percent) are concentrated in central cities, more than half of these live in poverty areas within those cities, and half of these, in turn, have incomes below the poverty line. Seventeen percent, or one out of every six black families with children under eighteen, are found in the most vulnerable ecological niche (low income in a poverty area of a central city), compared to less than 1 percent of all whites. Even though only 14 percent of all American families with children are black, among those living in poverty areas of central cities and having incomes below the poverty level, they constitute the large majority (66 percent).

The grossly differential distribution of blacks and whites in American society by income, place of residence, and other ecological dimensions that we have not been able to examine for lack of adequate data makes even more comprehensible the difference in degree of family disruption experienced by these two major classes of American citizens. Indeed, given the extent of the disparity in conditions of life, one wonders what keeps the figures for black families from running even higher than they do.

A possible answer is suggested by the data provided in Figure 1-11 that shows our measure of "extended families" separately for white and nonwhite families. It will be observed that this index is consistently and markedly higher for nonwhites. In other words, nonwhites are much more likely to be living in a household that includes more than two generations, with another relative besides the child's parent acting as the family head. To be sure, the decline since 1959 has been greater for nonwhites than for whites, but the former curve has shown an upswing in the last four years.

But there are other less favorable developments as well. If we examine, separately by race, the extent to which single parents head their own families, we observe the same trend toward greater isolation for both whites and nonwhites. As we see in Figure 1-12, these two curves are almost indistinguishable. Again, regardless of color, families in similar circumstances are affected in the same way for better or for worse.

What this means is that differences in the comparative well-being of black and white families are largely attributable to present societal patterns. Hence, if we chose to alter our social policies, and

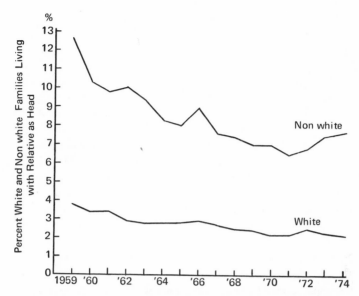

Figure 1-11. Percentage of white and nonwhite families with children under 18 living with a relative as family head. The base for the percentage is the total number of families for each race with children under 18. 1959–1974.

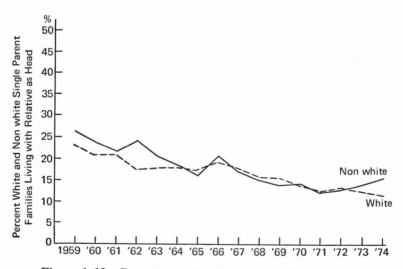

Figure 1-12. Percentage of white and nonwhite single-parent families with children under 18 living with a relative as family head. 1959–1974. The base for the percentage is the total number of single-parent families for each race with children under 18.

institute new arrangements, much of the disparity could be eliminated. The recommendations of Senator Schweiker in Chapter 7 regarding vocational competance might constitute a constructive policy alteration.

We have now completed our analysis of changes in the American family over the past quarter century. For the nation as a whole, the analysis reveals progressive fragmentation and isolation of the family in its child rearing role. With respect to different segments of American society, the changes have been most rapid among younger families with younger children, and increase with the degree of economic deprivation and industrialization, reaching their maximum among low income families living in the central core of our largest cities. But the general trend applies to all strata of the society. Middle class families, in cities, suburbia, and nonurban areas, are changing in similar ways. Specifically, in terms of such characteristics as the proportion of working mothers, number of adults in the home, single-parent families, or children born out of wedlock, the middle class family of today increasingly resembles the low income family of the early 1960s.

THE CHANGING AMERICAN CHILD

Having described the changes in the structure and status of the American family, we are now ready to address our next question: So what? Or, to be more formal and explicit: What do these changes mean for the well-being and growth of children? What does it mean for the young that more and more mothers, especially mothers of preschoolers and infants, are going to work, the majority of them full-time? What does it mean that, as these mothers leave for work, there are also fewer adults in the family who might look after the child, and that, among adults who are leaving the home, the principal deserter is one or the other parent, usually the father?

Paradoxically, the most telling answer to the foregoing questions is yet another question that is even more difficult to answer: *Who cares for America's children? Who cares?*

At the present, substitute care for children of whatever form—nursery schools, group day care, family day care, or just a body to babysit—falls so far short of the need that it can be measured in millions of children under the age of six, not to mention the millions more of school age youngsters, so-called "latch-key" children, who come home to empty houses, and who contribute far out of proportion to the ranks of pupils with academic and behavior problems, have difficulties in learning to read, who are dropouts, drug users, and juvenile delinquents.

But we are getting ahead of our story. We have seen what has been happening to America's families. Let us try to examine systematically what has been happening to the American child. Unfortunately, statistics at a national level on the state of the child are neither as comprehensive nor as complete as those on the state of the family, but the available data does suggest a pattern consistent with the evidence from our prior analysis.

We begin at the level at which all the trends of disorganization converge. For this purpose, there is an even better index than low income level—one that combines economic deprivation with every kind—health, housing, education, and welfare. Let us look first at children who are born to American citizens whose skin color is other than white.

Death in the First Year of Life

The first consequence we meet is that of survival itself. In recent years, many people have become aware of the existence of the problem to which I refer, but perhaps not of the evidence for its practical solution. America, the richest and most powerful country in the world, stands fourteenth among the nations in combating infant mortality; even East Germany does better. Moreover, our ranking has dropped steadily in recent decades. A similar situation obtains with respect to maternal and child health, day care, children's allowances, and other basic services to children and families.

But the figures for the nation as a whole, dismaying as they are, mask even greater inequities. For example, infant mortality for nonwhites in the United States is almost twice that for whites, the maternal death rate is four times as high, and there are a number of Southern states, and Northern metropolitan areas, in which the ratios are considerably higher. Among New York City health districts, for example, the infant mortality rate in 1966–67 varied from 13 per 1000 in Haspeth, Forest Hills to 41.5 per 1000 in Central Harlem.[4] One illuminating way of describing the differences in infant mortality by race is from a time perspective. Babies born of nonwhite mothers are today dying at a rate that white babies have not experienced for almost a quarter of a century. The current nonwhite rate of 28.1 was last reported for American whites in the late 1940s. The rate for whites in 1950, 26.8 percent, was not yet achieved by nonwhites in 1974. In fact in recent years the gap between the races, instead of narrowing, has been getting wider.

4. D.S. Kessner *et al.*, *Infant Death: An Analysis by Maternal Risk and Health Care.* (Washington, D.C.: Institute of Medicine, National Academy of Sciences, 1973).

The way to the solution is suggested by the results of the two-stage analysis carried out by Dr. Harold Watts for the Advisory Committee on Child Development of the National Academy of Sciences. First, Watts demonstrated that 92 percent of the variation in infant death among the thirty New York City health districts is explainable by low birth weight. Second, he showed that 97 percent of the variation in low birth weight can be attributed to the fraction of mothers who received no prenatal care or received care only late in their pregnancy, and the fraction unwed at the time of delivery.

Confirmatory evidence is available from an important and elegant study, published in 1973, on the relations between infant mortality, social and medical risk, and health care.[5] From an analysis of data in 140,000 births in New York City, the investigators found the following:

1. The highest rate of infant mortality was for children of black native-born women at social and medical risk and with inadequate health care. This rate was forty-five times higher than that for a group of white mothers at no risk with adequate care. Next in line were Puerto Rican infants with a rate twenty-two times as high.

2. Among mothers receiving adequate medical care, there was essentially no difference in mortality among white, black, and Puerto Rican groups, even for mothers at high medical risk.

3. For mothers at socio-economic risk, however, adequate medical care substantially reduced infant mortality rates for all races, but the figures for black and Puerto Rican families were still substantially greater than those for whites. In other words, other factors besides inadequate medical care contribute to producing the higher infant mortality for these nonwhite groups. Again these factors have to do with the social and economic conditions in which these families have to live. Thus, the results of the New York City study and other investigations point to the following characteristics as predictive of higher infant mortality: employment status of the breadwinner, mother unwed at infant's birth, married but no father in the home, number of children per room, mother under twenty or over thirty-five, and parents' educational level.

5. Kessner *et al., Infant Death.*

4. Approximately 95 percent of those mothers at risk
   had medical or social conditions that could have
   been identified at the time of the first prenatal
   visit; infants born to this group of women
   accounted for 70 percent of the deaths.

What would have happened had these conditions been identified and adequate medical care provided? The answer to this question has recently become available from an analysis of data from the
Maternal and Infant Care Projects of HEW which, in the middle
1960s, were established in slum areas of fourteen cities across the
nation and in Puerto Rico. In Denver, a dramatic fall in infant mortality from 34.2 per 1000 live births in 1964 to 21.5 per 1000 in 1969
was observed for the twenty-five census tracts that made up the
target area for such a program. In Birmingham, Alabama, the rate
decreased from 25.4 in 1965 to 14.3 in 1969, and in Omaha from 33.4
in 1964 to 13.4 in 1960. Significant reductions have also occurred
over the populations served by these programs in prematurity,
repeated teenage pregnancy, women who conceive over thirty-five
years old, and families with more than four children.

It is testimony to our perverted priorities that these programs are in serious jeopardy. Since the proposed alternatives
involving revenue sharing are not yet in the offing, the termination
of the projects will increase the mortality rate to earlier levels; more
infants will die.

The Interplay of Biological and Environmental Factors

The decisive role that environmental factors (alluded to by
Salk in Chapter 6) can play in influencing the biological growth of
the organism, and, thereby, its psychological development, is
illustrated by a series of recent follow-up studies of babies experiencing prenatal complications at birth, but surviving and growing
up in families at different socio-economic levels. As an example we
may take an excellently designed and analyzed study by
Richardson.[6] It is a well established finding that mothers from low
income families bear a higher proportion of premature babies, as
measured either by weight at birth or gestational age, and that pre-
matures generally tend to be somewhat retarded in mental growth.
Richardson studied a group of such children in Aberdeen, Scotland

6. S.A. Richardson, "Ecology of Malnutrition: Non-nutritional Factors Influencing
Intellectual and Behavioral Development," *Nutrition, The Nervous System, and
Behavior.* Scientific Publication #251 (Washington, D.C.: Pan American Health Or-
ganization, 1972), pp. 101–110.

from birth through seven years with special focus on intellectual development. He found, as expected, that children born prematurely to mothers in low income families showed significantly poorer performance on measures of mental growth, especially when the babies were both born before term and weighed less than five pounds. The average I.Q. for these children at seven years of age was 80. But the higher the family's socio-economic level, the weaker the tendency for birth weight to be associated with impaired intellectual function. For example, in the higher social class group, infants born before term and weighing under five pounds had a mean I.Q. of 105, higher than the average for the general population, and only five points below the mean for full term babies of normal weight born to mothers in the same socio-economic group. In other words, children starting off with similar biological deficits ended up with widely differing risks of mental retardation as a function of the conditions of life for the family in which they were born.

But low income does not require a biological base to affect profoundly the welfare and development of the child. To cite but two examples. Child abuse is far more common in poor than in middle income families,[7] and the socio-economic status of the family has emerged as the most powerful predictor of school success in studies conducted at both the national and state level.[8]

Nor does income tell the whole story. In the first place, other social conditions, such as the absence of the parent have been shown to exacerbate the impact of poverty. For example, in low income homes, child abuse is more likely to occur in single-parent than in intact families, especially when the mother is under twenty-five years of age.[9] It is also the young mother who is most likely to have a premature baby.

In terms of subsequent development, a state-wide study in New York of factors affecting school performance at all grade levels[10] found that 58 percent of the variation in student achievement could be predicted by three factors: broken homes, overcrowded housing, and the educational level of the head of the household. When racial and ethnic variables were introduced into the analysis, they accounted for less than an additional 2 percent of the variation.

7.   D.G. Gil, *Violence against Children: Physical Child Abuse in the United States* (Cambridge, MA: Harvard University Press, 1970).

8.   J.S. Coleman, *Equality of Educational Opportunity.* (Washington, D.C.: U.S. Office of Education, 1966); C. Jencks, *Inequality.* (New York: Basic Books, 1972); *Report of the New York State Commission on the Quality, Cost, and Financing of Elementary and Secondary Education* Vol. 1.

9.   Gil, *Violence against Children.*

10. *Report of the New York State Commission.*

Finally, and perhaps most importantly, low income may not be the critical factor affecting the development and needs of children and families. The most powerful evidence for this con- clusion comes from census data on trends in family income over the past quarter century. Even after adjustment for inflation, the level has been rising steadily at least through 1974, and for black families as well as white. A reflection of this fact is a drop over the years in the percentages of children in families below the poverty line, 27 percent in 1959, 15 percent in 1968, and 14 percent in 1973.[11]

Changes over Time

And yet, as we have seen the percentage of single-parent fami- lies has been growing, especially in recent years. And there are analogous trends for indices bearing on the state and development of the child. Although lack of comparability between samples and measures precludes a valid assessment of change in child abuse rates, an index is available for this phenomenon in its most extreme form—homicide, or the deliberate killing of a child. As shown in Figure 1-13, the rate has been increasing over time for children of all ages. Adolescents are more likely to be the victims of homicide than younger children except in the first year of life, in which the rates again jump upward.

Children who survive face other risks. For example, the New York study cited earlier[12] reports a secular trend in the proportion of children failing to perform at minimal levels in reading and arith- metic: each year "more and more children are below minimum competence."

One might conclude that such a decrease in competence is occurring primarily, if not exclusively, among families of lower socio-economic status, with limited income, education, and cultural background. The data of Figure 1-14 suggests that the trend may be far more democratic. The graph shows the average score achieved each year in the verbal and mathematical sections of the Scholastic Aptitude Test, taken by virtually all high school juniors and seniors who plan to go to college. The test scores are used widely as the basis for determining admission. As is apparent from Figure 1-14 there has been a steady and substantial decrease over the past decade—thirty-five points in the verbal section, twenty- four in the mathematical section. In interpreting the significance of

11. Unfortunately, the curve levelled off in 1969 and has shown no decline in the 1970s.
12. Report of the New York State Commission.

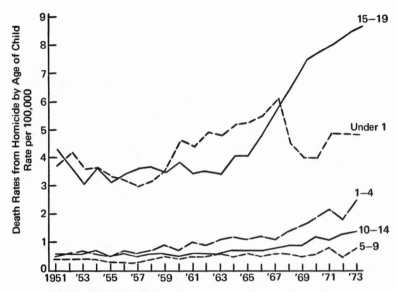

Figure 1-13.   Death rates from homicide by age of child victim. 1951-1973.

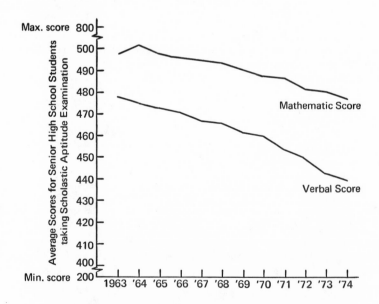

Figure 1-14.   Average scores for senior high school students taking the scholastic aptitude examinations. 1963-1974. Data provided courtesy of Education Testing Service.

this decline, Dr. T. Anne Clarey, Chief of the Program Services Division of the College Board, warned that it is incorrect to conclude from a score decline that schools have not been preparing students in verbal and mathematical skills as well as they have in former years. "The SAT measures skills developed over a youngster's life time—both in and out of the school setting. ...It is evident that many factors, including family and home life, exposure to mass media, and other cultural and environmental factors are associated with students' performance."[13]

Finally, the remaining sets of data shift attention from the cognitive to the emotional and social areas. Figures 1-15 documents the increase in suicide rates in recent years for children as young as ten. Figure 1-16 shows an even more precipitous climb in the rate of juvenile delinquency. Since 1963, crimes by children have been increasing at a higher rate than the juvenile population. In 1973, among children under fifteen,[14] almost half (47 percent) of all arrests involved theft, breaking and entering and vandalism, and, with an important exception to be noted below, these categories were also the ones showing the greatest increase over the past decade. The second largest grouping, also growing rapidly, constituted almost a quarter of all offenses[15] and included loitering, disorderly conduct,

13. Press release (College Entrance Examination Board, New York, New York, December 20, 1973). A report in *Time* (March 31, 1975) quotes Sam McCandless, Director of admissions testing for the College Entrance Examination Board, as refuting arguments that the decrease in SAT scores is not "real" but a reflection of changes on the tests or in the social composition of students taking them. According to McCandless, the reason for the drop is a decline in the students' "developed reasoning ability."

The same article reports two other developments that corroborate the downward trend in learning:

> The National Assessment of Educational Progress—a federally funded testing organization—reported last week that students knew less about science in 1973 than they did three years earlier. The test, which covered 90,000 students in elementary and junior and senior high schools in all parts of the nation, showed the sharpest decline among 17-year-olds in large cities, although suburban students' test scores fell too.

> The results of the third study, sponsored by the U.S. Department of Health, Education and Welfare and announced last week, showed that public school students' reading levels have been falling since the mid-1960s.

14. The figures that follow are based on the *Uniform Crime Reports for the United States* published annually by the Federal Bureau of Investigation.

15. It is noteworthy that the highest level and most rapid rise within this grouping occurred for runaways, an increase of more than 240 percent since 1964 (the rate has decreased somewhat since 1970). It would appear that the trend we have observed in the progressive break-up of the family includes the departure not only of its adult members, but its children as well.

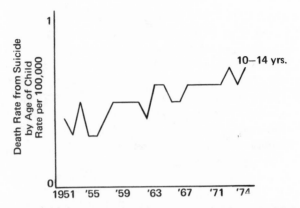

Figure 1-15. Death rates from suicide by age of child.
1951-1973.

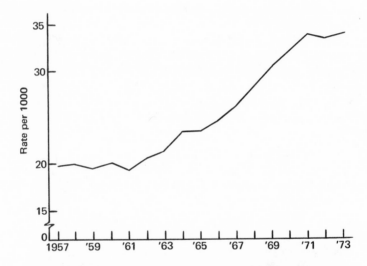

Figure 1-16. Rate of delinquency cases disposed of by
juvenile courts involving children 10 through 17 years of
age. 1957-1973.

and runaways. The most rapid rises, however, occurred in two other
categories, drug use and violent crimes. In 1973, drug arrests
accounted for 2.6 percent of all offenses by children under fifteen.
The precise rate of increase over time is difficult to estimate because
of inconsistant enforcement and reporting. In the same year, the
next most rapid rise was for violent crimes (aggravated assault,
armed robbery, forcible rape, and murder). These accounted for 3.3
percent of all arrests. While the proportion of children involved is of
course very small, this figure represents at least a 200 percent in-

crease over the 1964 level.[16] And the total number of children with a criminal record is substantial. "If the present trends continue, one out of every nine youngsters will appear before a juvenile court before age 18."[17] The figures, of course, index only offenses that are detected and prosecuted. One wonders how high the numbers must climb before we acknowledge that they reflect deep and pervasive problems in the treatment of children and youth in our society; problems that, as Tyler makes clear in Chapter 8, will take a substantial amount of time to correct.

THE ROOTS OF ALIENATION

What are the basic sources of these problems? The data we have examined point the accusing finger most directly at the destructive effect, both on families and children, of economic deprivation. In the light of our analysis, there can be no question that variation in income plays a critical role in accounting for the marked differences in the state of families and their children in different segments of American society. Hence, the keystone for any national policy in this sphere must insure basic economic security for American families.

But while income is crucial to the understanding and reduction of cross-sectional differences, our analyses indicate that the financial factor, taken by itself, cannot explain, or counteract, the profound longitudinal changes that have been taking place over the past quarter century, and that are documented in so many of our charts and figures. Other forces besides the purely economic have been operating to produce the present state of affairs, and will need to be invoked to bring about any desired improvement. These forces are reflected but not identified, in our data on the effects of urbanization. Available research does not enable us to pin them down with any degree of precision, but some indication of their possible nature is provided from studies of child socialization and development in other cultures.[18] These investigations call attention

16. We may take what comfort we can from the fact that the reported rates of drug arrests and of juvenile violence have dropped somewhat since 1970.

17. *Profiles of Children.* (Washington D.C.: White House Conference on Children, 1970), p. 79.

18. R. Berfenstam and I. William-Olsson, *Early child care in Sweden.* (New York: Gordon and Breach, 1974); U. Bronfenbrenner, *Two worlds of childhood: U.S. and U.S.S.R.* (New York: Russell Sage Foundation, 1970); M. David and I. Lezine, *Early Child Care in France.* (New York: Gordon and Breach, 1975); E.C. Devereux, Jr. *et al.,* "Child Rearing in England and the United States: A Cross-national Comparison" *Journal of Marriage and the Family,* May 1969, *31,* 257–270; A. Hermann, and S. Komlosi, *Early Child Care in Hungary.* (New York: Gordon and Breach, 1973); W.

to a distinctive feature of American child-rearing: segregation, not by race or social class, but by age. Increasingly, children in America are living and growing up in relative isolation from persons older, or younger, than themselves. For example, a survey of changes in child rearing practices in the United States over a twenty-five year period reveals a decrease in all spheres of interaction between parent and child.[19] A similar trend is indicated by data from cross-cultural studies comparing American families with their European counterparts.[20] Thus, in a comparative study of socialization practices among German and American parents, the former emerged as significantly more involved in activities with their children including both affection and discipline. A second study conducted several years later, showed changes over time in both cultures reflecting "a trend toward the dissolution of the family as a social system," with Germany moving closer to the American pattern of "centrifugal forces pulling the members into relationships outside the family."[21]

Although the nature and operation of these centrifugal forces have not been studied systematically, they are readily apparent to observers of the American scene. (Note Boulding's commentary in Chapter 2.) The following excerpt from the report of the President's White House Conference on Children summarizes the situation as seen by a group of experts, including both scientists and practitioners.

> In today's world parents find themselves at the mercy
> of a society which imposes pressures and priorities that
> allow neither time nor place for meaningful activities
> and relations between children and adults, which
> downgrade the role of parents and the functions of
> parenthood, and which prevent the parent from doing
> things he wants to do as a guide, friend, and companion
> to his children . . .

Kessen, *Children and China.* (New Haven: Yale University Press, in press); L. Liegle, *The Family's Role in Soviet Education.* (New York: Springer Publishing Co., in press); K.L. Luscher, *et al.,* Early child care in Switzerland. (New York: Gordon and Breach, 1973); M.K. Pringle and S. Naidoo, *Early child care in Britain.* (New York: Gordon and Breach, 1975); H.B. Robinson *et al., Early Child Care in the United States of America.* (New York: Gordon and Breach, 1973); R.R. Rodgers, "Changes in Parental Behavior reported by Children in West Germany and the United States," *Human Development,* 1971, *14,* 203–224.

19. U. Bronfenbrenner, "Socialization and social class through time and space," E.E. Maccoby, T.M. Newcomb, and E. Hartley, eds., *Readings in Social Psychology,* 3rd Edition. (New York: Holt, Rinehart and Winston, 1958), 400–425.

20. Bronfenbrenner, *Two Worlds of Childhood;* Devereux et al., *Child Rearing*

21. Rodgers, *Changes in Parental Behavior.*

The frustrations are greatest for the family of poverty where the capacity for human response is crippled by hunger, cold, filth, sickness, and despair. For families who can get along, the rats are gone, but the rat-race remains. The demands of a job, or often two jobs, that claim mealtimes, evenings, and weekends as well as days; the trips and moves necessary to get ahead or simply hold one's own; the ever increasing time spent in commuting, parties, evenings out, social and community obligations—all the things one has to do to meet so-called primary responsibilities—produce a situation in which a child often spends more time with a passive babysitter than a participating parent.[22]

Although systematically documented evidence is not available, there are clear indications that, outside the home as well, adults are deserting children. To quote again from the report of the White House Conference:

In our modern way of life, it is not only parents of whom children are deprived, it is people in general. A host of factors conspire to isolate children from the rest of society. The fragmentation of the extended family, the separation of residential and business areas, the disappearance of neighborhoods, zoning ordinances, occupational mobility, child labor laws, the abolishment of the apprentice system, consolidated schools, television, separate patterns of social life for different age groups, the working mother, the delegation of child care to specialists—all these manifestations of progress operate to decrease opportunity and incentive for meaningful contact between children and persons older, or younger, than themselves.[23]

This erosion of the social fabric isolates not only the child but also his family. As documented in earlier sections of this report, even in intact families the centrifugal forces generated within the family by its increasingly isolated position have propelled its members in different directions. As parents, especially mothers, spend more time in work and community activities, children are placed in or gravitate to group settings, both organized and informal. For example, since 1965 the number of children enrolled in day care

22. *Report to the President. White House Conference on Children.* (Washington, D.C.: U.S. Government Printing Office, 1970), 240-255.
23. *Report of Forum 15.* White House Conference on Children. (Washington, D.C., 1970).

centers has more than doubled, and the demand today far exceeds the supply. Outside preschool or school, the child spends increasing amounts of time solely in the company of his age-mates. The vacuum created by the withdrawal of parents and other adults has been filled by the informal peer group. A recent study has found that at every age and grade level, children today show a greater dependency on their peers than they did a decade ago.[24] A parallel investigation indicates that such susceptibility to group influence is higher among children from homes in which one or both parents are frequently absent.[25] In addition, "peer oriented" youngsters describe their parents as less affectionate and less firm in discipline. Attachment to age-mates appears to be influenced more by a lack of attention and concern at home than by any positive attraction of the peer group itself. In fact, these children have a rather negative view of their friends and of themselves as well. They are pessimistic about the future, rate lower in responsibility and leadership, and are more likely to engage in such anti-social behavior as lying, teasing other children, "playing hooky," "hurting others," or "doing something illegal."[26]

What we are seeing here, of course, are the roots of alienation and its milder consequences. The more serious manifestations are reflected in the rising rates of child homicide, suicide, drug use, and juvenile delinquency previously cited.

How are we to reverse these debilitating trends? If our analysis is correct, what is called for is nothing less than a change in our way of life and our institutions, both public and private, so as to give new opportunity and status for parenthood, and to bring children and adults back into each other's lives. Specifically, we need to develop a variety of *support systems* for families, and for others engaged in the care of the nation's children. And these support systems, in turn, should be based on the results of systematic research on the environmental forces, both actual and potential, that sustain and enhance the process of human development. Thus we are brought to the two final issues under discussion: the implications of our analyses for scientific work and for public policy.

24. J.C. Condry, and M.A. Siman, "Characteristics of Peer and Adult-oriented children," *Journal of Marriage and the Family,* 1974, *36,* 543–554.

25. J.C. Condry and M.A. Siman "An experimental study of adult vs. peer orientation," (Unpublished manuscript, Cornell University, 1968).

26. M.A. Siman, "Peer Group Influence during Adolescence: A Study of Forty-one Naturally Existing Friendship Groups." (A thesis presented to the Faculty of the Graduate School of Cornell University for the degree of Doctor of Philosophy, January 1973.)

IMPLICATIONS FOR RESEARCH

We began our discussion by asserting that the changes we would observe in the ecology of human development would lead to a new and more fruitful theoretical perspective for research. What is the new direction for investigation suggested by the results of our analyses?

One might expect from the nature and outcome of these analyses that we would now argue for systematic studies of the consequences for the child of the profound changes we have documented in the structure and position of the family in American society. But, desirable as such research would be, it does not in our view, represent the strategy of choice for the study of human development in context. Specifically, we propose a reorientation to theory and research in socialization based on two guiding principles.

The first is perhaps most cogently expressed in the words of Professor A. N. Leontiev of the University of Moscow. At one time, I was an exchange scientist at the Institute of Psychology. We had been discussing differences in the assumptions underlying research on socialization in the Soviet Union and in the United States. Leontiev's statement was the following: "It seems to me that American researchers are constantly seeking to explain how the child came to be what he is; we in the U.S.S.R. are striving to discover not how the child came to be what he is, but how he can become what he not yet is."

One reason why I remember Professor Leontiev's challenging comment is that it echoed the advice given me a quarter of a century earlier by my first mentor in graduate school Professor Walter Fenno Dearborn of Harvard. In his quiet, crisp New England accent, he once remarked: "Bronfenbrenner, if you want to understand something, try to change it."

In short, I propose that the strategy of choice for future research in human development is one that applies the experimental method to alter systematically the nature of the enduring environments in which children live and grow. The approach might be called: *experimental human ecology*.

The emphasis on systematic experimentation is prompted by two considerations. The first is painfully illustrated by the limitations of the kinds of data I have been presenting to you. They provide evidence of concurrent changes over time on the one hand, in the structure and position of the American family, and, on the other, in the abilities and character of American children. But as evidence for the existence, let alone the nature, of a causal connection between the two domains, the data are of course inadequate. There is confounding among variables not only within but also across domains, for one cannot be certain what is cause and what is effect. For example, a biologically damaged infant, or an aggressive child, could be a contributing factor in family disruption.

The second consideration that prompts an experimental approach arises not on grounds of science but of social policy. The trends we have documented are, I suggest, sufficiently widespread and destructive that we need to discover how they may be counteracted. And the best way to learn about change, is to try it. Thus considerations both of science and social policy support the validity and timeliness of Dearborn's dictum: "If you want to understand something, try to change it."

Criteria for a Program of Research

But knowing ends and means does not remove obstacles that stand in the way. In ironic validation of our ecological thesis, these obstacles also take the form of enduring environments—specifically, of established institutions, roles, and activities that resist alteration of the processes of socialization that prepare and perpetuate researchers in the prevailing mode. Accordingly, the first task to be accomplished if ecologically-oriented investigations are to be carried out in any substantial degree is to create institutional supports for such activity in the form of training, professional recognition, and, of course, research funds. At the present time, all of these are focused around success in implementing the traditional experimental model in laboratory settings. Unless this focus can be broadened, ecological research will paradoxically remain a purely academic exercise.

But there are grounds for hope. Over the past two years, with the support of a private foundation, the Foundation for Child Development, I have been developing a program of research in what we are calling "the ecology of human development." Recently, the Foundation made available funds for the support of small-scale investigations that approximate the distinctive properties of an ecological model as developed in this paper. As a convenient way of summarizing these distinctive properties, I summarize below the criteria that are being applied in the evaluation of research proposals under the Foundation's program.

These criteria are of two kinds: (A) those that are deemed *essential* and (B), *bonus* criteria, which are not regarded as necessary, but, if present, would give the proposal higher priority.

A. Essential Criteria

1. The proposed study must be concerned with the interplay between what is or could become some enduring aspect of the person's environment and the development of an enduring human activity that has social significance in that environment. In other words, the independent and dependent variables must be anchored in social reality, thus ensuring ecological validity at both ends of the causal chain.

2. A second criterion is that the study involve, as a basic element of the research design, the comparison of at least two different ecological systems or their components. This comparison may consist either of a true experiment in which subjects are assigned at random to different treatments, or of an "experiment of nature" in which subjects are found in different environments and some effort is made to control for possibly confounding factors. Thus this requirement rules out proposals of several kinds; for example: purely case studies of individuals, groups, or settings; exploratory studies designed solely to identify variables or hypotheses for future research, or projects restricted to the development of methods.

B. Bonus Criteria

The bonus criteria stipulate a variety of characteristics that could enhance the value of the proposal. The following are examples:

1. Proposals that examine the effect of different ecological systems as systems are given priority over investigations limited to single variables treated as separable in their effects.

2. Proposals that assess effects of innovation or deliberately induce ecological change are given higher priority than investigations of the status quo.

3. Priority is given to proposals in which outcome variables go beyond conventional measures of intellectual performance and academic achievement to include assessments of social and motivational orientations and behavior on the part both of individuals (e.g., children, parents, teachers, community

leaders) and social systems (e.g., schools, businesses, social agencies, communities).

4. Designs that go beyond the concrete contexts containing the person (e.g., family, classroom) to the higher order systems in which these contexts are embedded (e.g., the neighborhood, the world of work, health and welfare services, the legal system) are regarded as preferable to designs confined to the immediate setting only.

5. Proposals for research in which the social policy implications are apparent or made explicit are regarded as more appropriate than those in which practical and social implications remain implicit or unclear.

In addition to the foregoing substantive criteria, the program involves certain other distinctive features designed to encourage and assist research development along the indicated lines. For example, several leading researchers serve as consultants not only in the evaluation but also the cultivation and execution of research proposals.[27] The program also provides for expert critique of preliminary drafts of research papers to those grantees who desire such advice. The investigator is of course free to accept or reject such counsel as he wishes. Also, in the granting of funds, priority is given to younger scientists, including graduate students working on their dissertations.[28]

Proposals in Process

As an illustration of the kinds of research that the Program seeks to generate, I describe below two of the proposals we have funded to date that were judged to approximate the stated criteria.

Proposal I. Child rearing in home, family day care, and group day care. In this project the investigator, Moncrieff Cochran, takes advantage of a unique opportunity presented by contemporary Swedish society to investigate differences in socialization practices and outcomes as a function of three different child rearing settings.

27. These two functions are separated under the operating principle that no consultant can serve as the judge of a proposal that he has helped to develop.

28. More detailed information on criteria and procedures for submitting proposals may be obtained by writing to Joyce Brainard, Administrative Aide, FCD Program on the Ecology of Human Development, Department of Human Development and Family Studies, Cornell University, Ithaca, New York 14853.

To control for motivation, home-reared children are selected from families desiring day care but not receiving it because of a shortage of places. Children in the two continuous day care settings (family and group) entered at six to nine months of age. A longitudinal design will follow all children to age five, including one mixed group raised at home for the first two or three years but then placed in a center for the remaining two or three. Hypotheses based on preliminary work already completed posit the greater adult-child interaction and limit-setting in the two home contexts versus greater peer interaction and control at centers will result in greater competence in the child's dealing with adults in the first instance, and with age-mates in the second. Analogous predictions are made for conformity to adult versus peer norms. Also the child's tendency to resort to verbal mediation in peer conflict situations is anticipated to be greater for home-reared children. In general, youngsters raised in family day care are expected to fall in between home and group reared children, but to resemble the former more than the latter.

Proposal II. Effects of Parental Involvement in Teacher Training. Working in poor residential areas in Mexico City, the investigator, Eduardo Almeida, offered an eight-week training course in child development, in one case for teachers alone, in another for teachers and parents together. In each region, one sixth-grade classroom was assigned to the experimental treatment (parents plus teacher) and another to the control group (teachers only). The weekly two-hour training sessions were conducted by persons who live and work in the immediate neighborhood. The general hypothesis of the study is that parental participation will result in enhanced motivation and learning on the part of pupils as a function of increased mutual understanding and convergent value commitments on the part of parents, teachers, and children.

Almeida has begun the analysis of his data, and some preliminary findings are available that are instructive both substantively and methodologically. The difference between the experimental and control group turned out to be significant on most outcome measures when tested against individuals within treatments, as is typically done in our journals. But none of the treatment effects were significant when tested against an appropriate error term based on differences between experimental and control classrooms within neighborhoods. This is so because the treatment was effective in some neighborhoods but not in others.

Pursuing this matter further, Almeida found reliable correlations between the child's gain score over the eight-week period and various measures of social class (in particular parent's educational level and the presence in the home of such items as newspapers and encyclopedias). But the relationships were significantly stronger at the level of classrooms than of individuals. Specifically, a child's gain score was better predicted not by the socio-economic status of his own family but by the average social class level of the children in his classroom. In other words, what counted most was not his own background but the background of his classmates. Since, in Almeida's research, the classmates all come from different schools, they also reflect neighborhood differences. In checking on these differences, Almeida discovered that the schools exhibiting greatest gains were located in neighborhoods with well developed social networks, such that families were in some communication with each other. Moreover, under these circumstances, not only the experimental classrooms, but those in the control group showed improvement, presumably as a function of horizontal diffusion.[29]

Such findings illustrate a serious limitation of the conventional, nonecological research design typically employed in experimental studies in our field. Usually the sample is drawn from a few classrooms (often only one) in one or two schools all in the same neighborhood, and all main effects and interactions are tested against an error term based on individuals. This means that any generalizations though founded on statistically significant results, are in fact limited to the particular classrooms, schools or neighborhoods represented—unless one assumes that there are no reliable differences across these domains with respect to the variables being tested. In our own experimental and field studies,[30] all of which have been carried out cross-culturally, we have found this to be an unwarranted assumption. Differences among neighborhoods, schools, and even classrooms within schools are the rule rather than the exception. Therefore to establish the existence of experimental effects, of cultural contrasts or even of such mundane phenomena as sex differences, it is necessary to show that the observed differences override variations at the classroom, school, or neighborhood level. Otherwise the generalization is limited to the particular contexts in

29. S.W. Gray and R.A. Klaus, "The Early Training Project: The Seventh-year Report," *Child Development,* 1970, *41*, 909–924.

30. U. Bronfenbrenner, "Response to Pressure from Peers vs. Adults among Soviet and American School Children," *International Journal of Psychology,* 1967, *2*, 199–207; U. Bronfenbrenner, *Two Worlds of Childhood: U.S. and U.S.S.R.* (New York: Russell Sage Foundation, 1970); E.C. Devereux *et al.,* "Child-rearing in England and the United States: A Cross-national Comparison," *Journal of Marriage and the Family,* May, 1969, *31*, (2), 257–270; E.C. Devereux *et al.,* "Socialization Practices of Parents, Teachers, and Peers in Israel: The Kibbutz vs. the City," *Child Development,* 1974, *45*, 269–281); J. Garbarino and U. Bronfenbrenner, "The Socialization of Moral Judgment and Behavior in Cross-cultural Perspective," in T. Lickona, ed., *Morality: A handbook of moral development and behavior* (New York: Holt, Rinehart, and Winston, in press).

which the research was carried out. This means, of course, that many of the findings reported in our research literature, including some of those most often cited, may actually be situation-specific.

Recognition of this fact poses serious difficulties for the design of ecologically valid experiments, for it means that the minimum N necessary for statistical generalizability is defined not by the number subjects, but by the number settings (e.g., classrooms, schools, neighborhoods) that these subjects represent. From this point of view, the most efficient design for social psychological studies, may be an analogue to the paradigm laid down by Brunswik for research on perception in his classic monograph "Perception and the representational design of psychological experiments;"[31] that is, each subject would be selected from and thus be representative of a different setting (i.e., classroom, school, neighborhood) so that the sample reflects variation not only across individuals but over contexts as well, thus increasing the range of generalizability.

Some "Unproposed" Proposals

As additional examples of ecological experiments, I offer below a series of research problems and designs that have not yet appeared in proposals thus far received, but would be appropriate should they materialize.

Hypothethical Proposal 1. Student Volunteers as a Support System for Singleparent Families. The stresses experienced by families in which the father is absent[32] and the growing number of such families in modern societies, poses a need to understand and to alleviate these stresses. An experiment designed to achieve this two-fold objective involves the following elements. College students enrolled in courses in child development are asked to volunteer as aides to mothers who are single parents of a preschool child. There are two treatment groups. In one, the student offers to take care of the child in order to give the mother free time to do whatever she wishes. In the second, the student asks what chores he can do in order to relieve the mother, so that she can spend time with her son or daughter. In a control group, the student merely visits the home to provide resource materials in child development. Single-parent mothers desiring some form of assistance are assigned to one of the three groups at random. Outcome measures include the mother's attitudes toward the child and toward her role as parent, and pat-

31. E. Brunswik, *Perception and the Representational Design of Psychological Experiments* (Berkeley: University of California Press, 1956).

32. Bronfenbrenner, *Two Worlds of Childhood*; H.B. Robinson *et al.*, "Early Child Care in the United States of America," *Early Child Development and Care*, 1973, *2*, 350–581.

terns of mother-child interaction in the home. The general hypothesis of the study is that maternal attitudes and patterns of interaction will be more positive in the two experimental groups than in the control group, with higher levels achieved when the volunteer offers to relieve the mother of household chores, than when he takes over responsibilities for child care.

Hypothetical Proposal 2. The Impact of High-rise Housing on Socialization Practice and Effects.   In case studies in journalistic reports, high-rise housing is often described as an unfavorable environment for raising children. The frequent presence of both high and low rise apartments in the same housing project presents an opportunity for investigating this issue with reference both to patterns of parent-child interaction and the behavior of the child outside the home in school and peer group. For the latter purpose, the dependent variables would be similar to those outlined in the preceding proposals.

Hypothetical Proposal 3. Enabling Parents to be Home When their Children Return from School.   A growing problem in contemporary American society is posed by the increasing number of "latchkey children"—youngsters who come home from school to an empty house.[33] Such children are especially prone to academic difficulties, school absenteeism and drop-out, juvenile delinquency, and drug addiction. An experiment designed to illuminate and counteract such effects involves obtaining the cooperation of an enterprise employing a large number of workers to introduce, on an experimental basis, flexible work schedules that would enable parents who wish to do so to be at home when their children return from school. The time would be made up by working other hours. A control group would be offered similar flexibility in working schedules but not during the time when children come from school. Effects of this policy would be observed in the changing attitudes of parents toward their children and in the behavior of the latter, with particular reference to the deviant patterns described above.

Hypothetical Proposal 4. Introducing Children to the World of Work.   This experiment is based on policy and practice presently followed in the U.S.S.R. In that society, every unit of economic production, such as a shop, office, institute, or other workers collective, is encouraged to "adopt" as a civic responsibility some group of

33.   U. Bronfenbrenner, Statement to the Senate Subcommittee on Children and Youth. Congressional Record, September 26, 1973, Volume 19, #142; Robinson, *et al., Early Child Care.*

children such as a classroom, hospital ward, or preschool group. The workers visit the children wherever they are, and invite them to visit in return. They take the children on outings, get to know their teachers and their parents—in sum, the adults and children become friends. In the expectation that an American business could be interested in undertaking a similar program, it is proposed to gauge its impact on the children's attitudes and behavior along the lines indicated in preceding proposals.[34] A control group might consist of children who merely "tour" places of work without establishing friendly associations with the workers themselves.

Hypothetical Proposal 5. Family and Individual Development as a Function of Position in the Social Network. This research investigates the thesis that the existence, strength, and value focus of the informal social network play a critical part in enabling, or when weak or countervailing, in disabling the family to function in its childrearing role. The social networks would be mapped by interviewing both parents and, separately, their children to establish patterns of acquaintance, mutual activity, and assistance in time of need (for example, illness, emergencies, or perhaps simply advice on family problems). Attention would be focused on the extent to which resources for companionship or help are found within the immediate neighborhood, across or within boundaries of age, sex, occupation, and other social parameters. Of particular interest is the degree to which the social networks of parents and children intersect for different age groups.

There are two classes of dependent variables. The first concerns the attitudes and expectations of the parents toward themselves and their children. Assessment would be made of their sense of personal control not only over their own lives but also with respect to their child's development, their satisfaction with the parental role, with the behavior and progress of their children, and with their aspirations and realistic expectations for the child's future. The second class of dependent variables relates to the child himself, specifically, how well he functions in two contexts outside the home—the school and his informal peer group.

The analysis will focus on determining whether parental orientations and child behaviors do vary systematically as a function of the informal social networks in which parent and child are

34. At the author's suggestion a demonstration program of this kind was carried out at the *Detroit Free Press* by David Goslin of the Russell Sage Foundation (Goslin, 1971). The program is described in a documentary film entitled "A Place to Meet, A Way to Understand," which is available from the Federal government (The National Audio-Visual Center, Washington, D.C. 20409). Unfortunately, it was not possible to attach a research component to the project.

embedded. But a research design of this kind, unfortunately, poses a problem in interpretation, for the causal process may actually operate in either or both of two opposite directions. Specifically, the social network may in this instance be not only a creator but a creature of family life—the product of characteristics of the family or of the child derived from other sources, perhaps even biological, but more likely social—such as family tradition, religious commitment, or patterns of life in the neighborhood in which the parents themselves had grown up.

This last illustration is representative of potential experiments of nature that permit at least a partial resolution of the issues surrounding causal direction. Other forms of natural experiments, however, are also possible. One final example will perhaps suffice.

Hypothetical Proposal 6. The Developmental Impact of Moving to a New Neighborhood.   As suggested by the preliminary results of Almeida's project, the neighborhood may exert a profound influence on the child's psychological development. This phenomenon could be investigated in an "experiment of nature" by identifying children in a large city school system whose families will be moving in the following year to another neighborhood in the same city. In a two-stage longitudinal research, interview and observational data could be obtained on the socio-economic, motivational and behavioral characteristics of the target children and their classmates both in the original neighborhood and the new one with the aim of identifying the impact of particular features of the neighborhood that instigate behavioral change. Although each child serves as his own control, comparative data would also be obtained on children who continue to live in or newly move into the original neighborhood, as well as those who have been living for some years in the new one.[35]

35. The idea for this research was suggested by the author's reanalysis (U. Bronfenbrenner, "Nature with Nurture: A reinterpretation of the evidence." In A. Montagu, ed., *Race and IQ.* New York: Oxford University Press, in press of data from published studies of identical twins reared apart cited by Jensen (A.R. Jensen, How much can we boost I.Q. and scholastic achievement? *Harvard Educational Review,* Winter, 1969, 1–123) in support of his claim that 80 percent of intelligence is genetically determined. To arrive at the 80 percent figure, Jensen made the assumption that the separated twins grew up in "uncorrelated environments" (p. 50). To test the validity of this assumption, the present author analyzed statistical and case study data provided in the original twin reports. Among other findings were the following:
a. Among thirty-five pairs of separated twins for whom information was available about the community in which they lived, the correlation in Binet IQ for those raised in the same town was .83; for those brought up in different towns, the figure was .67.

All of the foregoing proposals, both actual and hypothetical, are of course presented in incomplete form. The purpose is not to describe the design in its entirety, but only to illustrate how the general ecological model outlined in the main body of this paper can be implemented in concrete scientific experiments. Also, I wish to make clear that the facts and ideas that I have presented here are, in substantial measure, based on the work of others. What I have done is to bring together data and thought that is dispersed over time and topic in the published literature of the past few years. It has been my purpose to identify these scattered elements, consolidate them, and consider their implications for the direction and design of future research in human development.

In confronting this new research perspective, I offer a caveat no less to myself than to my colleagues. Those of us who are now active and experienced researchers were of course trained and socialized to use and value the research models and methods that now prevail in our field. If our theories of socialization are valid, however, it should be rather difficult for us to break out of our established modes of scientific thought and action. Try as we may, we are likely to regress to the kinds of formulations and analyses with which we are most familiar. This means that, if the ecological approach is indeed a promising one for our science, the major breakthroughs, both theoretical and empirical, will be accomplished not by the present cohort of established scientists, but by the younger generation of researchers just coming on the scene. It is for this reason that the grant program that I described gives priority to younger investigators. Our function is to give them support, and such wisdom as we have.

IMPLICATIONS FOR PUBLIC POLICY

We stated at the outset that an ecological perspective in human development carries implications not only for science but

---

b. In another sample of thirty-eight separated twins, tested with a combination of verbal and nonverbal intelligence scales, the correlation for those attending the same school in the same town was .87; for those attending schools in different towns, the coefficient was .66.

c. When the communities in the preceding sample were classified as similar vs. dissimilar on the basis of size and economic base (e.g., mining vs. agricultural), the correlation for separated twins living in similar communities was .86; for these residing in dissimilar localities the coefficient was .26.

also for public policy. We turn in conclusion to an examination of this issue.

Our analyses revealed a progressive deterioration over recent years, on the one hand, in the structure and position of the American family and, on the other, in the behavior and development of the nation's children. The data point to an obvious question of social policy and practice: What can be done to reverse these trends?

To the extent to which this problem has been recognized and addressed in the recent past, the principal focus of attention and programmatic effort has been the child, and in the context not of the family but of the school. At both the local and national levels, a variety of educational programs have been instituted, beginning at the preschool level, through Head Start, and extending into the elementary years via Follow Through and similar compensatory efforts, all designed to enhance, or at least prevent decline in, the all-round development of children, especially from low income families.

As we now know, the results of these educational strategies have proved disappointing. By and large, early intervention programs were effective while they lasted, but gains tended to wash out once the children entered school.[36] The only exception to this general trend occurred with programs emphasizing the direct involvement of parents in activities with their children. But the success of this approach was qualified by the realization that the families who were willing and able to participate in these programs tended to be the least disadvantaged among those eligible.

With respect to the effects of school programs, an impressive series of investigations, notably the studies published by James Coleman in 1966[37] and by Christopher Jencks in 1972,[38] demonstrate that the characteristics of schools, of classrooms and even of teachers, predict very little of the variation in school achievement. What does predict it is family background, particularly the characteristics that define the family in relation to its social context: the world of work, neighborhood, and community.

The critical question thus becomes: Can our social institutions be changed—old ones modified and new ones introduced—so as to rebuild and revitalize the social context that families and children require for their effective function and growth? Let me consider some institutions on the contemporary American scene that are likely to have the greatest impact, for better or for worse, on the welfare of America's children and young people.

36.   U. Bronfenbrenner, *Is early intervention effective?* (Washington, D.C.: Department of Health, Education, and Welfare, Office of Child Development. 1974).

37.   J.S. Coleman, *Equality of educational opportunity.* (Washington, D.C.: U.S. Office of Education, 1966).

38.   C. Jencks, *Inequality.* (New York: Basic Books, 1972).

1. Day Care. Day care is coming to America. The question is what kind. Shall we, in response to external pressures to "Put people to work" or for considerations of personal convenience, allow a pattern to develop in which the care of young children is delegated to specialists, further separating the child from his family and reducing the family's and the community's feeling of responsibility for their children? Or will day care be designed, as it can be, to reinvolve and strengthen the family as the primary and proper agent for making human beings human?

As Project Head Start demonstrated, preschool programs can have no lasting constructive impact on the child's development unless they affect not only the child himself but also the people who constitute his enduring day-to-day environment. This means that parents and other people from the child's immediate environment must play a prominent part in the planning and administration of day-care programs and also participate actively as volunteers and aides. It means that the program cannot be confined to the center but must reach out into the home and the community so that the entire neighborhood is caught up in activities in behalf of its children. We need to experiment with putting day-care centers within reach of the significant people in the child's life. For some families this will mean neighborhood centers, for others centers at the place of work. A great deal of variation and innovation, as well as administrative finesse of the sort prepared by Scanlon in Chapter 4, will be required to find the appropriate solutions for different groups in different settings.

2. Fair Part-Time Employment Practices Act. Such solutions confront a critical obstacle in contemporary American society. The keystone of an effective day-care program is parent participation, but how can parents participate if they work full time—which is one of the main reasons the family needs day care in the first place? I see only one possible solution: increased opportunities and rewards for part-time employment. It was in the light of this consideration that the report of the White House Conference urged business and industry, and government as employers, to introduce flexible work schedules (for example, to enable at least one parent to be at home when a child returns from school) and to increase the number and the status of part-time positions. Specifically, the report recommended that state legislatures enact a "Fair Part-Time Employment Practices Act" to prohibit discrimination in job opportunity, rate of pay, fringe benefits and status for parents who sought or engaged in part-time employment.

I should like to report the instructive experience of one state legislator who attempted to put through such a bill, Assemblywoman Constance Cook of New York. Mrs. Cook sent me a copy of her bill as it had been introduced in committee. It began, "No employer shall set as a condition of employment, salary, promotion, fringe benefits, seniority" and so on that an employee who is the parent or guardian of a child under eighteen years of age shall be required to work more than forty hours a week. Forty hours a week, of course, is full time; Mrs. Cook informed me that there was no hope of getting a bill through with a lower limit. It turned out that even forty hours was too low. The bill was not passed even in committee. The pressure from business and industry was too great, and they insisted on the right to require their employees to work overtime.

(There is a ray of hope, however. In the settlement of the United Automobile Worker's 1973 strike against the Chrysler Corporation a limit was placed for the first time on the company policy of mandatory overtime.)

3.   Enhancing the Position of Women.   These concerns bring me to what I regard as the most important single factor affecting the welfare of the nation's children. I refer to the place and status of women in American society. Whatever the future trend may be, the fact remains that in our society today the care of children depends overwhelmingly on women, and specifically on mothers. Moreover, with the withdrawal of the social supports for the family to which I alluded above, the position of women and mothers has become more and more isolated. With the breakdown of the community, the neighborhood, and the extended family an increasing responsibility for the care and upbringing of children has fallen on the young mother. Under these circumstances it is not surprising that many young women in America are in revolt. I understand and share their sense of rage, but I fear the consequences of some of the solutions they advocate, which will have the effect of isolating children still further from the kind of care and attention they need. There is, of course, a constructive implication to this line of thought, in that a major route to the rehabilitation of children and youth in American society lies in the enhancement of the status and power of women in all walks of life—in the home as well as on the job.

4.   Work and Responsibility.   One of the most significant effects of age segregation in our society has been the isolation of children from the world of work. Once children not only saw what their parents did for a living but also shared substantially in the task; now many children have only a vague notion of the parent's job and have had little or no opportunity to observe the parent (or for that matter any other adult) fully engaged in his or her work. Although there is not systematic research evidence on this subject, it appears likely that the absence of such exposure contributes significantly to the growing alienation among children and young people. Experience in other modern urban societies indicates that the isolation of children from adults in the world of work is not inevitable; it can be countered by creative social innovations and as Rubin illustrates in Chapter 9, by a more shrewd approach to policy determination. Perhaps the most imaginative and pervasive of these is the common practice in the U.S.S.R., in which a department in a factory, an office, an institute or a business enterprise adopts a group of children as its "wards." The children's group is typically a school classroom, but it may also include a nursery, a hospital ward or any other setting in which children are dealt with collectively. The workers visit the children's group wherever it may be and also invite the youngsters to their place of work in order to familiarize the children with the nature of their activities and with themselves as people. The aim is not vocational education but rather acquaintance with adults as participants in the world of work.

There seems to be nothing in such an approach that would be incompatible with the values and aims of our own society, and this writer has urged its adaptation to the American scene. Acting on this suggestion, David A. Goslin then at the Russell Sage Foundation, and now at the National Academy of Science, persuaded the *Detroit Free Press* to participate in an unusual experiment as a prelude to the White House Conference on Children. By the time it was over two groups of twelve-year-old children, one from a slum area and the other predominantly middle class, had spent six to seven hours a day for three days in virtually every department of the newspaper, not just observing but participating actively in the department's work. There were boys and girls in the pressroom, the city room, the advertising department and the delivery department. The employees of the *Free Press* entered into the experiment with serious misgivings, but as a documentary film[39] that was made of the projects makes clear, the children were not bored, nor were the adults—and the paper did get out every day.

The Fair Part-Time Employment Practices Act and the *Detriot Free Press* experiment are offered as examples, one in the public, the other in the private sector, of the kinds of innovations in policy and practice that are needed if we are to achieve the objective of rebuilding and revitalizing the social contexts that children and families require for their effective function and growth. But even more fundamental are three basic family support systems that are now being provided in every modern society except our own:

---

39. "A Place to Meet, A Way to Understand." (Washington, D.C. The National Audio-Visual Center.)

1. The United States is now the only industrialized
    nation that does not insure health care for every
    family with young children.

2. The United States is the only industrialized nation
    that does not guarantee a minimum income level
    for every family with young children.

3. The United States is the only industrialized nation
    that has not yet established a nationwide program
    of child care services for children of working
    mothers.

The roots of alienation go deep. Their correction will not be easy. But, it is far from impossible. What matters, therefore, is that we care enough to try.

commentary on bronfenbrenner ·

Bronfenbrenner's findings constitute a sobering message. If the trends he has documented continue, we are unquestionably on a dangerous path. There is more cause for alarm when we acknowledge that the scene he paints is but a partial representation of the overall difficulties in which we now find ourselves. Bronfenbrenner, a respected scholar, is not given to hyperbole; therefore, our circumstances, with respect to the nurturing of children must be regarded as serious.

The phenomena accounting for these circumstances are plainly marked: (1) the percentage of working mothers among divorced parents has risen steadily, (2) more infants are being born to unwed mothers, (3) the number of single-adult families is rising, and (4) fewer adults are available in the home for essential child care. Thus, extraordinary numbers of children are being reared in comparative isolation.

The question of the appropriateness of divorce (and even of single-adult families) is one that does not lend itself to an easy answer. While many of the children referred to by Bronfenbrenner are not particularly well-off without the sustained attention of their parents, they would be far worse-off without food. In many instances, divorce and singleness may be preferable to an unworkable relationship. Many men and women are, in the opinion of some psychiatrists, psychologically unfit for marriage. And the number of women who evidence an extraordinary ability to both work and provide their children with parental sustenance is not small. However, the fact remains, that in a good many instances children are being deprived of adequate contact with the important adults in their lives.

While Bronfenbrenner, understandably, does not engage in a lengthy analysis of the existing cultural scene—since his objectives lead in another direction—his evidence demonstrates, once again, that the solution to one social problem will very often give rise to other sorts of entanglements. The long overdue drive for female equality and independence, coupled with the concomitant effort of many women to gain some of the perquisites traditionally reserved for males has, not surprisingly, generated a greater degree of sexual freedom resulting in a far greater number of unwed mothers. Similarly, as divorce, in recent decades, has come to be regarded as an acceptable solution to interpersonal problems among married couples, the percentage of single-adult families has risen correspondingly. As rising human expectations shifted into high gear, many women (already bored with the drudgery of home-

making) entered the work force both as a means to additional income and as a further affirmation of their feminine independence. Thus, a good many children are separated from their mothers for long hours. Finally, inexpensive transportation and the geographical spread of the population have virtually eliminated the accessibility of extended family assistance in child care. The result of these disparate developments is the current situation described by Bronfenbrenner wherein one out of every six children under the age of eighteen lives in a single-adult family.

Many would argue that the changing family structure and the rising popularity of free relationships, as opposed to marriage, are beyond the legitimate concern of the schools. However, to the extent that family instability is a threat to societal health, such arguments are debatable. As drug abuse and environmental destruction became more critical, corrective programs were added to the curriculum. Serious attention is now being given to a revitalization of moral-civic education because the young may have lost their faith in the democratic process. Precedents for dealing with social problems in the curriculum exist in abundance.

During the 1960s the number of household heads, living apart from their families and cohabitating with an unrelated adult, increased six times. This trend, like the declining birth rate, the easing of provisions for divorce, and the growing incidence of unwed parents is attributable to personal belief and choice. Such choices are, properly, private matters and should remain so. This does not mean, nonetheless, that the schools should not endeavor to clarify the long-range consequences of these trends. New forms of the nuclear family, for example, may develop but, as Plato noted long ago, they will necessitate a fundamental reorganization of the social system. We could dispense with legal marriage and rely upon de facto family arrangements. However, even in this event, we would still find it necessary to respect the basic assumption that people who produce children are responsible for their welfare.

Moreover, the high rate of remarriage after divorce would seem to suggest that it is not marriage as an institution that is faltering but rather the relationships between particular husbands and wives. And, in what may be a slight reversal of the falling birthrate, there is new evidence that young couples are again manifesting a renewed interest in parenthood. If this pattern continues, the importance of family stability will increase correspondingly if children are to be protected from the ravages of parental self-absorbtion and narcissism. For all of these reasons, the school may have a legitimate role to play in the advancement of family solidarity, as long as it abstains from interfering in private matters.

The main issues we are now concerned with, then, are these: (1) What ill effects are likely to arise out of ongoing trends? and (2) What can schools do to offset these effects?

With respect to the first of these, Bronfenbrenner provides us with a few preliminary clues. The trends clearly suggest that a progressive fragmentation of the family is underway. Fathers and mothers, to an increasing extent, are separating, or at least pursuing separate concerns, and proportionately less time is being devoted to parenting. Children—particularly very young children —are therefore deprived of adequate attention from those who are chiefly instrumental in their growth and care. It is not difficult to speculate about the malignant consequences that could occur. The young victimized by such isolation may lose essential role models, particularly that of male and father. They are almost certain to suffer from insufficient nurturing, since the single working-adult has substantially less time and energy for the obligations of parenthood. In addition, the tensions of the child-parent relationship may be aggravated, if only because the usual stress-sharing among parents, characteristic of intact families, is no longer possible. Most frightening of all is the specter of children being left to fend for themselves during an exceptionally sensitive period in their formative development when adult contact is critical. One can only conjecture about the psychic disorders that could afflict these children later in their lives.

The consequence of all this is that the second issue takes on extreme importance: What reforms should the public system initiate in order to help children who have endured a family experience that is deficient and perhaps traumatic? Because the issue is complex, a number of secondary questions must be considered.

The ancient dilemma, for example, as to whether the schools should serve as socially compensating agencies once again becomes germane. Bronfenbrenner's position on this count is anything but ambiguous. He believes that new policies and support systems must be devised to counteract the dangers that are now manifest. It is also clear that he wants the schools to be an integral part of these compensatory support systems. Yet conservative-minded critics of liberal education will undoubtedly question, first, the school's ability to neutralize the detrimental effects of defective family experience, and second, the propriety of even attempting such intervention.

Many of the arguments over compensatory education for disadvantaged youth that were voiced during the early-sixties are again relevant. The controversies failed to produce any definitive conclusions; the end results were viewed by some observers as a monumental failure and by others as a promising beginning. Even if the intended correctives were in fact ineffectual, one need not assume that all other compensatory endeavors would be equally inconsequential. Logic suggests that until there is incontrovertible evidence that the schools are powerless to alleviate social distress, efforts should be sustained. As matters now stand, there is no real reason to assume that the right kind of counter-activities would not make a constructive difference in the lives of secluded children.

Other questions relate to what can be done in the curriculum to (a) offset the pernicious effects already suffered by deprived children, (b) diminish family fragmentation in the future, and (c) instill among present secondary-school youth a receptive attitude toward nontraditional arrangements for child care. These issues, in a sense, are of a piece: there are not three problems but rather one problem with three dimensions.

Provision must be made, seemingly, to enlarge the socialization experiences of children whose preschool social development has been blunted. At the same time we must do something to interrupt the present tides of neglect. In short, there are both prophylatic and curative aspects to the dilemma.

With respect to a prophylatic curriculum (one that might help utlimately to reduce child neglect) there is much to be said for many of the tactics suggested in the other chapters; for example, learning experiences that strengthen commitments to family life and to the responsibilities of parenting. A heavier emphasis on interpersonal skills, on the humanisitic elements of schooling, and on efforts to clarify role misconceptions with respect to feminine equality and autonomy would also offer considerable benefit. Much can be done to extend the sophistication of secondary-school students regarding the developmental needs of children, and to stress the consummate importance of sustained child-adult interaction. A prophylatic curriculum would be relatively easy to construct and might offer some long-range utility as a preventive mechanism.

On the other hand a curative curriculum—one that counterbalances inadequate or negative family experience—requires a good deal more inventiveness. It may be, for example, that male and female teacher teams—used in the primary grades as parent surrogates—could prove useful. The research data on the virtues of early childhood education remain a subject of contention. But it can scarcely be denied that youngsters are better off in an organized care center than in a home where, because of the prolonged absence of significant adults, their early years are characterized by endless loneliness.

A curative curriculum needs to place broader emphasis on disparate socializing activities. Expanded opportunity for sustained interaction with older students and adults, as well as experiences simulating the maturescent aspects of a healthy family life, might help in filling socialization voids. These arrangements need to be relatively flexibile, since it is unlikely that all deprived children require precisely the same sort of compensatory experiences. It might, in fact, be possible to organize nurturing experiences spontaneously, readjusting them as home situation and developmental level require.

From the way Bronfenbrenner sees things, a more powerful solution may lie in the creation of supporting acculturation systems outside the formal school. It is significant that he saw fit to address a section of his chapter to the question "Who Cares for America's Children?" implying perhaps that it is not the conventional trap-

pings of family life that matters most but rather the fulfillment of the caring function. The children of many divorced and unwed working-mothers—through various provisions—sometimes receive care as good as, or superior to, that provided in the typical intact family unit.

The support systems mentioned in the chapter might be patterned after prototypes that operate elsewhere in the world. In fact, it can be argued that the United States is akin to an under-developed country when it comes to state-supported child-care centers. Sweden offers comprehensive infant programs for virtually all preschool youngsters; Hungary makes nurseries and creches available to most of its children between the ages of three and six; and Israel provides health care for 90 percent of its young through a national network of mother and child clinics. There is no serious imposition on either the family organization or the parent-child relationship in any of these programs.

In his other writings, Bronfenbrenner has described the custom in China wherein grandparents meet children at the close of school so as to provide inter-generational contact and custodial care for children whose parents are at work. If working mothers are to become a permanent feature of American life, some form of extra-familial child supervision will be essential. It may, of course, become more commonplace for fathers to play a larger part in the management of households, but a total role-reversal seems improbable. And, the fads of the moment notwithstanding, it is not entirely certain that the presence of a female is totally dispensable in child-rearing.

The climbing divorce rate and the rising incidence of unwed mothers pose a rather different dilemma. Here, not mere customs but fundamental alterations in belief are involved. Irrespective of one's attitudes toward marriage and divorce, parenthood and responsibility should be regarded as inseparable. Every social order is based on some form of doctrine, and the acculturative process demands at least minimal orientation to the established system. What, then, should a curative curriculum advocate with respect to orthodox and unorthodox family patterns?

In deference to the majority opinion, the schools probably should continue to stress the virtues of family life. Throughout history few societies have long endured without a stable family, whatever its character, as the basic social unit. Circumstances could change, but until they do the schools must keep with convention. It is thus imperative that we look closely at values education that encourage students to embrace whatever beliefs they assume fitting. Ultimately, all of us, to be sure, choose our own life patterns. But if the schools are to be charged with the perpetuation of the social order, the young must be helped to ponder the consequences, both personal and societal, of whatever variant attitudes they happen to find attractive.

One of the most delicate aspects of curriculum-making lies in establishing a sensible equilibrium between conservative and radical postures. There is a neutral ground, easily overlooked, from which it is possible to illuminate both the insolvencies of custom and the potential virtues of a different ideology. It is this middle ground that must be sought in classroom appraisals of divergent values. While disparate beliefs go hand in hand with cultural pluralism, there must be some degree of consensus out of which can be fashioned a generally accepted body of precepts for the young. Without this consensus, no system of public education can accomplish its purpose.

The social problems that Bronfenbrenner describes are influenced by social attitudes. In a curative curriculum, they can only be countered through instruction that develops a strong commitment to the importance of family, the enjoinders of responsible parenthood, and a social system that provides for neglected children. One might also argue that the scope and intensity of the difficulties are so great that, without both symptomatic and preventive therapy, major catastrophies could occur.

The society must therefore respond with as much intelligence as it can muster. For schools, the obvious need is to teach more efficaciously than in the past, about the virtues of stable family life and the psychological nourishment children should receive from their parents, or parent-surrogates. These teachings should not gainsay the right of mothers to work, denigrate the benefits of high-quality child-care programs, or liken divorce to sin.

Family disintegration—like the abuse of drugs, the ravagement of the environment, and the exploitation of women—may, in time, disappear of its own accord. Logic suggests, however, that until this happens, the existence of the above should be made known to those still in school. Elise Boulding's contention (in Chapter 2) that children be taught an a-b-c of social conflicts is thus reiterated.

I do not mean to argue that the schools should uncritically preserve the status quo, or that the present social order connot be improved on. I mean, instead, to argue that since profound tragedies can occur when children are fostered without adequate care, remedies must be found. As Bronfenbrenner demonstrates, one such remedy involves child-support systems that help to offset the detriments of massive urbanization. Another lies in making the citizenry, both child and adult, aware of unsuspected dangers. Such awareness is the essence of what was once called consciousness-raising.

Our historians tell us that few forces are truly inexorable and, therefore, human events are almost never immutable. Let us then tell the children, through a rational curriculum, about the problems humankind must combat. Let us teach that our old ways are not sacred and that new ones are needed. But newness alone is not enough; that which is different must also be better.

Finally, a word must be said about Bronfenbrenner's recommendations with respect to educational research. In educational writing, it is comparatively rare for a single essay to analyze a significant social problem, trace its etiology, explore implied modifications in research policy, and depict—through tangible illustrations—the kinds of experimental endeavors that are needed. In these regards, the author's own rhetoric speaks for itself.

Bronfenbrenner shows us that the structure of family life in America is changing; that enviromental factors are more important than racial ones in regulating the development of children; that our society badly needs some form of substitute care for the children of working parents; and that economic deprivation, age segregation, and inadequate medical services together impose a massive hardship on many of our young. He then speculates about a variety of ameliorating activities that might be undertaken by the scholarship community.

He suggests, for example, that research performed in artificial and constrained settings is of less utility than that conducted in the natural environment; that experiments incorporating the multiple variables impinging upon a problem are more useful than those that do not; and that the long-term potency of research depends on the extent to which it generates explicit social policy implications, and provides realistic comparisons of optimal solutions to real problems. He asks that research, rather than content itself with a detached and dispassionate inquiry into social dilemmas, become an active instrument for responsible social change. Thus, he describes an agenda of scholarly investigation, relating to family life, wherein researchers strive toward assessing the feasibility of flexible work schedules for parents of young children; perpetuating family development through experimental use of informal social networks; testing the potential of students as voluntary aides in a family support system; and generally measuring the impact of planned "ecological" changes. In his own apt phrase he asks for "experiments of nature."

The chapter's value is threefold; it documents forces contributing to a decline in family stability; it outlines a different conception of educational research that may offer greater efficacy than the traditional mechanisms; and, finally, to point the way, it sets forth the components of desirable support systems. All of which comes, by any measure, to a sizable contribution.

L.R.

Issues •

1. What kinds of research methodology facilitate the experimental investigation of significant problems in actual settings?

2. If, as the evidence seems to suggest, children are influenced by their peers to a greater extent than in the past, can peer-pressure be capitalized upon in constructive socialization?

3. What can be done to increase research that is designed, among other things, to initiate social improvement?

4. Since great benefit would derive from educational research in which the variables are based upon social reality, in which different ecological systems are compared, and in which there are efforts to extract policy implications, what modifications in the training of educational researchers are necessary?

5. In view of the impending enlargement of Day Care and Early Childhood Education, what, if any, curricular revisions will be necessary in the early primary grades?

6. Since the welfare of children is inseparable from the welfare of their families, needed improvements in the educational system cannot be accomplished without corresponding improvements in the social system itself. Therefore, should social experimentation and educational research occur in tandem, or should experimentation preceed research?

7. In a time when the schools suffer from diminished credibility, parental satisfaction with the educational system is crucial. Would it, then, be advisable (a) to fulfill existing parental expectations, irrespective of their rationality, (b) to take steps to clarify, for parents, the probable outcomes of alternative educational programs, or (c) both?

8. It is widely assumed that one of education's significant purposes is to enable the child to cope with present and future life-problems. As a consequence, the criteria for assessing educational effectiveness should, at least in part, relate to success in peer-groups and home-life. What evaluation techniques are most useful in this regard?

9. Can the traditional school pattern, wherein learners are segregated by ages, be altered without excessive or unmanageable difficulties?

elise boulding
university of colorado

2

LEARNING TO MAKE NEW FUTURES

Technological futurism and visionary futurism are two very different perspectives on the world. In these pages there is a very powerful presentation of visionary futurism at its best, but the euphoria it creates must not draw our attention away from the fact that educators in their daily work are far more affected by another breed of futurists entirely—the technological futurists. The technologists operate inside mega-bureaucracies and produce solutions to the problems of human welfare that frequently worsen human conditions.

Herbert Spencer warned nearly a hundred years ago against planning because whatever planners tried to do, things would always come out differently than anticipated. We now have a century of experience of this truth. Wars entered into as a matter of national policy have never come out as intended—not for any nation. Population policy has never affected to any noticeable extent, the behavior of society's child-bearers. Women reduce or increase the size of their families in response to promptings other than those of policy-makers. Urban planners are never more than one step ahead of disaster, while the human beings for whom they plan struggle on their own to find other ways to humanize the neighborhoods they live in—providing small but significant affirmations of another future. Some folk are exploring the countryside again. In 1976, for the first time in U. S. history, there was no further drop in the number of farmers, rather a slight increase.

The visionary futurists stand outside the social traps. They are listeners. They know intimately all the social sounds that technological futurists are too busy to hear. They have somehow escaped being insulated from primary social processes. There are community insulation systems that keep educators, planners and

57

policy-makers from knowing their own society. These insulation systems are the most tragic features of contemporary industrial society. Moving along on their own special tracks, administrators continually ask "What's new?" but don't stop to hear the answer. What is missing from technological futurism?

On the one hand, we have a sense of the cosmic event stream, the long, long view such as we get from a very few highly gifted visionaries and glimpse in these pages through the eyes of Buckminster Fuller and Jonas Salk, (Chapters 5 and 6). On the other hand, we have a recognition of the fragility of life, a reverence for micro-environments and the rich diversity of life that niches make possible; a reverence for intuitional knowledge about the human condition. Finally, what is missing is an understanding of the functions of solitude and withdrawal, processes that must take place from inside the social web, in order to create deeper and more meaningful bonds among humans.

Eloquence about the spaceship earth and the crowded planet has on the whole not opened up new vistas of how to think, feel and behave as humans. It has not led us to an exploration of the joys of frugality, nor to a personal recognition that the earth-family sits at one table and is fed from one farm, the earth farm. It has not increased our respect, to say nothing of love, for one another, nor our skill in getting along together. It has certainly not opened up new understanding about the inner spaces of the human spirit, that arena we are now urged to explore because outer space puts so many limitations on us.

In short, technological futurism has missed most of the key potentials for that other tomorrow. The potential in the development of an ethic of frugality is enormous, and is a logical extension of the realizations that have come with the limits-to-growth analysis of the planetary system. Yet we save frugality for holidays, when we go camping or backpacking, taking our joy in what we can carry on our backs, in needing so little. This we do only *for fun*. Or we send our emissaries to the moon, in a kind of space backpacking venture, thrilled to realize what a stripped-down existence human beings can live and work in. The desire to test our capacities at the very margins of the possibility of human life, in space, on mountain tops, at the bottom of the sea, is still strong. But for daily life, crude and foolish abundance is our preference.

By the same token, technological futurists encourage us to scorn labor-intensive activity in our work life. We save our joy in craftwork for the hobby shop in the basement and for the embroidery basket. We produce in leisure hours finely wrought objects by an expenditure of effort and skill we would reject for our regular daily work. We even buy more hours for leisure-time craftwork by installing increasingly automated push-button mechanisms in kitchen and office, carefully removing every element of craft from our so-called productive labor.

Another potential untapped by technological futurism is our delight in human-to-human love, in watching children grow, in helping another in distress—basic human traits expressed in every conceivable type of cultural setting. Instead of drawing on that potential for creating new planetary distribution systems that move food from over-full larders to empty ones, we draw national boundaries more tightly, and put our trust in deterrence systems and uptight diplomats.

Our centuries-old love affair with the universe, sung by poets, captured in movement, music, visual image and austere equations, is uncelebrated by blue-print style futurism. This enduring love affair points to a set of spiritual-intuitive capacities that keep welling up in us humans, capacities that cry out to be linked with our carefully husbanded cognitive and analytic skills that bring us into new kinds of social spaces. We squelch these impulses firmly, replacing them with programmed responses known as socialization, beginning with the very young child. Or, since they cannot be completely squelched, we sterilize them by a careful policy of apartheid: all such impulses shall be expressed in clubrooms, playgrounds, museums, concert halls, and occasionally in churches—very rarely in schools.

Planner-type futurists are not to blame for this. They are the victims, not the creators, of society. What has to be recognized now is the extent to which we have all, particularly educators, been confined by powerful but invisible insulation systems that have made it possible to ignore a vast realm of human experience, to be deaf to clamorous potentials. Technology has created this insulation, so that we feel neither heat nor cold, wind nor rain, love nor hate, and never know what phase the moon is in unless we look at a calendar. Technology lets us travel the world's jetways freely, seeing nothing. Perhaps the worst feature of the twentieth century is its pseudo-mobility—the constant movement through one-dimensional social and physical space without ever discovering the multi-dimensionality of reality. It is as if we are forever recreating the famous inspection trip of royalty down the Nile—all the cozy villages are pasteboard, all the cheerfully waving people are make-believe. The last time there was any major questioning of this insulation phenomenon brought about by technology was during the back-to-nature romantic revival in England a hundred years ago. At that time there was a whole spate of utopian novels that leap-frogged technology into a past or a future that brought people close to the earth again. Since everyone knew perfectly well that this was nonsense given existing population densities and existing new technological solutions to human problems, it was easy to reject the movement. The whole American counter-culture and "Greening of America" phenomenon was simply a replay of the earlier romantic revival (nothing new was added except to call the old art, art nouveau). This has made it all the easier to reject it.

The result of "seeing through" these romanticized attempts at breaking out of a technologized society has been an increasing acceptance of the insulation systems it creates. Only long habitation to such insulation can account for the kind of military subculture we have today, a subculture that goes on risking the future of the planet with its toys. Or account for the intellectual subcultures of our universities and research institutes, spinning thought webs that never connect with the daily subsistence reality of 99/100ths of the world's population. Or for the development expert's subculture, exporting industrial technology to nonindustrial societies to destroy existing labor-intensive productivities on farms and in craft-shops, to replace them with soil-destroying technology and a mode of organizing production that creates vast reservoirs of unemployment. Only a massive insulation from reality makes possible continuing mistakes of such magnitude on the part of intellectuals. No feedback on consequences of actions ever penetrates the technological shield to enter the minds and consciousness of the military, the intellectual, or the development specialist.

One structural feature of American society that is a key support of the social insulation system and one that is largely created and maintained by our educational institutions, is age-grading. Age-grading means that toddlers will be kept with toddlers, kindergartners with kindergartners, elementary, junior high and senior high with their own, college and young married with their own, young parents with their own, middle years and retireds and golden age folk with their own. We move right through life in lock-step fashion, with our own age group. We all dry out on our own little twigs, never nourished by the freshness of different perceptions of folk in other age groups, on other parts of the vine, never experiencing that we are all branches of the one vine.

An inevitable response in this century to conditions of increased population densities, it has now become a pathological condition. Age-grading produces a kind of social autism and mutual distrust between those who must be partners in the reconstruction of society—the adult and the young; it prevents the development of common images of the future and common definitions of social responsibility; it keeps each group from teaching the other what it knows.

The kindergarten through twelfth grade system provides the basic frame for societal age-grading and offers the rationale for all the other age-linked structural limitations we place on people. The administrative mentality that has created a market for schoolbooks using a tightly age-graded system also patterned our lives into a series of institutionalized age-segregated experiences that confines the wisdom of the aged to the shuffle board. In a school environment where every developmental phase in a child's life becomes the specialty of some adult on a payroll, it becomes an exciting new specialty to create a program in which sixth graders come in to help first graders with their reading. Yet this learning-by-teaching device was absolutely basic to the one room school house learning of the previous century. The age-graded classroom, no matter how well stocked with enrichment materials, is an environment of deprivation.

Not only is it an environment of deprivation for children, it absolutely guarantees, because of the basic power structure inherent in the classroom setting, that children are excluded from all significant dialogues about the changes that need to take place in the educational system. To talk of a child-adult partnership in shaping the future, though this is what we need, is under the circumstances empty rhetoric. Educators by and large (there are exceptions) do not intend that children and young people shall have any effect at all on the system within which they are educated. And even if they did there is the shadow behind them of the community power structure, which is even more committed to the nonparticipation of children in social change.[1]

What I am saying is that schools, acting on behalf of society, have effectively cut children off from society. This is a situation with terrifying implications, as Urie Bronfenbrenner (Chapter 1) has pointed out. It leaves the family, weak as it is, as almost the only institution left in society for cross-age communication, not structured by the impersonal authority relationships of schools and helping services.[2] Because the child-parent relationship has to bear the whole burden of communication between age sets, it often breaks down under emotional overloading and cannot carry out one of the most important functions left to it. Even with all the handicaps placed on the family, and all the strains and pathologies it is subject to, it remains a significant common experience for all its members,

1. The issue of community power structures, and the radical critique of what is wrong with our schools, deserves close attention but is not gone into here. Miriam Wasserman's *Demysitifying Schools: Radical Writings and Experiences*, (New York: Praeger, 1974) deserves a lot of careful thought.

2. Elise Boulding, "Familism and the Creation of Futures," (Paper presented to The American Anthropological Association, November 19, 1971); and "I and Thou: The Child-Adult Relationship in The Society of Friends," (Lecture presented at the Friends General Conference in Philadelphia, January, 1975)

and a place where perceptions are shared out of different perspectives determined by different decades of birth. Let us consider this phenomenon of family sharing of experience and compare it with the kind of cross-generation sharing that happens in the classroom. Inquiring year by year about the family experience of my own students at the college level, I find that more sharing goes on in these families than is reflected in the popular press or in research on families. Since both popular writers and researchers are usually oriented to identification of pathologies or of alternative solutions to the family as a primary living group, the positive experience fund of family life tends to be ignored.

In a Social Change class of fifty students that I am currently teaching, consisting of a typical population of young people, largely middle class, of the Southwest of the United States with a few Easterners and Far Westerners thrown in, only two students have never felt close to either parent, and only half of them have never been close to a grandparent. Some of them have been close to two or three, several to all four grandparents. When they reflect on the themes of the stories and communications that have come to them from grandparents and parents, it is a rich variety of life experience of pioneer struggle, surviving the depression, of life on the farm, at sea and of tales of family adventures. It is also a rich blend of philosophies of life—how to find fulfillment in a range of patterns including the extremely hedonistic, the compassionate service-oriented, and the driving work-for-success style. While these students have been through many crises with their families, crises of bereavement, serious illness, alcoholism, bankruptcy, unemployment, marital problems and divorce, most of them have found ways to stay in communication with their parents. A third of them mention special family gatherings as one of the greatest joys of growing up, and one of the most important continuing influences in their lives. A fifth of them have experienced three-generation households, at some time in their lives. And all of them have, at least occasionally, been listened to. Their experience has also entered the family knowledge stock. The richness of this shared familial experience, incidentally, is of another order of magnitude than the TV experience, which has been much inflated as a source of personal growth for the young.

What is the comparable sharing in the classroom? The authority of the teacher impedes an easy two-way flow of life experiences, though sharing can certainly take place. The philosophy of gearing the curriculum to "where the child is" hardly takes account of the need for the child to learn to articulate her inner knowledge in order to have the experience of contributing to the creation of the knowledge stock.

As teachers, we should reflect on the significance of the fact that the family is the one place where human beings are not, except in pathological cases, insulated from the human dimension of reality. There they experience reality, and to a far greater degree than generally recognized, they deal with it, accept pain as growth, and recognize the need for continuing human relationships and loyalties even in the face of great differences. The divorce and recombination rate, now the highest in American history and in the world, may be very misleading. It has been pointed out how often divorce and recombination in fact develop a kind of extended family with former spouses continuing to take responsibility for one another.[3] While marital struggles are painful, they do represent an attempt to deal with reality, and the family is almost the only part of the social system that provides immediate feedback to individuals in our society. What can the educator learn from this? For the teacher, parents are often the enemy, and the family the influence that subverts the work of the school, particularly in the case of minority families. Rather than abusing the family, the educator might find it productive to examine ways in which other parts of the social system including the school could also develop person-oriented feedback processes and thus take some of the load off the family for bearing the brunt of the technological society.

I have been hammering away on this point about insulation from reality because I think it is the greatest challenge facing our educational system today. Schools are supposed to teach about reality, not insulate from it. If, as Tyler suggests in Chapter 8, our schools must be responsive to a changing society, is it too extreme to suggest that they do not teach about reality? The easiest way to deal with that question is to define what we teach, or what we work with, as reality. Using that approach, any school curriculum comes equipped with a built-in justifying mechanism. The technological futurist and the planner use the same mechanism. The technological shell is reality. The cybernetic systems that tell us how the shell is doing are the only significant feedback systems in society, and the adjustments we make to keep the shell in working order or to improve it are the only significant reality-coping acts. It is an appealing argument, particularly because it is so obvious that the technological shell is indeed a reality. The problem comes when we ask how much of the larger reality that we need to take account of for human welfare, is included in the technological shell.

Is it significant that most people who have been through high school, a lot of people who have been through college, and a surprising number of people who have Ph.D.'s, feel that they never learned how to *do* anything? People of all ages, not just college students, will tell you that whatever they have learned to do, in the way of di-

3. Paul Bohannon and John Middleton, eds., *Kinship and Social Organization*, (New York: The Natural History Press, 1968).

rectly dealing with people, systems, production roles of any kind, they have learned outside of formal schooling. The drive to specialize is the drive to get a little corner on reality, to feel that one can *do* something, by manipulating that corner. We are all on assembly lines, and the experience of completion is rare. Even the small daily completion of household tasks available to householders are politicized and rejected because they are usually linked to an oppressive division of labor.

The despairing cry of the graduating senior, "What am I going to *do*?" is heard by every college teacher annually. Senator Schweiker's apprehensions regarding vocational incompetence serve as a case in point. Today not even teaching is left as a job possibility, except for a lucky few. The felt helplessness shows up in many ways. It begins with pre-teenage suicide. While the teenage suicide rate has more than doubled in the past decade, suicides at ages eleven and twelve have shown the greatest increase. We are all aware how the helplessness shows up in escape into the world of drugs. We may be less aware of increases in alcoholism. Homicide rates have also doubled in the past decade, and the old regional differences in homicide rates, which left New England a complacently nonviolent society compared to the urban south, are now disappearing in a homogenizing wave of violence. Homicide is of course one of the most pathological forms of helplessness a society can produce. It signifies helplessness both of the murderer and of the victim. Neither has found alternative courses of action.

There is really something odd about the widespread feeling of helplessness in our society. It is found both in those with the most, and in those with the least, education. We have covered it over with talk about competence, and tried to assuage the feeling with a philosophy of competency-based learning. Competence in what? Our capacity for self-delusion is almost infinite. In order to deal with an increasingly comfortless physical and social enviornment, and inner helplessness, we utilize our technology to project on our mental screens images of a continuous process of environmental construction and redesign. We think we are experiencing rapid change, that we are a progressive, creatively adaptive society, when in fact it is all done with mirrors, and we are instead becoming increasingly rigid. It is no accident that Plato's cave analogy is cropping up so often in writing today. All we see are the shadows on the wall. The reality is somewhere out there behind us. But we are protected from that knowledge because of the immediately persuasive character of the technologies we are developing. In fact, whether they deal with the prolongation of life, with moving us or our ideas more quickly around the planet, or with making it still easier to clean immaculate middle-class homes, they are about as useful to us in light of plane tary needs as the dinosaur's unwieldy skeleton was to her. While the technology of miniatures exists that could free us from this skeleton, in fact we utilize technology to develop ever-larger administrative systems and to reduce individual freedom. Will we go the way of the dinosaur?

Where do the persistent illusions of competence come from? In part, from a misreading of history. Every teacher carries somewhere in the back of her mind the image of the British Empire, and of the British school system preparing eager young men to go out and shape the world through the study of Latin and Greek. It is an elitist, anti-craft view of education, and it worked in places like India because these young men had countless skilled craftworkers, women and men, at their disposal. Even more, they had an existing infrastructure of administrative skill from a far older civilization to work with. It is the mandarin tradition in history, and it is odd that the most progress-oriented society in the world should have bought it. As long as the majority of young people went directly into the factory or apprenticed to a craft trade it did not matter, for only a few received the mandarin's education and their helplessness was shielded from view. Now nearly everyone goes to high school. The big battle today is to keep the expanding junior college system in the mandarin tradition also, not to let it become craft education. The resulting helplessness can no longer be shielded from view.

History has its own logic, and it is in China, the home of the mandarin system, that the first breakthrough has come in requiring a combination of craft and intellectual analytic training for everyone. The bureaucrat and the intellectual are now supposed to spend time in factory and field in regular rotation, and farmer and factory worker are to do their stint in the bureaucratic system. Impossible? Absurd? Let's wait and see. If they fail, we will only have learned that this kind of rotation is very hard to accomplish, that old social habit structures are very hard to break. In the meantime, we Euro-Northamericans must solve our own problems in our own way, and a major component of our problems is the feeling of helplessness of our school-trained population.

An educational system with classroom-based teaching as its major focus can do little to deal either with that helplessness, or with the social rigidities that make it so difficult to improve our urban environment and our welfare and health systems. It is the classroom model of the world that makes it possible for us to misallocate resources so that millions of dollars go into advanced medical research while we do not even provide the equivalent of the Chinese "barefoot doctors" for vast numbers of our population. The classroom model of the world is responsible for the funneling of millions of dollars into computer simulation of urban systems, while the urban poor remain persistently outside all the redistribution systems that administrators devise. The classroom model structures societal helplessness.

Few systems planners today would disagree that our models need to be improved. Decentralism and the associated problems of how to increase the number of decision points in the lower reaches of any system and how to increase local involvement in decision making are now important issues. There is experimentation with completely nonhierarchical systems of decision-making. This is a difficult area, because decentralist decision-making, the antidote to helplessness, vastly increases the amount of necessary social communication. We are still so impressed with the efficiencies of hierarchical organization that we are unwilling to face that increased communication load. Since those efficiencies are in fact fast disappearing in the face of new problems of scale with current population densities, we really don't have any choice but to reexamine the possibilities of decentralist, nonhierarchical social organization. The illusions of administrative efficiency in modern society can no longer be maintained.

The only hope of breaking out of the rigidities of hierarchical systems, based on patterns with centuries of societal role-models behind them, is to begin in the educational system, society's womb. Given the experience with educational experiment of our generation, it hardly seems the most promising place to start. Yet how else are we to work at the reincorporation of some of the best educational features of the craft society we have left behind into the new, mini-technology localist society that may hold the best promise for the future? The challenge is, how not to go backwards into the very real rigidities of the older craft society where every villager was a prisoner of the village guild association, but to go forward into a more fluid localist society where travel and communication keep open the doors that have been shut for the masses both in industrial and pre-industrial society. This is the Gandhian ideal of a world network of villages, and its details have yet to be explored.

The concept of the neo-village school, or the community-centered school, is hardly a new one. We have witnessed a number of efforts in this direction in the past couple of decades, particularly in our major urban centers. Philadelphia has been the home of some of the best of these efforts. They are for the most part one-school experiments, highly fragile and often short-lived. Perhaps the most successful versions of these efforts are in areas like the San Luis Valley in Colorado, where Spanish-speaking populations have simply withdrawn their children from a public school system that was educating their children to incompetence and failure by systematically forbidding those children to draw on their own hard-earned knowledge stock. Such parents have created their own community schools in which children and adults alike learn the skills they need to function productively, and with self-respect and joy, in the region in which they live. In situations like this every adult becomes both a teacher and a learner, every child both an apprentice and a teacher of those younger than herself. The school itself becomes a skills center, linked to the community in numerous ways. What would it mean for a larger town or city to recreate its entire educational system along these lines?

Archibald Shaw suggested this in a pioneering proposal entitled "The Random Falls Idea" as far back as 1956.[4] It has never gotten even close to actual trial, and yet it holds the answer to many of our most pressing problems. His proposal involves:

> Turning the school into a headquarters, and the entire community into a complex of learning sites. This would involve a substantial redeployment of personnel and resources in our public schools, as well as a substantial redefinition of the relationship between school and community, teachers and community persons, adults and children. The school headquarters provides classroom teaching for very specific skills, and the rest of the learning takes place in a variety of apprenticeship situations which are arranged between pupils and every adult in the community at his place of work. Figure 2–1 diagrams the school-community relationship in terms of learning sites. A substantial part of the school personnel, now engaged in classroom teaching or in-house administrative work, would be developing and coordinating the numerous linkages which would be needed to ensure that every adult in the community spent some time in a teaching relationship with pupils at his place of work.[5]

This of course could produce a horrendous new bureaucracy, unless the linkage persons themselves were also involved in community-based productive work. Previous experiments have broken down largely because linkage persons have remained outsiders, resented by the community. They have appeared as advocates of second-class education for minority children, (perpetuating the social discrimination Chisholm describes in Chapter 3) and have served as a

4. Archibald B. Shaw, "The Random Falls Idea," *The School Executive*, March, 1956.

5. Elise Boulding, "New Approaches to Learning," (Paper prepared for the Science Education Commission of the American Association for the Advancement of Science, 1971.)

force to deprive the already deprived of chances to enter the success system the outside innovator remains cosily esconced in. Part-time employment at various apprenticeship sites in the community for all persons associated with the educational system may be part of the answer here. This breaks down the specialist role of both the teacher and the administrator. There would naturally be enormous resistance to this. Think of the resistances, and also the potentials, in a project of turning all labor union headquarters, including teacher's unions, into learning sites for children. Only community-wide demonstration experiments can break down fears and show the potentialities of such an approach.

As community adults find themselves in teaching roles they never had before, new questions and problems arise from them, new curiosities will be stimulated, and they too will seek the special knowledge skills provided by the headquarters school. The apprentice system of the pre-industrial era, reintroduced in a much more sophisticated way with the aid of modern communications and coordination technology, could humanize both education and work. It could break down the age-graded social system which keeps young and old from participating jointly in the two-way communication and learning process every society requires for survival. The mutual mistrust of the young and the not-so-young today is proverbial. Most communities would be panicked at the thought of turning children and young people loose all over the community to "learn," and it will be years before a workable program along these lines can be developed in a form that will be usable by and acceptable to the average community. On the other hand, the work of Shaw in beginning to spell out the logistics in the Random Falls Idea is of incalculable value. Far-seeing school systems could begin now to reassign some of their staff, and find new staff, to begin the long slow job of analyzing the community as a potential learning site. New building programs will become irrelevant with the new minimum-type use of school as headquarters. The resources saved can be used in mapping the community to identify all the relevant sites as suggested in Figure 2-1, in working with the community to develop the new mechanisms for recruiting its adults as teachers in their own places of work, and in making provision for the numerous physical and coordination details involved.

When new headquarters space is needed, all types of existing buildings can be used in lieu of the large multi-purpose schools we now know. With the entire

community as the learning site, the headquarters can
be widely spaced, and communications technology can
facilitate the necessary information flow.[6]

This kind of approach to education is counter-intuitive, in
that it goes against all developments in educational specialization,
and against the basic concept of the highly differentiated occupation and service structure of the modern community. We get
glimpses of its possibilities in looking at the work of the Community
Technology group initiated by Karl Hess and associates in the
Adams-Morgan District of Washington, D.C.[7] Here is a group of
highly specialized scientists using their knowledge to create self-
sustaining communities, producing their own food and fuel right in
the midst of the city, and developing self-help social structures to
match their production skills. Residents are being gradually drawn
into a participatory town meeting that can reshape the local institutions to meet the needs of the residents. The community-based
school involving all residents as teachers becomes very natural
when the local carpenters and locksmiths and maintenance and repair people are already active in the community council along with
the white collar workers who commute to the desks of the nation's
bureaucracies. Such efforts are of course fragile, and highly subject
to distortion by acts of absentee landlords who stand entirely outside these participatory structures (by their own preference). When
the contradictions in the present system become great enough, such
community ventures will succeed, simply because they represent
the emergence of competence, and of problem-solving ability, in the
midst of helplessness. The irony is that such competence, our greatest resource in the helpless technological society, is perceived as a
threat by the supposedly innovative and forward-looking sectors of
society. The Foundation world has not supported this type of venture.

The whole issue of nonformal education needs to be reexa-
mined, in the context of the urgent need to learn of children and
adults. Johan Galtung's study of trends in nonformal education at
the University of Oslo, part of a general study of trends in Western
society, points to an increasing bureaucratization of all forms of
adult education.[8] All incipient learning opportunities are being captured into administrative systems that reduce the freedom to re-

6. Elise Boulding, New Approaches to Learning.
7. Nicholas Wade, "Karl Hess: Technology with a Human Face," *Science,* 187,
(January 31, 1975), 332-334.
8. Johan Galtung, "On Macro-history and Western Civilization," The Trends in
Western Civilization, Number 1 University of Oslo, Chair in Conflict and Peace
Research, 1974.

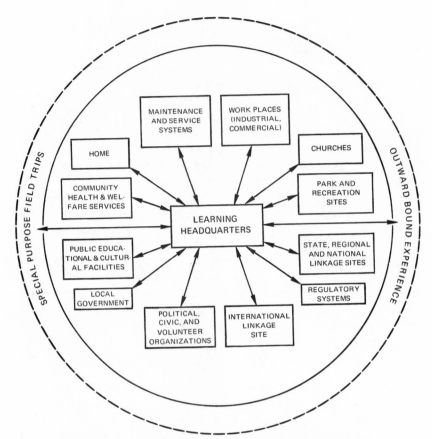

Figure 2-1.   Community Learning Sites. From Elise Boulding, "New Approaches to Learning," a paper prepared for the Science Education Commission of the American Association for the Advancement of Science, 1971.

spond to local needs. While it is happening faster in the United States, it is happening in Europe too. Administrators who are insulated from the realities of local teaching-learning situations organize systems that become increasingly expensive to operate, requiring increasing charges to would-be students, and making the curriculum offerings increasingly unrealistic in terms of local needs.

What is happening to nonformal education is happening to a far greater degree to formal education. The rationalization for this seems clear enough. Education is a highly complex specialization, and should be in the hands of professionals who possess the sensitivities and skills outlined by Scanlon (Chapter 4). It is understandably hard to take the idea of community-based learning seriously in light of the proliferation of free schools and alternative schools in the past few years that have confused nonstructure and freedom of movement with learning. What *is* the best way to structure the learning situation? Oddly, the dynamics of the learning process, in spite of decades of research on learning, still elude us.

The failure to teach competence and "copability," which I have been emphasizing here, is paralleled by the failure to generate moral development and consciousness of civic responsibility, whether at the local, national or world level. Keniston, Kohlberg and others have pointed out to us in a variety of writings that Western society, the most literate society in human history, is in a state of incredible moral underdevelopment. The average person cannot transcend the most limited interests, and altruism is considered an abnormal trait, fit for preaching but not for behavior. We do not lack research knowledge on the generation of altruism. The development of learning situations that take account of relevant genetic substrates and predispositions to nurturance and altruism in the child, is perfectly possible with existing knowledge. Educational approaches that take into account the whole range of human response potentialities can vastly increase the proportion of altruistic over aggressive responses in both children and adults, and this does not require the use of mechanically applied behavioral modification routines.[9]

Why is this aspect of pedagogy so removed from classroom practice? Much of the blame for this lies in the value orientations of the larger society, but part of it lies in the insulation of the classroom itself from society, and the narrow range of experiences that we define as appropriate formal learning. The general requirement that all children from kindergarten on deal with knowledge in the verbal-analytic mode, the mode used in class recitations, in examinations and essays, guarantees rigidity in the cognitive process, and compartmentalization of formal knowledge and human values.

I have begun only recently to realize what a straitjacket this mode imposes on the mind. Now in all my sociology classes, whatever the subject, I give assignments that require transforming concepts and theories and fact-clusters into a series of other modes, including metaphor, music, poetry, pictures, color, mathematical equations and diagrammatic and free-form visual presentations. The increase in levels of comprehension, in ability to handle complexity, and in general creativity in dealing with the subject matter, is so great that I am myself dumbfounded at the implications for general educational practice.

9. Elise Boulding, "The Child and Non-violent Social Change," in *Handbook on Peace Education*, Christopher Wulf, ed., (Oslo: International Peace Research Association, 1974).

Literacy has locked us into words in peculiar ways. Originally regarded as the great emancipator of the mind, freeing it from the burden of memorization, literacy has now become the great emptier of the mind. We know how to look things up, so we don't need to remember anything. Consciously building up an interior knowledge stock, and learning to play with knowledge combinations in the mind, run our own mental mazes, and test our own mental combinations in the environment, seems to be something that many nonliterates can do better than we. There have been some disconcerting discoveries in recent decades about the superiority of abilities of nonliterates compared to literates in a developing society, in terms of problem-solving and keenness of civic judgment.[10] This refinement of mental and intuitive capacities in developing and working with knowledge stocks that nonliterate societies at their best have achieved is very different from the immersion in visual images that has become so attractive in the post-McCluhan age. The "Media is the Message" kind of immersion is almost the opposite of the mental cultivation I am speaking of.

We actually have had many warnings about the danger of restrictive approaches to mental training. Huizinga told us that all culture and all knowledge is created through play.[11] We have just not assimilated that insight. The great achievement of modern society is the differentiation of work and play. Do we dare differentiate again? If we remove the verbal-analytic structure on which all our teaching technology depends (in computer-assisted learning, to an extreme degree) how will we know when learning takes place? How do we test the validity of a metaphor? The lure of the verbal-analytic is powerful because it is so easily tested, at least in the classroom. The test of the metaphor is in life, and then we are back to the issue of breaking down the walls in order to develop and test knowledge in community apprenticeship settings.

If we let community needs set priorities for educational agendas, as well as utilizing the community as a testing ground for the practice of knowledge, we would find items entering the curriculum that are not now there. One important item would be the development of skills of conflict analysis and of creative dealing with conflict situations. If there is one skill that every human being needs in every life situation she will face, from interpersonal situations in family and community to the entire range of occupational

10. Howard Schuman, Alex Inkeles, and David Smith, "Some Psychological Effects and Non-effects of Literacy in a New Nation," *Economic Development and Social Change*, October 16, 1967; and Jack Goody, ed., *Literacy in Traditional Societies*, (Cambridge, England: Cambridge University Press, 1968).

11. Johan Huizinga, *Homo Ludens: A Study of the Play Element in Culture*, (Boston: Beacon Press, 1950).

and civic settings she will move through over a lifetime, it is skill in dealing with conflict. Conflicts of interest, perceptual conflicts, preference conflicts, are ubiquitous in the human experience. We teach the three R's, we teach nutrition and hygiene, in every elementary school, yet we do not teach the ABC's of conflict. The fact that we are currently locked into what could be the final doomsday escalation of an absurd arms race with the Soviet Union, a decade and a half after carefully programmed and timed de-escalation procedures were agreed upon, certainly indicates a crying need for new kinds of conflict specialists at governmental and intergovernmental levels. Escalation in urban violence gives us the same message.

The field of conflict and peace studies, which is developing new curriculum approaches and materials at all levels from elementary school to the university, offers crucial new resources here. We are for the first time beginning to identify a whole new set of peace-making roles that students need to be trained for. Identifying the "holes" in society, where peace-making roles could be functioning, and identifying the relevant training for them, is one more illustration of the importance of community-linked education. The classroom teacher's experience is not adequate for these new needs.

The redefinition of the educational process that I am suggesting here also involves a redefinition of goals to include education for role-creation. Students are still looking for the "jobs out there"—the slots waiting for them plainly labelled and with job descriptions attached. When the curriculum begins to change towards developing skills of social mapping in children (teachers need to know them first, and usually don't), every young person will know first-hand what the gaps are in the social structure, from local to international; she will develop a feel for what doesn't exist, but should, and skills in social design. One of the final exam questions in every course I teach is: design a new type of career that does not now exist, that deals with some of the problems dealt with in this course; write a job description, and prepare an analysis of the community structure in terms of where the job will fit in, and who will pay for it.

Students can't do this who have not had some direct experience of the community structures they study. Some of the know-how of mapping social structures can be developed in the classroom, but learning to map happens on the terrain itself.

The overarching challenge to education in confronting the future is the problem of scale. The reason we don't manage our planetary society better is that we don't know how. We can't even manage a country the size of the United States very well. We cannot grasp the planetary present, so it is not surprising that the planetary future is beyond us. Yet as has been repeatedly suggested in this volume, there are new ways to learn to think that will help us into the future. Particularly, there are new ways to deal with complexity. The dedifferentiation I have several times spoken of is only an apparent dedifferentiation. Removing the boundaries between teaching and other community occupations, between work and play, between the child and the adult, is a necessary aspect of a kind of meta-differentiation that will be much clearer a hundred years from now than it is today. This meta-differentiation is related to the distinction that Jonas Salk (Chapter 6) makes between Epoch A and Epoch B. It is a process of social discernment that must involve us all across all the social boundaries that have ever been drawn in the past. We need all kinds of new partnerships, including teacher-student-community partnerships, to make better maps of the social terrain, drawing on all the hitherto excluded communities. Only this will make us more adequate problem-solvers. As women begin participating more fully in the public spaces of society, it will be seen that they know how to draw all kinds of maps that public sectors dominated by men knew nothing of. We are already beginning to learn from the maps drawn for us by blacks, Chicanos, and American Indians. Many spaces and terrrains in our society remain that we, mainstream America, know nothing of.

Mapping the spaces of our own society is only a tiny part of what we have to do as humans. We have another, far more important, identity as earthlings. There is another whole set of maps to be created showing the significant terrains of the earth-family. That is another set of challenges for school community partnerships at the world level that cannot be gone into here. If we add unexplored inner terrain to the agenda of unexplored social terrain, the problem of mapping the physical energy resources of the planet that we hear so much about is trivial. Yet it is out of this psycho-social diversity that our futures are to be made. We earthlings will need every minute of the two to five billion years left to our solar system to find out what we are, what we have, and what we can become.

commentary on boulding •

There is an extraordinary sweep to Boulding's chapter; thus, its implications for the future of schooling are somewhat eclectic. Clearly a revisionist educator, she fears the progressive crippling of social consciousness through an instructional curriculum that insulates the learner from reality. Consequently, she calls for a program of instruction that will encourage moral development. Such a program would kindle an abiding belief in the importance of altruism and open children's minds to new ways of thinking about social conflicts. Boulding is convinced that the major breakthroughs of the future lie in new approaches to non-formal education. The effect, if not the intention, of her arguments is to dramatize the problem of curricular obsolescence.

These arguments are drawn from the humanist tradition. Boulding believes that the critical balance between technological futurism and benefic futurism has been lost. Unless realignments are made, education will use the new technology, not to achieve more salutary goals, but rather to pursue existing irrationalities with even greater efficiency. Her suggestions for the improvement of education are firmly rooted in a new conception of what constitutes essential knowledge. She writes about the need to familiarize children with the ethical virtue of frugality, and with the increasing extent to which humans comprise a single earth-family. Her dominant concern is for the cultivation of skills that enable people to interact with mutual advantage.

Underlying Boulding's fears regarding the present educational system is the conviction that schooling is used to insulate the young from social reality. She contends that as things now stand, the socialization process is directed at the hypocrisies of convention rather than at that which is ennobling. Like Fuller and Salk (Chapters 5 and 6), she suggests that our preoccupation with enculturation has caused us to substitute empty catchwords for reality, and to ignore important dimensions of human potential. "What has to be recognized now," she writes, "is the extent to which we have all been confined by powerful but invisible insulation systems that have made it possible to ignore a vast realm of human experience, to be deaf to clamorous potentials." She asks for a curriculum that will more accurately depict the existing human predicament and at the same time open the student's mind to what would make for a better society.

Boulding shares Bronfenbrenner's anxiety about the steady decrease in intergenerational communication. She sees age-grading as a particularly damaging aspect of a curriculum that creates an "environment of deprivation for children." She believes a great deal could be gained if students participated in authentic dialogues about the kinds of changes that are needed, not only in the educational system, but in society as a whole. Such involvement would not only bring children closer to reality, but would also provide the best possible kind of socialization. She views socialization, not as mere enculturation or basic grounding in the rules of the system, but rather as an orientation to the kind of world that could be. In this regard, she enlarges on the views of Polak, a Dutch futurologist, who has argued that our images of the future heavily influence our actions in the present by establishing focus and direction. Boulding feels that the socialization process should take the child's vision beyond traditions, rituals, and mystique to a confrontation with reality and, ultimately, to an ideal valuational system.

Her arguments suggest that authentic socialization must be directed toward personal as well as societal awareness. She faults the schools for the scant attention given to enlarging children's insights into their own nature, for failure to acknowledge the significance of "inner knowledge," and for insufficient emphasis upon educational experiences that reinforce the nurturing aspects of family life. "The family," she writes, "is the one place where human beings are rarely insulated from reality." By contrast, schooling is artificial and contrived. Thus, Boulding supports the proposition that education's preoccupation with traditional forms of knowledge has now become counter-productive.

These indictments are obviously open to dispute. Depending on one's ideological persuasion they are likely to provoke either strong acceptance or vehement rejection. However, even if one chooses to disagree with them, the criticism is valuable if only because it prompts a reexamination of our present condition. Speculative thought is most useful when it forces us to question what we normally accept as gospel. And speculative thought about reform, in anticipation of the future, is particularly worthwhile because it draws attention not only to existing problems that could become worse, but to potential dilemmas not yet widely recognized but already in genesis.

Whatever objections we may have to Boulding's arguments, her suggestions for change clearly warrant serious consideration. She recommends more cross-age interaction, more direct focus upon transnational difficulties confronting nations, more orientation to the reality of our times, more classroom time for direct engagement in ongoing social issues, and more correspondence with school-related learnings that occur within family life. These recommendations cannot be easily dismissed; if implemented, they could produce an improvement over present practice.

The basic direction of Boulding's chapter stems from the fundamental assumption that the central mission of schooling is to enable youth to build a better, more sensible, more rewarding future for themselves. Reading between the lines, one suspects that Boulding believes the generation now in power is too enamored of its own self-deception to recognize, let alone embrace, a different scheme of social values. Consequently, reform must be left to those who have not been so seriously infected as to be beyond cure. Her thesis is that schooling aimed at indoctrinating youth with orthodox mystique will serve only to perpetuate orthodox mystique.

For example the pervasive sense of helplessness felt by so many of the young reflects our habit of confusing synthetic and real competence. Boulding argues that the existing curriculum leaves students with the feeling of not having learned anything worthwhile. The subject-matter reflects "an elitist, anti-craft view of education" and produces not only a sense of helplessness but an excessive worship of nonfunctional knowledge. Needed reform must introduce learning that develops the ability "to use mind and hand with equal effectiveness." She suggests that we fashion an instructional program aimed at craft skills and analytic thinking. A sociologist accustomed to anticipating potential problems and solutions, Boulding's vision centers on the eventual possibility of a world network of villages and, correspondingly, on a system of community-centered village-schools.

Those more concerned with immediate problems may find Boulding's ideas excessively remote. For example, most school administrators act on the premise that schools must prepare youth for the society they will enter, not for some hypothetical universe. They are inclined to believe that attention to a network of community-centered village schools should be postponed until their reality becomes more apparent. Still, one is reminded in this connection of a caption in one of Winston Churchill's books: "How the great democracies triumphed and so were able to resume the follies which had so nearly cost them their life." While the schools must indeed cope with their current problems, already complex beyond belief, Boulding's objective is to direct our attention beyond the here and now.

No two generations encounter the same experiences. In times of rapid social transition, it is entirely fitting for the adult generation to warn its young about a future that is certain to be different. Since the primary intent of social projection is to promote flexibility and adaptability, it does not really matter whether or not the anticipated difficulties are correctly forecast. What does matter is that we prepare the young, as best we can, to be resilient in dealing with whatever contingencies may arise. Our situation has been aptly summarized by Margaret Mead. Observing that those who matured before World War II entered an era for which they were not prepared, she says:

We are immigrants in time, who have left behind our familiar worlds to live in a new age, under conditions that are

*different from any we have known. Our thinking binds us
to the past—to the world as it existed in our childhood and
youth. . . just as the early Americans had to teach themselves not to daydream of the past but to concentrate on
the present, and, in turn, taught their children, not to daydream, but to act, so today's elders have to treat their own
past as incommunicable. . . . we must place the future, like
the unborn child in the womb of a woman, within a community of men, women, and children, among us already
here, already to be nourished and succored and protected,
already in need of things, for which, if they are not prepared before it is born, it will be too late.*[1]

*As humans, we are torn by contradictory impulses. Our creative
imagination permits us to conceive of new organizations and arrangements and to dream of better things. At the same time, we are
attached to existing ways, to custom and convention, because the
old is secure and the new is uncertain. Nevertheless, we must re-
mind ourselves that security may not, in time to come, be of any
particular comfort to our children. Conversely, what we see as
cause for alarm may not evoke any special anxiety in future generations.*

*Boulding's conclusions are suggestive of a natural symbiosis
between education and society. Although the point has long been
debated by theorists, there is not yet an unquestioned link between
what occurs in schools and the values that prevail in society two or
three decades later. If, as she argues, the connections are stronger
than we suspect, her recommendations are indeed logical. Actively
engaging students in the process of social change would help to reduce the insularity of schooling and enhance social commitment,
responsibility and altruism.*

*Acquired knowledge becomes more functional when the in-
structional curriculum is based on the societal stresses of the present, rather than on the history of the past. Conflicting precepts
and cognitive dissonance are diminished when correspondence between the experiental learnings of home, community and classroom
is strengthened. School life can be made more useful and more
satisfying when career and vocational education are joined with
other socializing endeavors. Educational benefits can be extended
beyond their existing boundaries. The incidence of learning failure
can be reduced by increasing the effort to accommodate individual
student natures.*

*When Boulding turns to ideological issues, one is again
struck by the consensus created by similar arguments in other chapters. Like Fuller, Boulding contends that children must be helped to
understand the pitfalls of excess. She also reinforces his contention*

1.   Margaret Mead, *The Future Is Now: Dimensions,* a publication of the Northern States
Power Company.

*that steps be taken to counteract the growing tendency of the youn-
ger generation toward pessimism. Both agree that we are unaware
of our true potential, and that the tapping of unsuspected reservoirs of creativity and imagination will elicit workable solutions to
emerging problems. Boulding's postulations also reiterate Salk's
beliefs that new modes of scientific and cultural education must be
devised; a more rational code of ethical behavior must be incul-
cated; and the spirit of futility that sometimes seems to overpower
the young must be contained through a deliberate emphasis on imaginative problem-solving.*

*Boulding's strongest attack is directed toward "the narrow
range of experiences that we define as appropriate formal learning" and our heavy reliance on verbal learning. Citing a number of
early studies on the limitations inherent in our conception of
literacy, she raises a fundamental question: Does a preoccupation
with literacy and traditional learning objectives serve as "the great
emptier of the mind?" Are, as some critics seem to imply, nonliterates more effective problem solvers because their mind-set has not
been conditioned by school-induced preconceptions? If so, we have
somehow misconceived the function of education. The accumulated cultural heritage consists of more than book knowledge
alone, and we may have underestimated the value of learning that
derives from other sources.*

*Perhaps illiteracy, in some instances, does offer virtue but to
say that its advantages outweigh its disadvantages would be irrational. It may be that the dilemma Boulding poses can best be resolved by discovering what aspects of formal training produce liabilities, and by finding ways in which the disadvantages can be offset. This is what she has in mind when she reminds us that "all
culture and all knowledge is created through play." Yet, the undeniable worth of knowledge acquired in community apprenticeship settings and through informal experiences need not militate
against a judicious use of the intellectual disciplines.*

*Admittedly, the terrain here is uncharted. A number of re-
searchers, particularly Eisner, have suggested that schooling may
be excessively reliant on verbal abstractions. Others have observed
that little attention in the classroom is given to reflective thought,
and that schools routinely stifle the creative impulse. But
Boulding's point is different. Her argument is that nonliterate
people frequently develop a special kind of "mental and intuitive
competency" as a consequence of their own self-acquired knowledge. Therefore, the critical question is whether such competencies
could also be developed by literate individuals so that a double advantage would be obtained.*

*Most human activity is impossible to analyze or even de-
scribe with any precision. Michelangelo, when asked how to carve a
horse, is reported to have said: "Take a block of wood and cut
away the part that is not the horse." Similarly, Boulding wants
education to eliminate the extraneous and superfluous elements
that contribute nothing to the larger goal and to give greater atten-*

tion to intuitive understanding. Many aspects of learning are not yet fully understood. Moreover, the presumption that a specific instructional tactic will guarantee the achievement of a specific outcome is little more than wishful thinking. Boulding believes education must make allowances for the beneficial learning that occurs when children are actively engaged in experiences they find stimulating, whether or not the exact nature of the learning can be described or assessed.

It is the intuitive and the imaginative, rather than the deductive, that she has in mind when she speaks of conflict resolution. Boulding states:

> *If there is one skill that every human being needs in every life situation she will face, from interpersonal situations in family and community, to the entire ranks of occupational and civic settings she will move through over a lifetime, it is skill in dealing with conflict. Conflicts of interest, perceptual conflicts, preference conflicts, are ubiquitous in the human experience. We teach the three R's, we teach nutrition and hygiene, in every elementary school, yet we do not teach the ABC's of conflict.*

People do not always choose to act rationally; the issues they dispute are frequently irrational, and the solutions they reach in settling dilemmas often defy logic. What is sensible behavior depends to a considerable degree on one's purpose. Consequently, it may well be that education for conflict resolution must go beyond the merely logical. The deliberate effort to break away from conventional attitudes may make it possible to think about common problems, and their solutions, in uncommon ways and to find better answers.

It hardly needs to be noted that many of Boulding's ideas must become popular before they can be implemented. The elimination of age-grading, for example, is largely a matter of generating desire and commitment among practitioners and sufficient acceptance among clients. The legitimization of nonverbal learning activities, in contrast, will be somewhat more complicated. New instructional procedures must be devised; educational expectations must be altered; and the processes through which we judge student growth must be modified accordingly.

Nothing of moment is likely to occur, however, until the educational values of the public-at-large change. The profession's failure to clarify for its constituencies the differences between good and bad education has, probably more than any other factor, prevented the results of useful research from making their way into practice. However right Boulding may be in her conception of education as a prophylactic against social disease, it cannot be imposed on unreceptive parents, unwilling professionals, and unresponsive students.

L.R.

ISSUES •

1. Can the curriculum be expanded to incorporate dimensions of human experience that are now ignored?

2. Age-grading offers organizational convenience, but it also restricts desirable cross-age communication. What provisions would be helpful in overcoming these disadvantages?

3. Undeniable benefits occur when children serve as the "teachers" of other children. However, will the routine use of student tutors produce concomitant disadvantages?

4. In view of the competing demands for curriculum priority, can children profit, in any constructive way, from active participation in the planning of desirable social change?

5. Should schooling take steps to increase inter-generational contact among children and adults?

6. Does the school have an obligation—in a time of social flux—to aid in the realization of those socialization objectives, traditionally reserved for the home, or should it restrict itself to its own designated responsibilities?

7. If the present curriculum insulates children from social reality, what correctives are (a) possible, and (b) desirable?

8. What problems relating to conflicts in values, are associated with teaching about social problems?

9. In an era of educational conservatism, characterized by a pronounced emphasis on the so-called fundamentals, what can be done to counteract the inner sense of helplessness felt by many adolescents?

10. In a changing world, reflecting inevitable shifts in beliefs and life-styles, what, in the educational system, is truly basic?

11. Would there be merit in adding craft or technical skill development to the *general* curriculum?

12. Can advantages be derived from a greater reliance on nonformal educational experiences, and, if such advantages are substantial, how can formal and nonformal learning best be conjoined?

13. What learning modes other than the verbal-analytic could be incorporated into the instructional program?

14. What congnitive skills, taught through what processes, most enlarge the student's capacity for conflict analysis?

shirley chisholm
congresswoman, state of new york

3

RESCUE THE CHILDREN

A democratic society depends upon the intelligence and wisdom of the mass of the people to keep the country moving. A government of the people, by the people and for the people necessarily depends upon the peoples' judgment to make decisions that affect the growth of the country. In America, we delegate to the schools the responsibility to train the minds of those who will continue to be the guardians of this society. We have a strong commitment to public education. To see public education broken up into sectarian and, therefore, possibly antagonistic compartments within our society weakens the fabric of the common school educational basis on which this nation was founded. The truth of the matter is that our large cities are not going to survive unless we have a reasonable system of public schools that people have confidence in and one of the ways we build a reasonable system of public schools is to put children in them and teach them.

"Public education is failing millions of children who are from racial and language minority groups or who are simply poor," according to a study of elementary and secondary education undertaken during a three-year examination by the United States Senate's Select Committee on Equal Educational Opportunity, headed by Senator Mondale. This committee heard 300 witnesses, visited classrooms across the country, commissioned research and issued 13,000 pages of printed record. It acknowledged that "public education has been successful for most Americans" but then added that "full educational opportunity has been denied to millions of others who were born poor or nonwhite. It is not that children fail. It is our nation that has failed them."

Some of the elements of inequality in education are: (1) minority and disadvantaged children are isolated from the rest of society, segregated by race, economic and social class; (2) these children are often treated unequally in the classroom. Schools are not responsive to their needs and their backgrounds. Before they have a chance to prove otherwise, they are labeled as being inferior and failures; (3) school districts have unequal finances, and depend largely on the taxable wealth of each district and its citizens and the cost of unequal education is a lifetime of lost opportunities. The report recommended that schools be made more responsive, more a part of their communities and that communities be involved in their schools. It called for reform of financing so that financial and human resources for education are raised and distributed more equitably. It said no education reform can really succeed unless we also deal with a host of connected issues—inadequate health care and nutrition, unemployment, substandard housing, and discrimination. "What is missing," said Senator Mondale, "is a deep and strong national commitment to justice for disadvantaged children." Mr. Bronfenbrenner's explanation in Chapter One of how our society fails its children, also speaks for itself.

Today in many of our schools a climate of alienation exists among students, an atmosphere of unrest fostered by overcrowding, student resentment against use of security guards in schools, an unrealistic curriculum that does not allow for differences in student abilities, etc. A British authority on primary education making her first tour of the United States, indicated that there is a tendency in American schools to view children "as material waiting to be molded" rather than as distinct individuals. Ms. Yardley, a principal lecturer in education at Nottingham College of Education, feels that "the standardized achievement test is one of the main devices American schools use to force students into a mold. Rather than allow children to be people, you impose behavioral objectives thought up by adults," she concurs. Ms. Yardley has had twenty-seven years of experience in British infant and junior schools including fifteen years as a principal. She also criticized the tremendous emphasis on learning through memorizing in the United States. "You can produce testable results this way and the students will play the game, but it is hollow. Memory is the weakest faculty of the mind—it doesn't involve imagination and creativity. A child can learn what is needed to pass a test and then immediately shed what he has learned."

Why is our educational system not responsive to the demands of our society? Why does our educational system continue to be so reluctant in implementing new policies that would effect positive change and meet the demands of the people? Who are the keepers of the educational policy establishment?

The vast majority of the public in our nation live by a familiar vision of our public schools and they do believe that our schools have traditionally fulfilled a dual function—preparing young people for a career in adult life as Schweiker suggests in Chapter 7 and serving as transmitters to the culture.

Today's educational systems are in most cases related to classroom instruction. An educator is conceived of as one well versed in one discipline or another with a degree of sophistication about his mind. The true educator attempts to orient his teachings towards the life situation of the society in which the student will live but this concept involves a real understanding of the nature of the present society. The true educator will always encourage his students not to be satisfied with what they have achieved.

Parents, teachers and supervisors should form a coalition and demand an educational system that serves children. Today, children are processed and they tend to be dealt with in terms of homogeneity. There is a need for more humanity in many of our schools and more serious concern for the emotional lives of the children than we presently hold.

We must recognize that our community school boards have been handed a failing school system and it now becomes their responsibility, along with the parents, to help feed the children's minds as well as their bodies. The thrust for community control is the one most important development thus far in the transmutation of black and Puerto Rican local, indigenous power from rhetoric into a force for effective social change. A business has to show results or it becomes bankrupt; it has to be accountable. If a business were run the way many of our schools are operating, it would have gone bankrupt a long time ago.

The urban child experiences failing in reading and other academic skills because the quality of his life often lacks the social nourishment necessary to develop a curiosity for learning and doing. The effects of having a heritage of slavery and oppression plagues many black children with poverty, low-skilled parents and deep rooted feelings of insecurity. The endless assault of television, radio, and noise attacks the senses of the urban black child, weakens his attention span, interferes with his listening ability and depresses his desire to communicate with others. Added to this noise and confusion in his daily environment are the problems of living too near too many people and being too poor to escape into another setting. The school then becomes in many instances a part of a hostile world that offers little meaning to the child who lacks a path to follow in search of a meaningful future. It is difficult for the child to believe reading and study will produce real differences in his life.

Schools in urban areas do not plan effectively for the provision of increased communication among children and adults and between children of different age levels. Bronfenbrenner (Chapter 1) and Boulding (Chapter 2) make this quite clear. Crash programs designed to teach reading by machines rather than through teacher-individual methods do not produce significant gains in reading levels. This is to be expected because electronic equipment can not respond to the variety of thoughts that the learning of new words triggers in children. In reading laboratories, children learn words but often fail to relate these words to other growth experiences.

Since these words are learned in isolation from other experiences, they are soon forgotten. The learner cannot use them effectively in his speech and writing. The schools in the urban areas are seeking magic methods to teach the basic skills and to date no substitute has been found for the warm, competent teacher whose class is small enough to permit individualized instruction for the students. Students would profit more from an increase in teacher service than from the talking typewriter. Educational gadgets are not to be completely eliminated. They can be valuable teaching aids when used to stimulate and supplement the lessons presented by the teacher. They cannot replace the teacher because human beings are still the best teachers for other human beings.

Traditional educators are not noted for their willingness to create change. They have to understand the need for a built-in motivation system that can make students want to learn and read. One reason that students are now getting into junior and senior high schools with reading handicaps is because they have no interest in their school work. However, if a practical education contains areas that students are interested in, we could use it for reading motivation. If a youngster is interested in auto repair, we could teach him to read with auto repair manuals. We must give students skills; things they can do to give a person confidence so that they can cope with the real world.

Communities have made up their minds that another generation of their children are not going to be wasted and they will not accept the conventional educational wisdom that it is their fault that their children fail. The urban league took high school dropouts who were years behind in the conventional reading levels, and trained them into successful college undergraduates. Community control is not an overall cure, a panacea. It is one of the most effective means of achieving some of our goals.

We have the responsibility, as parents and as a community, to demonstrate through our commitment to our children that there is a very real reason for being in school and that real reason is to be taught, to be educated, to be led out of low income, high unemployment, poor health care, inadequate housing—to be led out of ghetto life.

The bitter fight over school bussing, to which no end seems to be in sight, is really a fight, on both sides, for quality education. Blacks, no less than white ethnics, still perceive education as the way for their children to make it. They both want "good schools," whatever they may be, and they are in agreement (this has seldom been remarked on) that the city schools most black children attend are not good schools. I was once a strong advocate of urban-suburban cross-bussing, because I felt it would produce immediate improvement for at least a few black city children, and most of all it would bring pressure on the entire white community to improve the wretched inner-city schools. It has not worked that way. Some bussing experiments have worked very well but only for a limited number of children.

There are those who are opposed to bussing on racial grounds. There are also parents who are opposed to having their children bussed to schools they consider academically inferior. It is clear that everyone understands that inner city schools do not have the financial resources that the suburbs have. Unfortunately, the anger aroused by the bussing controversy has not been directed at the condition of the poor, rural and inner city schools, as some of us had hoped it would be. It has taken a more direct form: "I fought my way up and now they're trying to take what little I have away from me." Blacks, too, have become angry. When a few city children are transported to the cool, clean suburban campuses, it does no good for the majority who are left behind, still attending their under-supplied, run-down neighborhood schools. Sometimes even those who are bussed out are not helped. Children come home and plead with their parents, "I don't want to go there again. They don't like me." This has been the case especially in those communities where the bussing issue has been allowed to polarize the black and white communities.

I do not see bussing as a panacea but I do believe that anti-bussing laws are unconstitutional and wrong. If bussing, in a particular situation, for a period of time, helps to improve education for all the children involved and speeds the breakdown of artificial barriers between groups, then it should be permitted. After all, bussing has been going on for a long time in this country. Something like 65 percent of our children are already bussed.

Clearly, all groups involved have the same goals. If they unite to press for their attainment, they may succeed. If they waste their energies in hostility and unprofitable action, they will fail. The solution to the school problem must start with steps to revise the systems of state and local financing (a process already being started under the pressure of court decisions) and to increase federal support for local schools. With greater and more fairly-collected support, increased community control must be allowed. This will violate one of the axioms of taxation, that where the money goes control must follow, but this axiom like many others has long been due for reexamination.

More support for schools, a program on which black and white ethnic citizens can agree, is only part of a greater need on which they can also agree—a reallocation of our national resources to achieve long-neglected social goals.

Community control is a way of providing that much needed link between the school and the area residents that it serves. By involving parents in this type of endeavor, it forces the curriculum to become relevant. Relevant in terms of reflecting the culture of black and Puerto Rican communities and relevant in terms of no longer being influenced by those who refuse to reach out to the community. How can black and Puerto Rican children have images in a school to emulate if they are nonexistent? Children need models of different races to emulate. If integration is to live, it must be seen not only in terms of "Race," but in terms of culture—a coming together of different peoples in a social, esthetic, emotional and philosophical manner—in terms of pluralism rather than assimilation. It must be based on a respect for differences rather than on a desire for amalgamation. "It must be seen as a salad bowl rather than a melting pot" (from NEA Task Force on Urban Education: Schools of the Urban Crisis). The integration of our day was deferred in terms of giving a white child a locker next to a black child, hiring a public relations staff member to improve the image on the school. To me, this concept of integration was lifeless even before it took on its present form.

No self-protective jargon such as "culturally disadvantaged" will be acceptable from the educational powers any longer in terms of the learning power children grasp under the tutelage of concerned and committed teachers. The black parent knows his child is "educable" in spite of all the funded programs and studies to the contrary. Mr. Rubin's chapter shows how easy it is to make mistakes in determining educational policy.

The time for rationalizing is well beyond us. We have all too often made the cry that as teachers our power is minimized by our prinicipals; as principals by our superintendents; as superintendents by our school boards; and as school boards by our Legislature. The cries are true, no doubt, in some instances, and permit us some justification in viewing ourselves as being not totally at fault: our educational system must not take creative, spontaneous young people and make them into dull, stupid adults. So often we have pounded our young into a system that makes them dull but we have never thought to challenge the system. Instead, we blamed the children.

Finally, we know that institutions resist change and if we forget this, all that we believe in and strive for will be lost. The challenge is here and all of us together have been so concerned with *teaching* that we forgot about childrens' *learning*.

Let us together feed our children's minds as we feed their bodies! From books come *truth* and *freedom*. The child brings to us his *whole* being; use this whole being and educate the child. If we are really to affect eternity, let it be to our credit.

No longer must we mutilate the spirits of millions of American children every day—it is surely a sin!

commentary on chisholm •

Congresswoman Chisholm writes as a representa-
tive of the people, particularly the poor and the deprived in the
nation's ghettos. Her anger is directed toward those aspects of the
educational system that leave some children at a great disadvantage. "Public education," she writes in reference to a Senate
committee study, "is failing millions of children who are from
racial and language minority groups or who are simply poor." She
believes the survival of our great cities depends on our ability to
reform and to improve the schools.

Chisholm's indignation over the current state of affairs
leads her to ask for a balanced curriculum, one that both "trains
the mind" and reflects a "serious concern for the emotional lives of
the children." Her criticism is based squarely on the conviction that
the ghetto schools are, at best, inefficient, unrealistic, and uncaring
and, at worst, deliberately designed to favor some children and dis-
favor others. Such schools, she contends, outwardly profess a
strong desire to eliminate inequality and reduce the plight of the
disadvantaged, but inwardly, these same schools steadfastly resist
change, and try to preserve the traditional imbalance between the
poverty-line schools of the cities and the affluent schools of the
suburbs.

Chisholm's indictments are cast in the form of sweeping
generalities, mainly, one suspects, to dramatize her concerns. That
the charges are not applicable in every instance is of less significance than the fact thay they are valid in too many instances. These
generalizations may kindle resentment in those who have worked
tirelessly to diminish the inequities to which Chisholm refers. The
Congresswoman would undoubtedly acknowledge, in this regard,
that heartwarming exceptions do exist, but it is the general rather
than the exceptional that must concern us.

A wide array of implied malpractices arouses her ire:
teaching methods are inept in many instances; policies are determined haphazardly and sometimes malevolently; the curriculum is
frequently unrealistic; administrators take refuge in placing the
blame elsewhere, rather than facing up to failures; in the most
serious of the failings, equality of educational opportunity simply
does not exist.

In regard to these allegations, it is perhaps fair to note that
even though the indictments are levied against the schools, many of
the difficulties stem, not from administrative mismanagement or

incompetent teaching, but rather from fundamental inequities in the social system. This distinction is important for two reasons: (1) it has become commonplace to fault the schools not only for their own imperfections but also for society's ills, and (2) the solutions to many of education's problems must emanate from sources over which the schools themselves have no control.

This is not to say that the educational system is without blemishes. But schooling, of necessity, is a compromise between the professional convictions of educators and the constraints of society. In some instances, educational failure stems from policy shortcomings; in other instances it is a byproduct of social disintegration. The low ebb we have reached in public credibility is thus unfortunate and somewhat unfair—unfortunate because badly needed resources are being withheld in implied retaliation and unfair because to assume that all educators are radically corrupt in their values, thereby depriving children of a first-rate education, is simply not consistent with the facts.

Chisholm's observations regarding educational inequality serve as a case in point. She suggests that there are three factors contributing to the problem. One, children are segregated by "race, economic and social class;" two, children are sometimes treated differentially in schools, particularly in the sense that classroom events are incongruous with their cultural background; and three, variable amounts of money, "dependent largely on the taxable wealth of each district and its citizens," are expended for educational purposes. Of the three, only the second can be counted as a professional liability. Segregation arises out of the hypocrisies of convention and out of parental preference. Dollar imbalance in school expenditures, in contrast, is the direct result of our existing tax structure. To hope that either of these defects can be overcome through visionary school management or inspired teaching is to delude ourselves.

A similar complication occurs in connection with Chisholm's concerns regarding educational policy. It can scarcely be denied that her impulses are altruistic and that she wants, desperately, to save children from urban blight. She asks for a brand of education that is both humane and efficient. There are, she says, no "magic methods" with which to teach basic skills, and "to date no substitute has been found for the warm, competent teacher whose class is small enough to permit individualized instruction for the students." One suspects that few professionals would quarrel with her contentions on this score. At the same time, however, Chisholm is mindful of the fact that black children of the ghetto are victimized, not only by their heritage of slavery and oppression, but also by a social environment frequently involving unemployed parents, endless television, human clutter, and low motivation. "The school then becomes," she says, "in many instances a part of a hostile world that offers little meaning to the child who lacks a path to follow in search of a meaningful future." Here again the real power to improve matters lies not with school personnel but elsewhere in the social system.

Although Chisholm's chapter is oriented toward the social and educational injustices that exist in the inner city, whereas the volume's other essays are more concerned with the societal scene in general, one cannot help but be struck by the parallelism that exists. Like Scanlon (Chapter 4), Chisholm fears that many of our existing policies may be in error. In concert with Bronfenbrenner (Chapter 1), she deplores the lack of inter-generational contact that has become a hallmark of our time. Similarly, she shares, with Boulding (Chapter 2), a belief that a sharp decline in social competence has occurred and that age-grading may have deleterious consequences. She notes, as does Salk (Chapter 6), the rising sense of futility among youth and the indispensable need to provide children with rich intellectual stimulation at appropriate points in their maturation. Concurring with Schweiker's apprehensions (Chapter 7) regarding a surreptitious "cooling-out" process, Chisholm thinks the schools must provide the young both with a respectable general education and with prerequisites for satisfying employment. Finally, she joins with Fuller (Chapter 5) in questioning whether the present system may already be paralyzed and moribund.

In view of the continuing controversy over bussing it is of special interest to note Chisholm's position on this issue. Once a staunch advocate of bussing, she is now inclined to take a somewhat more moderate stance. In a sense, her sentiments are mixed. On one hand, she reflects a basic conviction that anti-bussing laws are clearly unconstitutional. On the other hand, however, she is mindful that bussing has not only failed, but failed spectacularly, to accomplish its mission. Observing that blacks and whites alike recognize that inner-city schools serving black children are clearly inferior to suburban schools serving white children, Chisholm suggests that bussing be used whenever and wherever it seems beneficial. Yet, she warns, it cannot be relied on as the total solution to educational inequality. The definitive corrective "must start with steps to revise the systems of state and local financing." Moreover, we must have more federal support of schools and greater community control. It is through local autonomy alone, she reasons, that a culturally relevant school will develop. Of course, it is hard to quibble with the concept of educational pluralism, and the curricular preferences of parents and students (where they do not conflict) must be respected. Still, it also seems clear that Chisholm would object to instruction that, howsoever culturally relevant, failed to teach the learner how to cope successfully in the adult world.

There are two major implications to be derived from Chisholm's rationale. The nation's educational system does not do right by all of its youth and reforms are needed. These reforms must improve the educational provisions for those children who, for one reason or another, now suffer from serious learning disadvantages. The accomplishment of these reforms will require substantial modifications in the educational system as well as in the social system. Neither more money, better teaching, a changed curriculum, or the elimination of racial isolation alone, will suffice. It will take all of these, fused into a powerful and coherent thrust, to make a difference.

Our understanding of the intricacies involved in systematic social change, moreover, may not yet be sufficient to assure success in curing these infirmities. What is most needed is a sustained period of experimental reforms based, not only on new educational policies, but also on political and economic ones. It is certain that the traditional remedies will not work. We cannot turn to educators, bureaucrats, social scientists, and politicians for solutions because none of them have sure answers. In short, no one appears to know exactly what must be done to guarantee reasonable academic achievement, healthy social development, and vocational competence for American youth.

Now is the time for further research and experimentation. Without these, any attempted reforms are likely to be fruitless. In sharp contrast with past explorations, however, the new experimental endeavors must be governed by knowledgeable specialists and by the clients themselves. Child and parent, teacher and administrator, social scientist and civil servant must all, through collaborative endeavor, become involved in the search for a better system.

A committee of the Social Science Research Council concluded that social experimentation is an essential ingredient in the formula for a flourishing social order.[1] The committee further stated that there are a number of purposes in such experimentation: evaluating a promising idea; testing a potentially useful hypothesis; devising specific components of a projected program; contrasting alternative solutions; exploring the utility of a theory; regulating the "fit" among different program elements, and so on. It is this sort of experimentation that must occur if we are to deal effectively with the problems Chisholm identifies. If the solution to a problem is unknown, two primary courses of action are available: (1) abandon all hope and endure whatever hardships develop, and (2) intensify the efforts to search out at least partial answers. In view of the catastrophic penalties attached to a do-nothing policy, there is only one real course open to us.

It is of great importance that the new vintage of educational-social experimentation be holistic, pursued on multilateral rather than unilateral fronts. Much of our past difficulty has arisen out of efforts that were excessively fragmented. One

1. Riechen and Borah, eds., "Purposes of Social Experimentation," A Committee of the Social Science Research Council, *Educational Researcher,* December, 1974.

cannot help but wonder, for example, what might have happened if the Headstart programs had been carefully co- ordinated with home-based learning games, parent-motivation clinics, corresponding modifications in the early primary grades of the formal school, aptitude-treatment interactions that helped to enhance learning capacity, individualization procedures that accomodated learning idiocyncracies, repeti- tive reinforcement activities that compensated for early failure, joint community development that improved housing and reduced unemployment, special teacher in-service educa- tion agendas that furnished insight into the subtleties of childrens' cultural backgrounds, television fare that was educational as well as recreational, community learning activi- ties that expanded the learner's horizon, a more relevant and more humanistic curriculum—one aimed at affective as well as cognitive objectives, a school environment that induced pride in ethnic identity, and simultaneous urban development pro- grams that alleviated the ravages of poverty, extended children's social experience, and kindled healthier self-concepts and a stronger sense of optimism.

Public education has fallen into a crisis that is without precedent in recent times. The faith of the citizenry has dwindled; monetary support, resultingly, has been reduced to the point where many children are deprived, not only of luxuries, but also of basic essentials, and criticism, both thoughtful and thoughtless, flows from all quarters. Some blame the schools for preserving the social status quo; others attack them for perpetuating the economic hierarchy; and still others contend that they not only waste money but produce a poor product. The resulting vendetta, in the form of curtailed funds, is now of such proportion that school districts, large and small, may close their doors a month or so ahead of schedule because of budgetary deficits. Once again, as in the depression, some teachers are being paid in promissory script.

The schools, to be sure, are not without their liabilities. The record of debit is hardly unknown. Large numbers of child- ren still do not gain an adequate mastery of basic skills; bore- dom is commonplace; student and community interests are not sufficiently respected in the instructional program; and in many classrooms the principles of affective education have been perverted into mindless ritual. It is fair to say, in fact, that perhaps 20 percent of the nation's youth leave school with less than a satisfactory education. But it is also legitimate to observe that fully 65 percent of America's youth benefit from an education infinitely superior to that of their parents and grandparents.

Scores on standardized tests have slipped somewhat, but a reversal is almost certain as the shift in curricular empha- sis and the modernization of test vocabulary take effect. More-

over, the tests do not show the massive improvements that have occurred in other aspects of children's learning—in, for example, reasoning ability, decision-making capacity and information-processing skills. Beyond this, public institutions should not properly be held responsible for difficulties stemming from external empediments. The schools, it must be remembered, are but one of many elements in the education of children. Fifty-one percent of mothers with children in school participate, directly or indirectly, in the work force, and parental reinforcement of educational objectives has in a great many instances all but disappeared. Similarly, if children in their formative years spend as much time watching television as they spend in school, the impact of what they view and what they lose in the way of nonvicarious experience becomes extremely significant.

Finally, the achievement of the highest 15 percent of American high school graduates is extremely impressive in relation to the achievement of students in other nations. An infrequently publicized fact is that the test scores of our best students are substantially better than those of comparable students a decade or two ago. Thus, for many of the school's graduates, the criticism may be exaggerated. The real tragedy exists in the situations described so forcefully by Congresswoman Chisholm.

We hope that the regrettable tendency to think of the schools as an undifferentiated entity will give way to a more precise focus on particularized problems in particularized contexts. The educational defects of many inner city schools are one such particularization of a situation badly in need of repair.

L. R.

ISSUES •

1.   Can the schools act to reduce the societal isolation suffered by minority and disadvantaged children?

2.   If conventional curricula are incongruent with the cultural backgrounds of disadvantaged children, would it be better to (a) design alternative curricula, (b) initiate compensatory learning experiences that would make the conventional programs more usable, or (c) test, experimentally, the virtues of both procedures?

3.   The educational achievement of poverty-belt children is impaired by sub-standard health care, housing, and nutrition. Since modifications in schooling cannot overcome these deficiencies, should educational reform and family welfare reform be initiated in concert, or can one precede the other?

4.   Do children from disadvantaged backgrounds learn effectively from ordinary instructional procedures, or are alternative learning modes likely to be more efficacious?

5.   If greater community involvement in the control of education is inevitable, what advantages and disadvantages can be anticipated?

6.   Inner-city children frequently are handicapped by the absence of routine contact with significant adults. Could innovations in the organization of schooling help to counteract this defect through the more extensive use of para-professionals, and a larger number of informal learning activities in the outside community?

7.   What educationally valid alterations in the curriculum might increase the relevance between the in-school and out-of-school experiences of disadvantaged children?

8.   Limited incentive to learn remains a major impediment to successful educational achievement among socially deprived children. What countervening tactics offer the greatest viability?

9.   Few tragedies rival that wherein children are compelled, by law, to attend schools in which they feel unwanted and unloved. At the same time, the hostile behavior of children, maligned by a harsh environment, can easily breed teacher rejection. What selection criteria and special training are essential for adults who work with disadvantaged youth?

10.   True integration, implying an authentic social intercourse among children of diverse cultural backgrounds, must go beyond the mere congregation of ethnically and racially different children in the same school facility. What might be done to facilitate increased interaction?

robert g. scanlon
executve director,
research for better schools, inc.

ADMINISTERING FOR REFORM

The capability of school administrators to improve the quality of education is constrained by the complex pressures being exerted on public education today. The prevailing educational-effectiveness and cost-efficiency crisis is symptomatic of public frustration over the perceived low-productivity and the high-cost of our educational system.

That schools need to change is no longer a point of dispute. Administrators are beleaguered on all sides by angry critics demanding that something be done to reform the present educational system. A sharp difference of opinion does exist as to how schools should reform and who should be responsible. Tangled management systems involving state education departments, city and local governments, school boards, teacher associations and school administrators have, with very few exceptions, hindered rather than enhanced meaningful reform. The host of regulatory and contractual constraints that work against effective education and exaggerate cost, often prevent chief school officers from maintaining an effective cost-benefit ratio.

Local communities, although vocal about their dissatisfaction, are seldom sufficiently well-organized to foster constructive changes. Universities, the natural leaders of reform, have seldom exercised their leadership.

The reform problems confronting the public school administrator clearly demonstrate the need for separating policy-making from management, revising antiquated school codes, simplifying organizational structures, increasing adeptness in the negotiation of union contracts, harnessing the best of technology, and adapting schools more fully to the needs of the individual child.

In one of the largest privately-supported efforts to improve the American public schools, the Ford Foundation's Comprehensive School Improvement Project (CSIP) efforts were focused on ways to make school systems adaptable, flexible, and open to change so that they could more easily incorporate effective new procedures. Because the 1960s were a decade of innovation, there was a general assumption that "with more money, more buildings, and more teachers, our nation's schools could indeed make a few adjustments and changes to produce a better society."[1] But in many instances, the innovations put into effect were no longer in use by the end of the decade.[2]

One of the important implications stemming from CSIP, and from other change efforts in a wide variety of educational experiments, was that the concept of a "monolithic" American education system is a myth. In today's pluralistic society, education must respond to fundamental individual differences among the population or face increased public criticism and further loss of credibility.

The CSIP experience indicates that capable leadership and administrative continuity are as important as organizational structure, sound policy, level of commitment, innovative attitude, and adequate funding, in facilitating school improvement.[3]

The school principals who are most successful in dealing with the problems of low achievement, teacher disinterest, community hostility, pupil apathy and bureaucratic inertia, tend to make use of nontraditional styles of leadership.[4] They seem, more than anything else, to be catalysts and thus the need to alter the training of administrators correspondingly is an urgent one.

A close examination of the school environment reveals major stresses, ranging from mediating student confrontation to fulfilling unclear state mandates that demand new kinds of administrative skills. Large urban schools now require an in-school police force to control vandalism, physical assaults on teachers, rapes, extortions and burglaries. The dilemma of establishing racial balance in schools can frustrate even the most astute and sophisticated administrator. Few issues today have aroused more anger in parents than those surrounding the forced bussing of their children. The concerns, as many battle-scarred superintendents can attest, center upon the movement of students from one school to another, fears regarding the quality of education students will receive, potential

1. *A Foundation Goes to School—The Ford Foundation Comprehensive School Improvement Program*, 1960-1970 (New York: Ford Foundation, 1972), p. 3.

2. "Brief notes on A Foundation Goes to School," *Educational Researcher*, 2:2 (February, 1973), p. 14.

3. *Ibid.*, p. 42.

4. Gordon J. Klopf, "The Principal as an Educational Leader in the Elementary School," *Journal of R & D in Education*, (Spring, 1972), pp. 119-125.

racial conflict, and the basic physical safety of bussed and resident students.

Another new dimension of educational leadership arises out of the furor over relevance. The term has become a rallying point for taxpayers who want more for their money, for school boards who set particular expectations, for parents who reflect particular leanings, for state legislators who appropriate funds and influence policy, for the federal government that champions special new projects and programs, and significantly, for students themselves. The administrator, situated in the center of the battle-lines, is caught-up in a hopeless entanglement of contradictory demands. Obviously, he is accountable for providing quality education. But, as Chisholm asks in Chapter 3, what is quality education? Like most other standards, quality education is defined by the beliefs and values of the observer.

On a different front, the growing power and militancy of teacher organizations is becoming a major force in redefining the role of the school administrator. Traditional administrative functions involving the assignment and transfer of teachers, program development, and determination of class size are becoming items for collective bargaining along with the more conventional bartering-points of salaries, work conditions, and fringe benefits. In fact, the teacher contract has become one of the crucial elements in the determination of school policy.

It takes, moreover, extraordinary courage and resolution to withstand the long and bitter teachers strikes that have become standard procedure in the negotiation process. As angry teachers march shouting on one side of the administration building, irate parents often picket the other. The administrator is caught between opposing, sometimes irrational forces, and his ability to act is severely constrained. It is tempting to forget the ordeals of the present and seek relief in conjecturing about the future. The sad fact, however, is that the old problems have not gone away and the solutions still evade us.

To cite some of the "continuing business" of administration, one could mention the following:

1. Declining enrollments and inclining costs engender opinion differences among educators and taxpayers. Educators view smaller enrollments as an opportunity to improve the quality of education by, for example, reducing class size. Taxpayers see decreasing enrollments as an opportunity to reduce costs primarily by eliminating staff positions.

2. Dollar expenditures and instructional payoffs are primary considerations in all educational program-

ming. Technology, including both hardware and software systems, frequently can be used to lower costs while maintaining or even extending instructional effectiveness. The use of technological systems, however, is anxiety-provoking. Teachers fear the elimination of human teachers and parents fear the depersonalization of education.

3. Increased emphasis on basic skills, howsoever desirable, constrains the instructional time available for other important educational objectives. As a result, priority determination becomes crucial. What, then, represents a proper balance among basics, citizenship, values, the affective domain, career education, and so on.

4. Theorists contend that every student can learn when provided with a learning program that is appropriate. To use diverse instructional materials and methods, nonetheless, teachers must have substantial opportunity to enlarge their technical repertories.

5. Racial integration in schools, as a means of improving the quality of education, is an unrealized goal! An effective, generally acceptable, and manageable method of accomplishing desegration does not yet seem available.

6. The personalization of the educational process must become common practice, at least in certain areas of the curriculum. Accomplishing this personalization, nonetheless, will require a major reorientation in the attitudes of many practitioners.

7. Teacher associations will continue to bargain "hard" for improved working conditions, lower teacher-student ratios, and control over the curriculum to be taught. These views, however, may not be acceptable to other groups who also have a large stake in education.

8. As larger portions of school revenues come from state and federal sources, the political aspects of educational control will lead to increased confrontation.

To achieve solutions to these problems, and to reduce the unique pressures that exist in school administration, we will require a new kind of administrator, certainly an administrator who understands the techniques of conflict resolution and who is committed to the "art of the possible." Furthermore, an increasingly pluralistic society, rising human expectations, declining resources, and the growing assumption that education should provide a passport to satisfying adulthood, mandate that school administrators acquire new management skills through which diverse expectations can be met.

The reform of the schools depends in large part on whether administrators are willing to abandon existing systems and make greater use of change technology. The traditional paths to innovation—more money, more buildings, and more teachers—have obviously failed to produce a better educated youth. Administrators must become catalysts for improvement, particularly where conspicuous inadequacies exist, such as educational programming, personnel supervision, staffing patterns, community relations, and the use of facilities. There is no doubt that the administrative role, rather than diminish, will grow in both scope and complexity. This enlargement will, in turn, require more specialized technical skills in analyzing organizational deficiencies and developing plans for their remediation.

No longer will ad hoc "top-of-the-head" solutions suffice. What is essential, is the self-renewal of leadership, that is, the acquisition of coping behaviors that facilitate task-oriented organizational arrangements, greater staff involvement, broader power redistribution, better human relations, and more skillful conflict management. To achieve self-renewal, administrators must be able to:

1. Assess alternative values, goals, and objectives.

2. Evaluate the adequacy of existing programs.

3. Delegate power so as to increase organizational strength.

4. Mobilize resources.

5. Promote staff growth.

6. Ensure stability.

7. Initiate and reinitiate change strategies.

1. Administrators must be willing to assess educational values, goals, and objectives in relation to possible alternatives. Far-reaching social changes, as Salk makes clear in Chapter 6, mandate a reexamination of both the immediate and long-range goals of education. The administrator must ask: What knowledge and skills will be of most use to students now and in the future? Clearly, the ability to read, write and use practical mathematics will remain essential. However, such problems as a mounting dropout rate, growing student apathy, increasing group conflict, and the lack of

internal control among large numbers of students mandate new curricular objectives that deal not so much with specific knowledge of fact as with knowledge of self, and the capacity for critical thinking, responsible decision-making, and constructive action. The administrator must conceive of an educational program that enables students to achieve goals, interact effectively with others, and interpret information intelligently.

2. Administrators must be able to assess the adequacy of present programs and available alternatives. Measuring the extent to which current practices contribute to accomplishing established goals and objectives provides a basis for determining what changes are necessary. However, for reliable measurement, the right data must be collected and analyzed. Such data can be collected from the perceptions of students, teachers, and the community. The right data, however, is data that is indicative of the overall performance of the school and provides clues to necessary change.

3. Administrators must be able to redistribute power with a view toward the establishment of new roles and new organizational structures. The continued use of antique bureaucratic procedures, with their obsolete ideologies and out-of-date norms is difficult to defend. Effective reform will require a revitalized school organization suitable to the new needs. As administrative functions become more complex, more sophisticated competencies will become essential. The administrator must inventory these competencies and develop them in the organization's personnel. Teachers, for instance, have often criticized school administrators for restricting their involvement in determining policies and procedures. Their restricted involvement can, in part, be attributed to classical organizational structures that prohibit the division of authority. The capable administrator of the future will need to be adept in managing the dynamics of group interactions, redefining role expectations, assessing organizational health, and correcting role dysfunctions. All of these things, moreover, will need to be accomplished through humanitarian rather than authoritarian readjustments.

Many past reforms have failed simply because they proceeded on the assumption that only minor modifications in role structures and organizational patterns were needed to support the introduction and maintenance of new programs. We now know that the administrator seeking to effect improvements must be sensitive to three major aspects of organizational adaptiveness:

1. changes in external conditions

2. changes in the internal school structure

3. changes in the relationship between the individual and the organization

A management orientation to educational administration also will become increasingly important. As new projects emerge, administrators will have to become skilled in their own self-direction. Thus far, the potential application of management techniques to educational administration has been little explored. The next generation of administrators will need to become familiar with the benefits and limitations of management technology, for example computer programming, and develop the capacity to use these techniques in their tasks. In particular, a general orientation to project management procedures will be essential. Skills with which to formulate, develop, and operationalize a functional project-control system; to develop and conduct in-service training programs for project personnel; to evaluate and improve the effectiveness and efficiency of the system itself; to develop problem-solving methodologies; and to establish a project information system that provides valid, reliable, relevant and timely information for decision-making will all be required.

The primary purpose of management is to bring the various parts or units of an administrative system together in a proper relationship. The administrator should, in addition to providing leadership for reform, serve as a coordinator whose function is to insure unity and consistency, to avoid contradictions, conflicts and unnecessary duplication of efforts, and, by doing so, facilitate the achievement of objectives. This approach to management and coordination will be indispensable in future efforts to design better schooling.

There are many ways to achieve the essential coordination. It is often facilitated, for example, through better communication and information exchange, through formal or informal discussions on organizational purpose, through the initiation of joint coordinating machinery and through central planning by representative groups.

4. Administrators must be able to mobilize essential resources, particularly those in the community, for enhancing goal attainment. One of the major tasks of the administrator is to mobilize support for organizational objectives and to provide an environment that will encourage the use of creative human energies and potentials in pursuit of those goals. To achieve this, the administrator will need a better understanding of the behavioral sciences, human motivation, and interpersonal relations.

For the administrator seeking reform, the community can be a rich resource. The level of community support for schools generally parallels the extent to which the schools are responsive to the needs and interests of the community. Crisis conditions emerge, more often than not, when public confidence turns into public doubt.

Traditionally, communities have felt a strong sense of ownership regarding their schools. When this proprietary sense weakens, and public identification with education wanes, support tends to dissipate. If, in turn, the school administration fails to recognize the insufficient support base, reforms are frequently rejected.

The administrator who skillfully involves the community in district policy-making structure acquires an effective weapon against public discontent. A clear understanding of what it is that parents and other citizens want from their schools is a critical factor in assessing school and district goals, determining priorities, and projecting changes. Thus, community involvement is more than good public relations—it is, more fundamentally, giving parents the right to choose the kind of education they value for their children.

A number of school reforms are occurring in various locales across the country. There is a much-heralded program in Pontiac, Michigan where an elementary school has been transformed into a Human Resources Center housing not only classrooms for the young, but also health clinics, employment offices, child-care facilities, adult education programs, and senior citizen drop-in centers. Arlington, Virginia provides another example. There, a junior high school has been converted into a public service center that offers facilities for recreation, arts and music, health, and contains, as well, a community library.

Reform takes place in a political environment. Political machinery is instrumental in setting national, state, and local objectives, determining critical policies, formulating development plans, and allocating resources. The success or failure of a reform effort, and of the school system as a whole, furthermore, depends to a great extent on the amount of politically engendered state support, both financial and technical, available. It is the educational leaders reponsibility to ensure that the essential political forces are brought to bear. Conversely, administrators are also participants (directly and indirectly) in the making of policy. Political leaders are coming, more and more, to expect knowledgeable and practical advice from designated school leaders. The ways in which administrators define problems, interpret information, and reach conclusions can therefore influence political decisions.

This political significance of school administration is not a new phenomenon. Many administrators, over time, have helped to improve education by using a powerful political base to affect educational policy. For all of these reasons, consequently, some expertise in the fine art of politicking is a considerable advantage to the administrator interested in reform.

5.   Administrators must be able to establish and sustain continuous opportunities for staff growth. Teachers are, of course, the key to successful innovation. The task of ensuring effective in-service training for teachers rests with the administrator. It is un-

realistic to assume that teachers will (to reinforce a point in the Tyler chapter), without some special provision, automatically acquire the new teaching skills related to an educational change. Yet, few administrators are genuinely skilled in planning and managing an adequate staff development program for their teachers. In the development of a staff training program, the administrator must first be able to identify the teaching competencies required by an innovation and then specify the training materials and activities that are most useful in developing those competencies. Local training programs should go well beyond the usual efforts of publisher-consultants, teacher manuals, and university courses. They should, in addition, be directed toward a particular facet of professional renewal. Collaborative undertakings with teacher associations, particularly in teacher centers, are likely to become more commonplace and thus administrators must also master the requisite negotiating skills.

6.   Administrators must be able to stimulate change while maintaining stability. One of the constraints on planning for change is that shifts must occur in the midst of an on-going operation that must continue its function. This, in fact, is one of the principle implications of Salk's recommendations for the gradual evaluation of a new conception of schooling. The administrator organizing for change must plan these shifts so that the accomplishment of the basic objectives is not impaired. An incremental approach to change that sustains equilibrium while improvements are initiated must be devised, situation by situation.

One of the mandatory steps in implementing a reform is the elimination of the overlapping web of authority that exists in most school systems. The responsibilities of the various authority roles must be clearly defined if planning, implementation, and evaluation are to proceed smoothly.

Ideally, school boards set policy and administrators manage it. Conflicts between the two, common in most big-city school districts, can be reduced when both parties understand that the roles are complementary, not contradictory. Too often, administrators are required to secure board approval for even the most routine management decisions. Their power to lead and to reform, under these circumstances is severely restricted. When the Board agenda is filled with trivial items, valuable time is lost by both the policy-makers and the managers.

7.   Administrators must be able to revitalize the reform process when conditions indicate that redirection is necessary. Continuous study and evaluation must be carried out to insure that an innovation is, indeed, achieving its desired effects. Evaluation, in this sense, is a comparison between what is intended and what is

actually happening. The leader must, on the basis of such evaluation, detect failure and discuss the problem with teachers, students, and other administrators. If, in fact, the reform is not progressing as anticipated, revision and reinvigoration are in order.

If administrators are to fulfill these new kinds of roles, training programs need to go far beyond what is being taught today in educational administration at most of our colleges and universities. Some administrators do, of course, acquire a certain amount of sophistication through experience, but this kind of on-cite learning should not be left to chance. If we expect leadership from our administrators, we must see to it that they are professionally equipped with the tools of leadership.

Training administrators for America's schools is a complex business. Not only is an intimate, first-hand, knowledge of the classroom a must, but special training programs, *based squarely upon job-related skills*, are also crucial. If the administrator is to assume and meet management responsibility, he or she needs capabilities in business management, in personnel management, in human relations, in political maneuvering, and in the fine points of staff motivation. These capabilities moreover must be the result of didactic exposure in university classes, inter-disciplinary study, internship experience, and independent study. Most school districts assume, unfortunately, when they hire a school administrator that earned credentials guarantee expertness. Hence, few school districts plan and operate leadership development programs for their school administrators. We must move, as soon as possible, to offer not only service specialized university training for school administrators, but an active in-service training program at the local level as well.

Extensive grounding in the social sciences is mandatory. Leadership is rarely isolated from the practical concerns of political negotiation, establishing community consensus, budgeting, and conflict mediation. To cope effectively with these issues the leader must have book knowledge and practical sophistication. As a result, school districts and universities must seek new collaboration in providing training that fits real-world responsibility.

Entry into administration should be dependent upon the successful completion of training that combines formal classwork, including interdisciplinary seminars, and internships. Formal classwork should focus, primarily, on the technical aspects of managerial responsibility. Interdisciplinary seminars should integrate formal concepts from a variety of fields with the problems of administration. Above all, the preparation of administrators must be directly relevant to the complex world "out there," particularly with respect to problem-solving skills, strategy-building techniques, and the art of inspiring others to higher achievement.

commentary on scanlon •

Though Scanlon's chapter does not say explicitly that better administration and better schooling are inseparable, there is little doubt that his convictions run in this direction. Through their actions (and their failure to act) the managers of the nation's school systems have a profound impact on what does and does not occur. It is significant that this essay is neither a denunciatory attack, nor an impassioned defense, of present administrative practice. Rather, Scanlon's intent is to outline the central problems of reform that management must resolve. He offers us a thoughtful analysis of the current administrative landscape and an overview of the examination of major reform priorities.

An impediment of major proportions, perhaps the cardinal impediment, is brought to focus at the very outset of the essay. The existing mechanisms for the control and governance of schools are so enormously complex, so hopelessly muddled, and so imprecise, inconsistent, and inchoate that a desirable reform is virtually impossible to achieve with any expediency. Policy provisions overlap; the objectives of teachers and administrators sometimes conflict; antiquated legal requirements often prohibit the use of more efficient procedures; and the bureaucracy of the system itself can create a morass from which there is little escape.

For example, consider the hurdles and hazards created by judiciary intervention. In the present system, the courts are empowered to interpret the law and compel school districts to comply. However, these interpretations may (1) evoke enormous citizen antagonism, (2) be impossible to comply with in the existing school structure, (3) pose devastating financial burdens, (4) prohibit other educationally desirable policies, and (5) mandate instruction that contradicts the fundamental values and beliefs of teachers. It is not surprising, consequently, that many of the nation's school administrators consume an above-average quantity of headache remedies and that many intended reforms are aborted, early-on, because of the attendant turmoil.

Mindful of these circumstances (and aware that public educators must serve many taskmasters) Scanlon concludes that the capacity to mediate between opposing forces is an indispensable requirement for successful leadership. Among the many issues that must be resolved through sensitive mediation are the following:

1. Contradictory solutions for eliminating deleterious segregation.

2. *Disparate views among various factions regarding essential basic skills.*

3. *Proper balance in the curriculum between affective education, personological skills, and general knowledge.*

4. *Procedures that best ensure dollar efficiency in school operations.*

5. *Administrative strategies that can most effectively accomplish the readjustments necessitated by declining enrollments.*

6. *Policies that govern teacher bargaining.*

7. *Expeditious means of dealing with inconsistencies in federal, state, and local expectations.*

Michael Katz, after analyzing the structure underlying the educational bureaucracy, observed that it is based, to a considerable extent, on the requirements of an economic system that is dependent on racial exploitation and artificial status hierarchies.[1] *In a similar critique, Virginia Kidd deduced, from a close examination of a standard Basic Reading series, that the content contrives to inculcate a distortion of reality, sexist attitudes, acceptance of racism and blind obeisance to questionable cultural values.*[2]

Martin Carnoy, in a study that provokes a good deal of uneasiness, contends that human conditioning, through doctrinaire and manipulative schooling, is a basic tactic in capitalist societies. He then proceeds to the thesis that schools prepare children for differentiated social roles within the capitalist system, thus perpetuating a form of imperialism and colonialism. Carnoy suggests (as Chisholm does in Chapter 3) that economic inequities, more than anything else, account for the differences between the good schools of the suburbs and the bad ones of the inner city. He argues, therefore, that educational inequality is an indisputable fact of life.

In another indictment of current educational policy, David Tyack conjectures that the schools, as a result of their own inadequacies, have become totally unmanageable.[3] *He faults public education for its elitist postures, its mindless devotion to mass values, its obsession with conformity, its reliance on competition and standardization, its segregation*

1.   Michael Katz, "Bureaucracy and the Individual" in *Demystifying Schooling: Writings of Experiences* Miriam Wasserman, ed., (New York: Praeger Publishers, 1974).

2.   Virginia Kidd, "Now You See, Said Mark," in *Demystifying Schooling* Wasserman, 1974.

3.   David Tyack, *The One Best System: A History of American Urban Education* (Cambridge: Harvard University Press, 1974).

and degradation of students, and its anti-community philoso-phy.

All of these critics see the curriculum, in the language of Bowers, *"as a conspiracy to perpetuate myths about social reality and the 'taken-for-granted' middle class orientation."* The central theme of the criticism is that schools are engineered to turn out students who have a biased conception of their social and political environment. The schools orient youth toward behavioral patterns that reflect a prejudicial society, train them accordingly, and instill in them an indiscriminate obedience to authority. Even worse, they believe the educational system promotes a tacit acceptance of social injustice. Through cumulative indoctrination to established political procedures societal defects are camouflaged, open consideration of other alternatives is carefully avoided, and, in time, the minds of the young are permanently co-opted.

If the scholarly criticism continues, which seems likely, the issues may gain high currency and become the subject of widespread debate. Questions will be raised about the validity of the evidence, the accuracy of the inferences, and the legitimacy of the conclusions. Many will argue that the existing social order, though less than perfect, is at this point the most workable that human intelligence can devise, and that it is therefore perfectly appropriate for the schools to do exactly what they have been accused of doing. Tempers will become inflamed, disagreements will rage, and the mediating role to which Scanlon refers—that of bringing dispassionate judgment to bear upon the problems and securing general endorsement of the resulting implications—will ascend in importance.

Scanlon believes that the new demands of a new day will require a different breed of administrator. As paternalistic and authoritarian decision-making give way to due process decision-making and the present power base is diffused somewhat more broadly among the educational partnership, the tasks of leadership will grow in scope and complexity. At the same time the management cadre (the dominant catalyst for reform) will need to muster support among the citizenry for whatever changes are in order. Greater community involvement is of course highly desirable, but the experiences of the past few years have shown that community councils and other representative citizen's groups, such as school boards, do not come equipped to function effectively. These groups are likely to be most effective when the school superintendent acts as a sensitive facilitator and systematically develops a sense of mission and workstyle. He or she must, for example, give the group due respect as well as solicit and respect their opinions. It is essential for the leader to ensure that the group is made aware of the school district's pivotal problems so that attention is focused on the significant rather than on the trivial. When *deliberate "leading" of this sort is absent, those representing community interests are often unable to fulfill their intended function with any degree of potency.*

Several other factors are also germane to Scanlon's "new kind of administrator." Management theory, for example, has not kept pace with the emerging crises and it therefore is of limited help on the extraordinary leadership obligations that are characteristic of the time. For example, affirmative action, collective bargaining, and the demonstration of due cause, once remote abstractions, are now administrative facts of life. Moreover, because an increasing number of variables have begun to impinge on many management problems, administrative prowess is taxed even further by the subtle complexities of the interplay among these variables. In the typical school district a variety of political subcommunities compete. Each is directed by its own vested concerns and uses competitive tactics, such as an organized communication network and special defenses against the opposition. Consequently, in those hazardous arenas where administration is akin to political war, the administrator must be able to do battle on a number of fronts and draw on a multiplicity of maneuvering strategies.

Additionally in a tightening economy many desirable programs must vie for limited resources. Leader sophistication regarding the politics of money and the fine art of frugality become critical. A systematic program of continuing professional education for leaders therefore becomes increasingly important.

Referring to education as a "declining industry," March has suggested that the training of administrators must "attend to the problems posed by the context of decline and by the nature of educational organizations." [4] *That these organizations, and the managerial behavior they necessitate, are in a period of rapid evolution is not longer a point of debate. Today's schools are responsive to the demands of the present scene. They are markedly different from schools of even a half-decade ago. March, in speculating about the kinds of administrative finesse that must soon become standard technique, has developed five requirements:*

1. *skills associated with determining the administrative behavior most appropriate to a problem*

2. *skills associated with "sensing" the intent of political subcommunities in order to mediate internecine conflicts*

3. *skills associated with the reduction of goal ambiguity and the sharpening of priorities*

4. *skills associated with tactical timing and the other devices through which public support can be won*

---

4.   J. G. March "Analytical Skills and the University Teaching of Educational Administrators," *The Journal of Educational Administration, VII* 1, May, 1974.

5. skills associated with inferring useful leadership insights from the analysis of accumulated evidence

These skills blend easily with the "essential administrative tasks" outlined by Scanlon: the reassessment of educational goals; the development of alternative techniques for problem solving; the invention of methods for equitable authority delegation; and, generally, the establishment of administrative provisions that strengthen the internal organization of school systems, increase the correspondence between individual and organizational goals, and facilitate a sharper perception of the external conditions that will continually affect the course of education.

There is a certain freshness to the way Scanlon views the coming era of school administration. Although he grants the fundamental importance of basic leadership skills, he is more interested in the subtleties and fine points of leadership. This inclination toward an elevated state of the art is also shared by several other theorists. In a comparatively recent work on management, for example, Mintzburg offers an interesting synthesis of peer skills (working effectively with colleagues), leadership skills (the capacity to use authority and power), conflict-resolution skills (coping with ideological differences), resource-allocation skills (selecting priorities in the use of organizational resources), and entrepreneurial skills (the engineering of change).[5]

While Scanlon would find little at fault in these propositions, in his own analysis he centers on the mobilization of community resources, on the "art of politicking," and on negotiating a balance between change and stability. However, he places his strongest emphasis on leadersip persistence. Concerned about the growing tendency of administrators to avoid risks and to abandon whatever does not gain immediate acceptance, Scanlon believes that resilience and willingness to redouble effort in the face of failure are essential ingredients of authentic leadership.

At the close of the chapter, Scanlon advocates definitively different programs of professional preparation. In outlining these departures from present convention, he is chiefly interested in practical internship experiences that balance the study of theory, and in interdisciplinary exposure. The administrator "needs special skills in business management, in personnel management, and in the fields of psychology that deal with aspects of motivation." It would be shortsighted to assume that administrators are above or beyond the continual need for renewal and repair. For as the reform of schooling progresses, we shall need a changing administrator for a changing season.

L. R.

5. H. Mintzburg, *The Nature of Management and Work* (New York: Harper and Row, 1973).

ISSUES •

1. What can be done to eliminate the deleterious confusion that exists between the educational policy-making and management functions?

2. From an administrative point of view, is a quality education absolute, or, rather, does it vary from constituency to constituency, and from situation to situation?

3. Collective bargaining between teacher organizations and school boards has become a fact of life. Increasingly, however, matters of educational policy have become subjects for negotiation. Should legal restrictions be placed upon what should, and should not, be determined through negotiation and arbitration?

4. What administrative problems, stemming from declining school enrollments, can be anticipated and accommodated?

5. The aims of the schools are heavily influenced by public opinion. What procedures might promote community agreement as to the proper balance between individually-relevant and societally-relevant education?

6. Are alternative, yet untried, approaches to the objectives of school desegregation available?

7. In view of the current controversies regarding sensible approaches to educational evaluation, how can professional and public conceptions of acceptable educational outcomes be brought into closer accord?

8. What new administrative procedures will be required as a greater degree of decision-making power is delegated to students, parents and teachers?

9. Can better opinion-sampling devices— which would provide a sharper insight into alleged public discontent with the schools— be devised?

10. The processes of effective educational change are not yet well-understood. What kinds of research and development activities, added to that already on record, would most enhance our grasp of the intricacies involved?

11. Are the essential conditions for the continuing professional growth of administrators similar to those for teachers, or do significant differences exist with respect to both means and ends?

r. buckminster fuller
University City
Science Center

5

HUMANS IN UNIVERSE

The biases of all political ideologies are predicated upon the economic theorem that there are not and never will be adequate physical resources to accomodate all vital needs of all humanity; ergo, large numbers of humans must perish either by the deprivations of poverty or by the weapons of war. As first deduced by Thomas Malthus in 1810 when, as professor of Political Economics of the East India Company College, he was the first economist in history to have all the vital statistics from all countries around our closed system spherical planet. All empires prior to the "British Empire" had been only closed perimeter empires centrally occupying a flat world that extended omnilaterally to infinity, ergo an open system.

All political ideologies also assume that survival is only for the fittest, as stated circa 1845 by Charles Darwin as the raison d'etre for biological evolution. Though Darwin protested that his "survival only for the fittest" did not apply to economics, political ideologists adopted the concept—only those having the fittest political systems for most efficiently coping with the largely lethal conditions obtaining on our planet will survive; ergo, each political system says, "You may not like our way but we are convinced that we have the fairest, most logical and effective scheme for dealing with the fundamental inadequacies of life support, and since there is not enough for both of us and it has to be 'mine *or* yours,' great numbers of humans are going to have to perish either by war or starvation; ergo we must give highest priorities to preparing for war."

In the behavioral sciences human beings study the way animals behave; animals have brains so behaviorists feel that animals may be a proper information source for the way human beings behave under various conditions. The behavior of the animals has been disclosed through varying conditions and rates at which and by which the animals may acquire the metabolic essentials to support the life of the various animals. There are the inputs of food, air, water and light, giving the animal what it needs within a tolerable limit. Scientists are thus able to find out a great deal.

The metabolic support of humans themselves shows that if it is available they take in two pounds of dry food each day, five to six pounds of water, and fifty-four pounds of atmosphere from which they extract seven pounds of oxygen. Humans can go approximately thirty days without food without dying, but only a few days without water, and for less than two minutes without air. With respect to the oxygen of which humans consume the most, they have the least delay tolerance, therefore nature has seen to it that humans have lots of air. They have so much air that it has always been socialized, taken for granted, not even thought about.

The vital metabolic requirement that humans can do without the longest is food. This thirty day tolerance has given humans a chance to do something about themselves that has taught them much and has induced much scientific invention, as well as most wars. Humans say, "We're going to starve if we don't get something soon, and we had better do something about it." So gathering together all the starving neighbors they invade the domain of a more successful tribe that has growing foods. Wars have been primarily waged when man had the time to do something about the dilemma. What he did was to invent weapons and their means of production.

It is also relevant to comparative behaviors of animals vs. humans that human beings have something that the other creatures with brains do not have, and that is a mind. It is the more intelligent use of this mind that Salk asks for in Chapter 6. Brains are always and only dealing with each special case experience, putting in storage each piece of information that the senses detect, often recalling the items for further consideration. Mind, and mind alone, has the capability of discovering relationship variables existing between the brain's special case items that varying interrelationships are not in any way indicated by any of the constant characteristics of any of the special cases taken by themselves. As, for instance, Newton's discovery of mass interattraction, gravity. The Moon and the Earth each had their unique masses. Multiplying one times the other gave the relative interattraction of the Moon-Earth set as compared with that of an orange and apple set, but Newton found that when halving the distance between the two their interattraction increased fourfold. There was a second power, an exponential rate of increase, of the set's interattraction as they neared one another. But there was nothing in one of the bodies by itself, such as its mass, that said its interattraction with another body was going to vary *and* exponentially at that! It has been mind and mind alone that has first intuited and then, faithful to physical data, has been able to discover these mathematically generalized principles.

An enormous amount of observational data had been accumulated by Kepler and Gallileo before Newton could intuit from their work (as compounded with his own) just how to discover what was going on. Taking hints from Kepler and Gallileo, Newton made measurements of the rate at which the Moon was falling into the Earth away from the line that the Moon would travel away from Earth if the Earth were suddenly annihilated, and could no longer restrain the Moon. Newton found that the rate of the Moon's fall away exactly corresponded with Gallileo's accelerating rate of falling bodies. This gave him his clue to the exponential rate of change in the interattraction relationship. But it took humanity an enormous amount of study of the planetary system's whole behavior to intuitively sense and then discover what was going on. The relationship was not implicit in the parts, it was synergetic. Synergy means "behavior of whole systems unpredicted by behavior of any of the system's parts where considered only separately." Synergy is the only word having that meaning.

Now we find that mind, and mind alone, has the capability to discover such synergetic relationships. It is the absence of synergy, for example, that causes the problems described by Bronfenbrenner (Chapter 1). All the great generalizations of science are just such synergetic discoveries. And there is nothing that indicates that dogs will ever discover the theory of covarying functions as have the minds of humans.

Whenever I am confronted by the behaviorists saying that animals have innate aggression, I point out that animals behave with aggression only in desperate conditions when the life support has been reduced below the critical tolerance minimum whereafter they go mad. I'd have to point out then time and time again, I'm sad to say, they have so much of it that human beings have without thinking about it, assumed that air is socialized. However, once in a while there are catastrophic fires in theaters. The fire in the theater consumes all the oxygen. The people are not usually incinerated, they are suffocated by lack of air. Going into this horrible scene afterwards, of all the dead people we find that fathers and mothers who would gladly give their lives for their children, suddenly suffering, have gone mad, i.e. out of their minds "have blanked out" and have stampeded over their own children. Humans have no experience in passing the critical limit of respiration. After they blank out, their conditioned reflexes take over. Not having any such consciously recalled experience, they have been unable to train their reflexes in preparation for such moments.

While human's brains and nervous systems are similar to all animals, none of the animals have the extraordinary capability of the mind to discover relationships unpredicted by parts and thereafter to train their brains to reflex appropriately. Therefore, I can't accept a fundamental behavior of madness and aggression demonstrated by animals as a normal operative characteristic.

I don't know whether you have ever been personally in a lethally critical predicament, as a flier for instance, when something has gone wrong in flight. What does the flyer do? If he panics, he is lost. He will panic if he has had no experience and training. Time and again (I have had three such instances, two on the sea and one in the air) with split second awareness of being on the threshold of panic, I found suddenly that great clarity came to me because I reflexed from training and experience. There were principles involved, and you had just a split second to do first this then that exactly right. If you do so everything comes out all right. Panic and it's all over. Use your beautiful mind and fall out into safe level flight again. The clarities that I've experienced mentally under such critical conditions have been extremely revealing. So we have a recourse other animals do not have. Growling, shouting, roaring and clawing will not recover you from a tail spin.

Because iron rusts and seems to deteriorate, humans have long misassumed that our Earth's metals were being consumed and that we would soon be left without any. That turns out not to be true. We find that all metals that have been introduced into the functioning of our technology are continually recirculated as designs become obsolete. Each time th. y are recirculated they are used to produce much greater performance per capita, per hour, per pound, and per unit of energy effort than before. The way we use the copper and the numbers of messages we get over a cross-section of telephone wire is continually increasing. We went historically from one message per cross section to two m.ssages per the same cross section of copper wire, then to 12, 28, 200 and 2,000 and then went wireless. We now have one communication satellite weighing one quarter of a ton out-performing the transoceanic communication capability of 175 tons of copper cable—a seven hundred thousand fold improvement.

I found, as I began to study, that where humans are using the synergistic principles discovered by applying them to their survival problems that they then get their material resources to do more with less.

Again I began to say, "What are some of the evolutionary patterns that are taking place?" I began to study all kinds of long time trends from the earliest known data histories of each category.

Thus I discovered in the mid-1930s that the metals that we used to think were being consumed and exhausted were being recycled at various rates. Originally used in various kinds of technology, when those special technologies become obsolete metals are melted and reformed. There is no secondhand metal. When melted the metals are once more the same cosmic chemical elements. They are the same elements that have been melted and solidified eternally. I found in 1936 that the average rate at which all of the metals were being released from obsolete designs and returned to raw metal resources was twenty-two years. The turnover lag varies from industry to industry and the amount of various metals used in those industries varies. The electronics industry has the swiftest turnover rate, aeronautics comes next, then automobiles, ships, railroads, big city buildings, and at the slowest end private dwellings. This altogether averages at twenty-two years. The bulk of the metal comes back at this rate. Every twenty-two years there is a new generation of technology. In that twenty-two years interim, humans have learned so much more that they are able each time they use that metal, to get a very great deal more performance for a great many more people out of the same amount of metal.

I began cataloguing all such technological, economic and anthropological trends hoping to be able to see what their integrated effect might tell us. One of the most important integrated effects was discovery of precession operative in the ecology of biological life on our planet. In order to successfully support human life each of the creatures in life are programmed to do certain 180° inputs (the honey bee going after his honey at 180° and inadvertantly knocking off the pollen that would cross fertilize the vegetation at 90° to his polar axis of operation). I found ultimately that all biological drives were inadvertently accomplishing 90° side effects that made the whole system work; I saw the ways in which we could begin to look at things in the terms of the circumferencial of 90° instead of 180° and this began then to be a great clue to being able to put together the information that I needed. The effect of all bodies in motion upon other bodies in motion is always precessional, that is they result in 90° directions. The pull of the sun upon the Earth makes the Earth orbit around the sun at 90° to the line of pull. Thus I discovered that ecology is precessional.

I found that on the sea and in the sky, where the ship had to float, the doing more with less became obvious. But on the land, humanity throughout all history had been building great walls; the bigger and heavier and higher the walls, the bigger the grain bins, the more secure humanity felt.

So when I began to look into what was needed to keep all humanity living very healthy and prosperously, I went into high performance structures and living per pound, kilowatt, and second of resources invested. This brought me to geodesic structures.

With over 100,000 around the world, and many of them really very large and doing quite heavy tasks I now have enough experience to be able to say, "I can now give you fast environmental controlling for given stresses and for essential functions as well as proof against earthquakes, hurricanes, and snow loadings." This for only about 1/200th of the weight of materials we are now using in our comparable buildings.

Continually using recirculated world metals (Japan gets on without any mines whatsoever) I can now say to you that with the metals we now have mined, with the knowledge we now have, it is highly feasible to take care of all of humanity at a higher standard of living than anybody has ever known.

This is absolutely contradictory to the working hypothesis of all great governments.

In the time of the Pharoah, 99 percent of humanity was illiterate and only the Pharoah had information. There was a time when the nobles came into the information. There was a time when the middle class came into the information. That was as yet less than 1 percent of all humanity. Suddenly everybody in the world today is being informed about everything. Everybody is in on the information. Everybody is in on the decision making. That's why, as Scanlon (Chapter 4) points out, our administration processes must become more modern. Everyone is concerned about how to make the whole of humanity a lasting success.

Therefore, I can say, I now know that we do have an option that humanity didn't know it had. We do have the capability, and that I can also document. This can be accomplished by 1985. In other words, this is a very immediate kind of capability.

I see evolution manifesting progressively increasing information advantage on the part of each child being born. I think about all the misinformation that I was taught in my childhood. Until the Wright brothers flew when I was nine years old, I was taught that it was inherently impossible for man to fly. I was completely surrounded with misinformation.

Now every child being born is being born in the presence of less misinformation and an enormous amount of increasingly reliable information. It is really universe information. I find each of these children spontaneously saying if we can go to the moon, we can organize things on our planet to make it work.

commentary on fuller ·

Fuller's words convey a dual message: first, in coping with the social problems that now confront us, we must at all costs use our rational intelligence and avoid the sort of imprudence that is frequently born of panic. And second, we must, in attacking the problems, seek composite rather than simplistic solutions. Fuller, in voicing these sentiments, joins forces with those who are hopeful, rather than pessimistic, regarding civilization's survival. He is convinced that the answers to our riddles lie in our creative imagination and in our ability to invent a new order of things. History, he suggests, has repeatedly demonstrated the capacity of resilient minds to overcome seemingly insurmountable difficulties.

The force behind his optimism is his faith in the human ability to learn. "Evolution," he says, "manifesting progressively increasing information advantage on the part of each child being born" provides a strong weapon that can be used against the human predicament. Thus, Fuller feels strongly that new knowledge and the correction of misknowledge, if broadly disseminated, can set us free. Our conception of what is possible, Fuller contends, is chiefly constrained by misinformation. Perhaps reflecting his own dynamic pattern of problem-solving, developed over the course of an extraordinarily inventive life, he seeks a school that will unleash the creative powers of the young.

There is an inspiring optimism to his arguments yet, at the same time, they convey firm impressions regarding the course education should take. The essence of these impressions forms a reoccurring thread throughout Fuller's rhetoric (a legendary rhetoric, it might be said, that has caused endless nightmares for a good many editors). Fuller wants a school that operates with a fixed purpose. While his conception of good education is anything but conservative—the exercise of intuition, the nurture of creativity, the cultivation of receptivity to different social goals—it is prescriptive and constrained in scope. One suspects that although Fuller clearly favors the development of an open mind, he would not favor an open school.

His themes also reinforce, as do those of the other writers, the supreme importance of instilling an optimism in children about their ability to prevail over problems they will encounter. In particular, he shares with Salk the conviction that stress and problem-facing are indispensable elements of a sound education. Fuller's dominant quest is for a confident new younger generation whose self-assurance has been conditioned, not through baseless exhorta-

*tion, but through cumulative and successful experience in sur-
mounting obstacles. This survival ability, he suggests, is best
accomplished by making students genuinely knowledgeable, and by
giving them repeated practice in synergistic reasoning.*

*While his expectations are unquestionably defensible, they
are not easy to conceptualize, and they are even more difficult to
operationalize. For example, Fuller's ideas as to what constitutes
information and misinformation will undoubtedly provide curriculum designers with considerable cause for concern. He contends that education's ancient and time-honored ambition—passing accumulated wisdom from generation to generation, and perpetuating the societal organization—will not help youth to deal
with future problems. Since the dominant lesson of history is that
man is adaptable, we must now teach children to use their intuition,
intellect, and creativity in the engineering of social change.*

*Fuller wants a curriculum that supplies learners with a dif-
ferent kind of factual information and with repeated activity that is
aimed at increasing their ability to combine these facts in new and
novel ways. Similarly, when he speaks of "teaching children to
think synergistically," Fuller again emphasizes his basic supposi-
tion that the systematic acquisition of ideas is insufficient. The
ideas must be examined from a fresh point of view, probed
endlessly for new meaning, and fashioned into original, yet un-
tested, prospective solutions to social problems.*

*Fuller's premises, however, give rise to general questions.
Can colleges, parents and legislators be persuaded that synergistic
thinking is of greater worth than the accumulation of standard
knowledge? What guides can be used to separate the necessary
information for synergistic thinking from extraneous information?
And, of greatest importance, how are the skills of synergistic thinking best cultivated?*

*For the average educator, Fuller's advice may border on
impossible idealism. Not only is he an iconoclast, but his conceptions of what constitutes a good education are almost certain to be
controversial. Moreover, the cognitive activities incorporated in his
"synergistic thinking" are extraordinarily difficult to program. For
example, in the 1960s when there was considerable interest in classroom encouragement of creativity, teachers found it hard to
prompt divergent thinking among their classes and even harder to
evaluate the merits of the ideas generated. Protagonists of creative
education have long argued that since its chief virtues lay in the
process, not the product, appraising the quality of children's creative efforts should be avoided. Antagonists, in contrast, contended
that little good, and perhaps substantial harm, would be the predictable consequence of inept or nonsensical thinking.*

*Viewed from another perspective, however, Fuller's re-
marks can be construed as a more easily managed solution. If the
curriculum were organized, subject by subject, so as to afford con-*

tinuous opportunity for analytical thought, something akin to Fuller's synergetic thinking might take place. In this curriculum the student (1) would learn about the critical factors surrounding a particular human problem, (2) would analyze the problem from a variety of vantage points, (3) would acquire new information from diverse sources that had immediate relevance, and (4) would form- ulate a number of prospective solutions to the problem.

It is of considerable interest, in this connection, that Fuller favors teaching that takes the child from the general to the specific. While we are not told whether or not he thinks facts or general- izations are more useful, it is clear that he wants the student to apply generalized principles to specific problems. This point is important because instructional planners are already worried about devising effective procedures through which information overload can be constrained. Facts multiply endlessly, but the days and hours of schooling remain finite. The problems of selection and priority are therefore great, and generalizations, because of their great efficiency in organizing knowledge, have high appeal for curriculum specialists. Yet, it is precisely on this storehouse of information that Fuller bases his hopes for survival:

> *I see evolution manifesting progressively increasing infor- mation advantage on the part of each child being born. I think about all the mis information that I was taught in my childhood . . . . Now every child being born is being born in the presence of less misinformation and an enormous amount of increasingly reliable information. It is really uni- verse information.*

Fuller would like the student to distill significant informa- tion into operational principles and bring these principles to bear on human problems. He speculates that future education will be concerned less with the everyday living, and more with discovering how man can function in his evolving universe.

To a far greater extent then most of the other writers, Fuller cuts across the total educational enterprise. A celebrated eclectic, he offers us a free ranging set of observations on what should be taught, and when, where and how it should be taught. Like Boulding (Chapter 2), he believes that education must teach children how to do more with less, and like Salk (Chapter 6), he feels the time is ripe for a new concept of instruction. Convinced that the present system is already moribund, and that its last rites are only a matter of time, Fuller reasons that technologically facil- itated home study is likely to characterize a new educational era. Federally funded education, he argues, will yield high returns and will prove, in the long run, to be an excellent investment. But among his assorted opinions two dominant themes keep appearing: (1) our progress in solving human problems is inhibited because we continue to labor under conventional misconceptions of reality, and (2) education is most productive when it is conceived of as synergistic experience.

When Fuller's recipe for a school of the future is viewed in its entirety, it becomes obvious that he wants far more than a technologically improved way of doing the same old thing. Instead, he is interested in a radically different educational philosophy wherein teaching objectives and methods are the natural outgrowth of changed aspirations. In considering his arguments it is necessary to ask: What are the real possibilities of altering society's educational intent? In short, can we part with custom and reorganize the present school system so as to better meet the needs of present and future? The call for reform, after all, is hardly sudden. In recent times no fewer than five working groups, drawn from the ranks of the profession, have examined current practice and concluded that a minor revolution is necessary.

For example, The National Panel on High Schools and Adolescent Education, convened by the United States Office of Education has stated:

> *Major problems exist in the Secondary Schools as a consequence of changing patterns of adolescent growth and development—manifest unrest and frequent racial conflict; a growing drug problem; inadequate preparation for work or for higher education; alienation from the rest of society and lack of motivation to enter adult life.*

As a result, the Panel contends, a new approach has now become essential: education must enable students to learn by "doing what is socially needed, personally satisfying and health supporting for the individual and the community."

In much the same vein, the Kettering Commission on the Reform of Secondary Education suggests that the existing high school is in the process of rapid decay and must be reconstituted "as an establishment striving to meet the complex demands of a society in the throes of social change, at a time when the school system has become too large as an institution and is literally overrun with a mix of young people from inconsistent backgrounds." In yet another report, The Greening of the High School, *the text reads: "Though youth is no longer the same, and the world is no longer the same, high schools are essentially unchanged from what they were at the beginning of the century." In all of the reports nothing can be found that even remotely resembles an unconditional defense of the present system. Nonetheless, despite the general consensus that all is not well with the schools, the prospects of definitive change seem as dim as they were at the turn of the century.*

It might be noted that Fuller's convictions agree, in places, with the language of the reports; elsewhere, of course, they tend to follow their own unique conformation. However, similarities and dissimilarities aside, few of the recommendations are likely to be put into effect in the immediate future, largely because little real effort has been made to meet the fundamental requirements of institutional reform. The schools are a societal tool designed to serve the social system, and they therefore cannot change unilaterally—in detachment from other phenomena in the social scheme—they can only change as the overall system itself is modified.

By way of illustration, a few years ago, as the irrelevance and unsuitability of ongoing instructional programs became apparent, considerable interest in alternative schools began to develop. In due course, a number of such schools were planned and tested. While the results yielded varying degrees of success, some demonstrating greater merit than others, the movement as a whole ultimately began to lose its appeal—not so much because of programmatic inadequacies—but because the students from the alternative schools found it troublesome in some ways to enter the social mainstream. Some were handicapped by lower scores on college entrance examinations (attributable, in the main, to the nontraditional ideologies embraced in the alternative schools). Others were handicapped, as well, by fear among prospective employers that their unique schooling experience was in some way inferior to conventional education.

Consequently, it seems reasonable to conclude that irrespective of its other infirmities (or perhaps because of them), the present school system does socialize a majority of its students, enabling them to penetrate and fit within the existing societal order. Presumably, the kind of school Fuller describes, would be confronted with similar resistance. Unless the rules of transition were realigned, the graduates of a "Fullerian" school could not easily enter either a college or a vocational specialization.

The logical implication of all this is that school reform and societal reform must work as one. Inasmuch as the two interact and are interdependent in their present form, they must operate in similar tandem in any new form. If, as the evidence seems to suggest, the growing educational conservatism of parents is primarily a reaction against interference with "rites of passage," generated by new approaches to schooling, further chaos must be prevented before the public can be expected to look favorably on other alternatives. In this regard, the present is not unlike the past.

Hence, if the historical record is any indication, we cannot initiate a major reorganization of the schools without corresponding societal reinforcement. Therefore, we are unable to pursue Fuller's goals, the goals of the secondary school study groups, or the goals of any other group until the atten-

dant aspects of the social system are also readjusted. If all the interlocking elements are not rearranged together, so that they intermesh symbiotically, the old story of futile planning, premature abortion, and predestined failure will once again be written.

In view of these circumstances, it is somewhat astonishing that a comprehensive and systematic approach to school change on a major scale has never been tried. In all probability, only the government is in an adequate position to orchestrate the experimental testing of a new socialization process. For this reason, one is led to wonder why some state or federal agency has not seen fit to mount an exploratory program of one sort or another.

For example, a national group—involving students, parents, educators and social scientists—could identify a set of socialization goals and combine many of the traditional objectives and some objectives expressly addressed to the requirements of the future. Loosely defined, these might include such things as commitment to social responsibility, rational attitudes toward material consumption, altruistic values, interpersonal skills, and so on.

Once these goals had been incorporated into instructional units and tested to the point where their merits were generally accepted, programs to inform the public might be launched so that parents might be helped to understand and esteem such education. While the organizational problems would admittedly be somewhat complicated, colleges, universities and a broad cross section of representative employers could perhaps be persuaded to accept, on a trial basis, public school graduates who had undergone a curriculum specifically based on the redefined socialization goals. Given some assurance that a different, and more suitable, program of schooling would not impede postschool advancement, parents and students might be willing to participate in the experiments. Finally, with a cooperative clientele at hand, it would be comparatively easy to design a course of study that constituted a definitive departure from tradition and provided a better orientation to essential life skills.

I do not mean, by this example, to champion any particular educational aim, or to advocate specific policy. I mean, instead, to argue that our failure to achieve a consequential and lasting overhaul of the curriculum may be attributable to the fact that, as an acculturing agency, the schools must socialize for the world that exists rather than for a mystique.

There is, therefore, an additional message inherent in Fuller's main themes. They underscore the great need for renewed attention to the mechanics of educational and social change. However, it is not the Fuller prescription alone, but all of the major ideas and recommendations in this volume that will have little significance if ways cannot be found to activate reform in the overall societal organization.

L. R.

ISSUES •

1. What kinds of instructional designs, in anticipation of technologically facilitated home study, could now be explored?

2. Where, in the curriculum, are concepts relating to environmental conservation and human interdependence best taught?

3. Since children are influenced by attitudes acquired in the home, the community and the classroom, how can the beliefs resulting from these separate experiences become joined into a synergistic whole?

4. If there are instances in which children should be taught to reason from the general to the specific, *and,* instances in which they should be taught to reason from the specific to the general, what are the determining criteria?

5. Is there any virtue in a deliberate effort to nurture social creativity in the classroom?

6. In view of the shifting societal currents, should we alter the balance among general, humanistic, and career education?

7. Is it essential for the federal government to provide a proportionately greater share of educational costs considering economic restraints on the schools?

8. The schools, traditionally, are charged with socialization and transmission of existing cultural values. If major alterations in the social system will soon be inevitable, what kind of "mix" must exist with respect to the perpetuation of the status quo and the inculcation of receptivity to change?

jonas salk
director, salk institute
for biological studies

6

ANTICIPATING TOMORROW'S SCHOOLS

During my first year in medical school, I began to recognize that the students who were brilliant in terms of their capacity to repeat what they had learned by rote were not those who were distinguished. A new kind of capability was beginning to be recognized—problem-solving capability. Along with this trend was a developing concern for the nature of the problem-solving process itself—the reasoning behind human decisions and actions. The nature of the mind, the nature of the person, and the influence of the changes that have been taking place in the world have a bearing on the approach to education both now and in the future.

After my work on polio was completed, I became very much aware of certain phenomena regarding the nature of man through the reactions of colleagues, scientists, the medical profession, the lay public and politicians. Underlying the creation of an Institute for Biological Studies, there existed a strong assumption that man is a valid subject for study from a biological point of view. An even more appropriate name for it may have been an Institute for Biological and Humanological Studies, to identify the human as the unit of interest (man, woman, child) not merely cells and molecules such as are the unit of interest to experimental or molecular biologists, atoms and molecules such as are in the realm of interest to the chemist, and particles and atoms that are the units of interest to the physicist. We have reached a degree of understanding of the nature or order in the universe, in the physical and the chemical realm, and in the biological realm, so that it now seems quite appropriate to begin to search for a basis for understanding the nature of the order that must exist in the human realm. If disorder exists, order must exist—along with disorder. The dialogue between the biological and the human is constantly going on in my mind, and using biological and human metaphors in each realm, I find that each enriches the other, opening vast areas of imagination that, when pursued, have proved to be exceedingly fruitful.

It has been my feeling that in due course the physical ills of humankind would eventually be dealt with, to the extent that it is possible to do so. In any case, the problems of human disease would be reduced to a minimum, permitting us to then deal in the future with the problems of Man's relationship to Man and to himself.

In the realm of educational purpose[1] there is correspondence between the educational process and what goes on at the molecular-cellular level in living organisms throughout the process of evolution. An understanding of how living processes work in adapting and in coping with life can be applied to some of the human problems involved in the field of education.

THE IMMUNE SYSTEM

The immune system has evolved to maintain the integrity of the organism against outside invaders. Without it we would be invaded by every microbial parasite and consequently could be instantly consumed by any and all organisms. The immune system, that has enabled us to evolve this far, has developed into an elaborate, sophisticated network that deals with all kinds of problems, including the distinction and recognition of the difference between self and nonself. Without that ability the organism would attack and destroy itself. In fact, there are some diseases called auto-immune or autoallergic diseases in which the immune system erroneously recognizes something as self that is not self—an imperfection in the system for which some means of correction is necessary. But, by and large, the system works satisfactorily. In some instances, that system is turned off, as in the case of cancer. Cancer cells, which are recognizably different from normal cells, are tolerated in spite of the measurable presence of certain kinds of antibodies capable of destroying them. Cancer results in death when the cancer cells seem to emit a substance that smoke screens the immune system, preventing it from acting. In some instances there can be one or another kind of defect in the immune system that could be responsible.

The immune system has a character of its own and learns by experience. An earlier experience results in immunity. An immunity

---

1. Education in the sense of the Latin word *educare*, "to draw out," rather than "to put in."

is nothing more than a rapid response of defense and rejection. That is all vaccination does. It simply activates the immune system so that, upon a later exposure, there will already exist a capacity to defend quickly against an outside organism. Therefore, we have learning and we have memory.

There are fascinating analogies between the immunologic system and the nervous or psychologic system, or between immunologic and psychologic phenomena. There are such things as immune tolerance and intolerance, as well as psychological and sociological tolerance and intolerance. Although it is possible under special circumstances, to induce tolerance where there is intolerance, in most cases, once intolerance or immunity is established it is very difficult to break. By the same token, in the formation of the young individual, it is much easier to prevent a state of intolerance from developing in the first place than to break it once it has developed.

Thinking analogically in this way, it seems that some very fruitful ideas could be applied, not only to the field of immunization against infectious diseases, immunotherapy of cancer, or immunotherapy of auto-immune disease, but also to the field of education and to the problems inherent in man's relationship to man and to himself.

THE GENETIC SYSTEM

We understand chromosomes are made up of giant molecules called DNA. DNA makes up the numerous genes that exist in all organisms; and the genes, in turn, code for the making of the protein of which the cell is composed. Consequently, the very proteins that are made under the influence of the DNA code in turn, make the DNA itself. We begin to see a structure of the natural order in living systems, an order that can be understood in rather precise ways. The nature of the relationships between these independent and interdependent systems suddenly becomes clear.

We are now at a higher order of complexity that allows the imagination to begin the leap to what goes on in the human realm—the realm in which we do not as yet see the nature or structure of order. We are left, consequently, with an inability to cope with certain kinds of problems in the human realm, although we have been doing so for the last two decades in the biological realm. With increased knowledge, the insights that have developed in biology have become a part of our culture, our thinking, and our understanding of the nature and function of the universe. For this reason we can see the analogy between what goes on at the biological level and what goes on at the human level—an analogy that we would not be able to conceive due to the magnitude of size and the time span during which observations can be made. Relationships can be understood when reactions occur very rapidly in living systems. Reactions develop very slowly in human systems. Nevertheless, there is a correspondence that suggests that, although the time scale and the order of complexity are different, the essence of the relationships may be the same.

The way in which a bacterium produces an enzyme to digest a nutrient, and is then used by the bacterium for building up its own substance, serves as an example of the nature and function of this genetic system. There are two kinds of E. coli (bacteria of the intestinal tract). One has the genetic capacity to form an enzyme to digest a given sugar; the other one does not. In the first instance, the enzyme is not present in that bacterium, but the genetic capability to form that enzyme exists. But, if that bacterium is in a culture medium in which the substrate (the given sugar) exists, the sugar acts upon an inhibitor that is constantly operating to keep the enzyme from being formed by that gene and the enzyme is produced. The capacity to express this function is in place and ready to act. A stimulus, which acts as an inducer to remove an inhibitor, sets the process in action.

The other bacterium does not have the capacity to form that enzyme and digest the sugar, no matter how much sugar is put into that medium. Therefore, we have the analogy that there are genetic capabilities for expressing and learning. Imagine a relationships of this kind between what children are capable of learning and the learning function to determine what they are ready to learn.

THE "S" CURVE

The population in the world today is tremendously larger than it was centuries ago. During the 14th century, about one-fourth of the world's population was decimated by the bubonic plague, but was quickly restored to a number that the ecosystem could tolerate. Because of advances in science and technology in the 20th century (originating in the 17th and 18th centuries) our world population grew enormously. This great success in survival has obviously brought about a set of problems that require great ingenuity for their solution. However, the population curve will not continue to rise exponentially, as can be illustrated through inspection of a chart showing the curve of the fruit fly population in a closed system.

In a closed system, fruit flies have some kind of a signaling mechanism that tells them at a given point in time that they ought to stop multiplying exponentially. The sigmoid curve, shown in

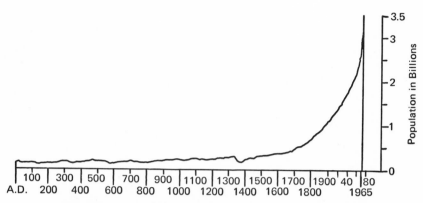

Figure 6-1. World population estimates, A.D. 0-1965. Adapted from *World Facts and Trends,* by John McHale. Copyright © 1972 by John McHale, published by the MacMillan Publishing Co., Inc.

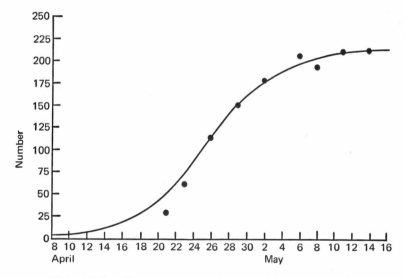

Figure 6-2. Growth of fruit-fly population. From *The Biology of Population Growth* by Raymond Pearl. Copyright © 1925 by A.A. Knopf, Inc. and renewed 1953 by Maude deWitt Pearl. Reprinted by permission of the publisher.

Figure 6-2, reflects the existence of the mechanism in the system related to the survival of that population.

The same thing can be seen in the yeast culture shown in Figure 6-3. At the end of eight hours, the growth rate of individual cells is eighty-eight, whereas in eighteen hours it is three. What

Population Growth of Yeast Cells in Culture

Time (hours)	Population Size (number of individuals)	Growth Rate (individuals per hour)
0	10	0
2	29	9.5
4	71	21
6	175	52
8	351	88
10	513	81
12	594	40.5
14	641	23.5
16	656	7.5
18	662	3

Source: Adapted from *The Biology of Population Growth*, Raymond Pearl, A.A. Knopf, Inc., Copyright 1925. Renewed by Maude de Witt Pearl.

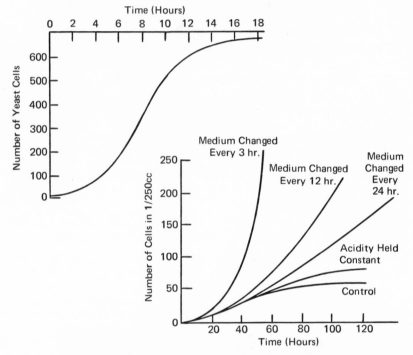

Figure 6-3. Adapted from *The Biology of Population Growth*, Raymond Pearl. Copyright © 125 by A.A. Knopf, Inc. Renewed by Maude deWitt Pearl.

The upper graph depicts the growth curve of yeast cells grown in a laboratory culture and refers to the table immediately above. The lower graph shows the growth curves of yeast cells grown under varying environmental conditions. From CRM Books, *Biology: An Appreciation of Life* © 1972 by Communications Research Machines, Inc.

happens is clearly reflected in the curve and also in the actual numbers that are produced at each point in time. It is rather interesting to look at the graphs in Figure 6-3 where the controls have a sigmoid-like curve. In the others, which reflect changes in the medium where the acidity is held constant (the medium is not allowed to become too acidic), more organisms grow. If the medium is changed every twenty-four hours or twelve hours, or every three hours, the numbers of individuals increase. In other words, if we produce more food, we could have more people on the face of the earth. However, there are other problems with which we would then be concerned. The graphs serve to illustrate the relationship between the environment and the organism, both individual and species.

This sigmoid curve is seen, not only in fruit flies, yeast and bacterial cultures, but also in molecular systems. Figure 6-4 shows that the antibody level tends to flatten after primary vaccination. The secondary or booster response occurs more rapidly and from a higher level to a higher level finally reaching a plateau. (See Figure 6-5.) Here we begin to see evidence that there is built into living systems some kind of a feedback mechanism that says too much is enough.

Figure 6-6a illustrates a more complex organism— sheep —that was introduced into a given area. In the course of the following century, the population growth curve has a sigmoid-like character with the evident fluctuations.

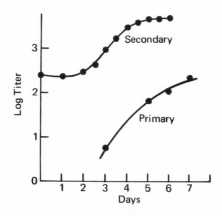

Figure 6-4. The primary and secondary antibody responses of two rabbits to intravenous injections of a "vaccine." From F.M. Burnet and Frank Fenner, *The Production of Antibodies,* published by MacMillan and Company Limited. Melbourne, 1949.

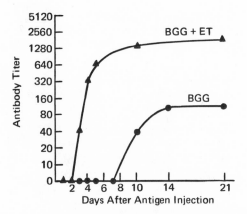

Figure 6-5. Primary antibody response in mice injection with bovine gamma globulin (BGC) with and without the reinforcing effect of another substance, endotoxin (ET). From Maurice Landy and Werner Braun, *Bacterial Endotoxins*, published by the Rutgers University Press, 1964.

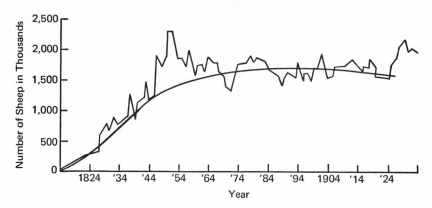

Figure 6-6a. Growth curve of sheep following their introduction to an area. Note initial sigmoid pattern followed by approximate equilibrium.

The brown lemming evidences a different pattern, as shown in Figure 6-6b and serves to illustrate that in nature there are a variety of patterns of behavior.

Paul Ehrlich in his book, *The Population Bomb,* has conveyed the notion of the population explosion, as illustrated in Figure 6-7 without offering any notions of future possibilities. I am confident that, whether we consciously do anything about it or not, nature will intervene. Whether she intervenes in the manner here discussed, as in the case of the brown lemming, or in other ways, remains to be seen. In any case, we have a tremendous obligation

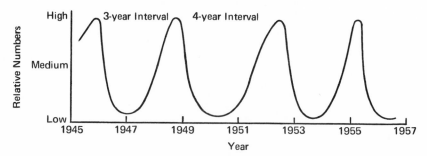

Figure 6-6b. **Generalized curve of the three-to-four year cycle of the brown lemming population. From CRM Books,** *Biology: An Appreciation of Life,* © **1972 by Communications Research Machines, Inc.**

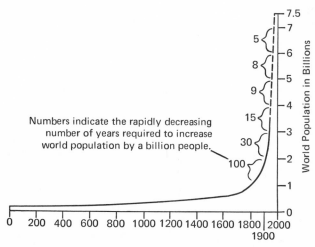

Figure 6-7. **Adapted from** *The Population Bomb* **by Paul R. Ehrlrich** © **1970 by the New York Times Company. Reprinted by permission.**

and responsibility for realistically viewing options for dealing with the future.

Two different sets of processes are operative (which can be illustrated by the sigmoid curve in Figure 6-8) with a break at the point of inflection—one curve up to the point of inflection and the other subsequent thereto. Separating them by a gap, as shown in Figure 6-9 we can call one curve A and the other curve B. These can now be referred to as Epoch A and Epoch B. We are now at the end of Epoch A and at the beginning of Epoch B. Values and value systems that are appropriate and relevant in Epoch A must be

Figure 6-8.

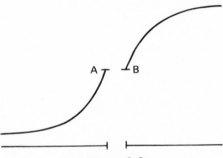

Figure 6-9.

different from those in Epoch B, since they are part of the control and regulatory mechanisms giving shape to curves of this kind. An individual born in Epoch A had quite a different future to look forward to than one born in Epoch B and would, of necessity, behave differently. Unlike the fruit flies, in whom all is genetically programmed, we are sentient and capable of this kind of consciousness although to differing extents. I am convinced that many of the changes occurring today are the result of an intuitive response of individuals to the changing circumstances prior to intellectual awareness. Therefore, the enormous changes taking place in our culture can be explained through symbols like these curves, that have far more meaning than simply two curves reflecting population growth and size. They can be meaningful in all aspects of human life, past and future.

What was of positive value in Epoch A could be of negative value in Epoch B, as is illustrated by the position and direction of the arrows in Figure 6-10. It is obvious that unlimited population growth was of positive value during a period of time when survival was of the greatest importance. Now it is of negative value. Likewise, what is of positive value in Epoch B would have been of negative value in Epoch A. Therefore, the notion that what we should do now we should have done before is not altogether correct.

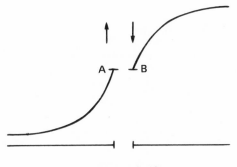

Figure 6–10.

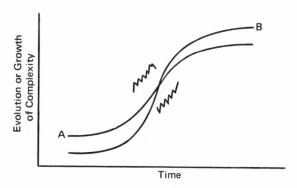

Figure 6–11.

Epochs A and B can further be distinguished through some of their identifying characteristics. Epoch A was possessed with an anti-death attitude, because infant mortality exceeded births. In Epoch B, the attitude now seems to be pro-life. In Epoch A it was anti-disease; now we think in terms of pro-health. Death control in Epoch A and birth control in Epoch B clearly are the dominant influences. Self-repression in Epoch A becomes self-expression in Epoch B. These are simply code words conveying a qualitative difference in the two epochs.

Our present point in time is often viewed in one of two ways, illustrated by Figure 6–11. Some people cannot imagine that A will continue other than exponentially, and others, abhoring the idea that B was connected with A in any way, desire to separate themselves from it and begin again. These are two sets of unrealistic attitudes. It must be emphasized that this is all part of a continuum. We must continue by making the changes that are necessary and appropriate to our present point in evolution.

In order to have a curve of this shape, at least two sets of factors must be operative or else things would go on in only one direction. First, there is a counterbalancing force. What tends to

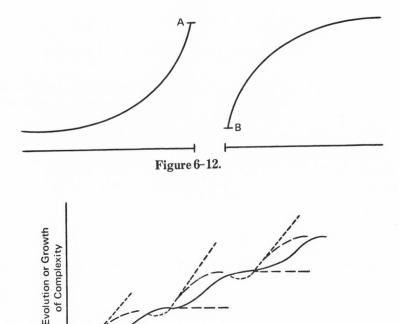

Figure 6-12.

Figure 6-13.

happen in living systems, where we understand the molecular events, and, very likely in human systems, is that what seems to have been dominant in the A period yields to the tendency for the domination of B characteristics. This shift, producing the curves illustrated in Figure 6-12, is applicable, not only to numbers of individuals, but also to shifts in values. Transposing from a quantitative to a qualitative image, we can consider the evolution or growth of complexity rather than numbers, as the ordinate and time as the abscissa.

The evolution or growth of complexity is clearly not so simple as either a single sigmoid curve or two curves. Rather, it results in a series of sigmoid curves, as shown in Figure 6-13, because there is a tendency on the part of some to want things to be constant, others to want things to change, and still others to wish change and then to revert back into the mainstream.

Imagining people in these respective positions, exercising these different ways of proceeding, it is obvious how those of the extreme right and left become mortal enemies and how wars of all kinds originate.

COMPLEMENTARY DUALISMS

We have a pretty good idea of physics and the structure of physical matter, of chemistry and the molecules we deal with, and of biological systems. We are beginning to understand socio-biological systems. In an attempt to approach an understanding of the nature of order in the human realms, I have utilized a complex diagram to illustrate structures and relationships. I have used the word meta-biology to refer to the human realm. Metaphysics is included and is to be distinguished from metabiology. Metaphysics deals with the cosmos. Physics deals with matter, chemistry with synthesis, biology with life, sociobiology with survival, and, I think, meta-biology with transcendence. Proceeding further, metaphysics deals not only with the cosmos but with order. Likewise, physics deals with the beginning of evolution, chemistry with structure, biology with function, sociobiology with relationship, and metabiology with creation. (In subsequent writings, I intend to add another term, sociometabiology. This is still in the process of development.) The boxes in the diagram have been utilized to represent the stucture of the matter that manifests these phenomena. In the box for biology I have two words, "gene" and "soma," referring to, let us say, the DNA (gene) and then the remaining structure of the cell (soma) made by the DNA. The DNA, which is the code, and, the somatic constituents, or proteins made under the influence of the code, in turn make the DNA. Here we have an example of a complementary dualism, where two independent systems are interdependent in the sense that, if one did not exist, neither of them would exist. There-fore, in the unit of life, we see that it is composed of two elements that are complementary and inter-dependent and, therefore, essen-tial. We see a unit that has a dual structure.

In the box for chemistry the dualism is between protons and electrons. In physics, it is energy and mass. These are inextricably related. The units of the chemist and the physicist are revealed.

The two elements of the dualism of the sociobiologist are the species and the individual. For the metabiologic unit (the human) I have chosen two words that I am defining analogically. I call one the "being" and the other the "ego." They correspond analogically to "gene" and "soma," and the relationship is the same. This has evolved and become evident as a result of the higher order of comp-lexity of the evolutionary process. I think that the terms "being" and "ego" come very close to something that is of tremendous importance for education and for the human beings that we would like to influence in a positive, constructive and pro-evolutionary way. When I attend to sociometabiology, I will probably speak of a collective being and a collective ego.

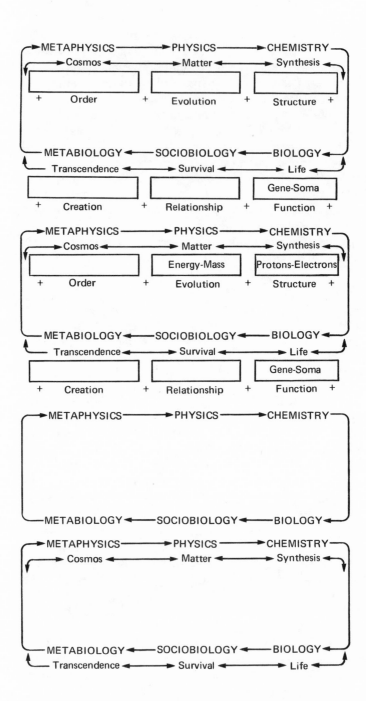

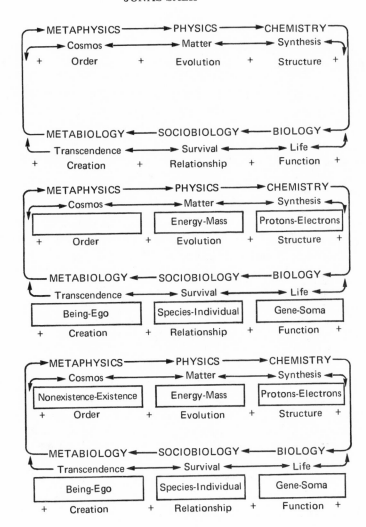

Figure 6–14.

Finally, in the box for metaphysics, I have changed my mind as to the words. Instead of speaking of nonexistence-existence, I now speak of nonmanifest and manifest. It is implied that in the metaphysical realm, where we are thinking of order in the universe, there must have been a nonmanifest order. This order then proceeded to evolve form physical matter (particles and atoms) on to molecules, cells, and organisms, and then, finally, a break and a leap to the metabiological realm with the emergence of man.

I will illustrate some of the ideas or terms of reference to somatic, genetic and individual species, to ego and being, and the analogic equivalence of ego and being. Parts of the ego system and parts of the being system are interlocked in intuition: reason and feeling, objective, subjective, morality, reality (ethics), differences, differentiation, competition, cooperation, horror, influence, win, lose, and double win. There are different strategies and there are different uses of power and influence, metabiologically, and, clearly, these also have extensions when we move into the sociobiological realm and the sociometabiological realm.

Some of the problems with which we are going to have to be concerned in education, and in our own conceptions, are the relationships between being and becoming, the absolute and the relative, the parts and the whole, extremes and balance, quantity and quality, and present and future.

Figure 6-15 is an attempt to suggest what the idea of the future might be if we assume that we are dealing with complexity of this kind. If the future will allow the intertwining of these two sets of forces, I suggest that A is the ego system that has been dominant in the past, and B is the being system that has been, I think, somewhat subservient.

Figure 6-16 is included to represent graphically one of the alternatives to what could be if we were to deal with two components of the complementary dualism of which man is composed, namely the being and the ego. Of recent interest are the studies on the differences in the role and function of the right and left halves of the brain. It had occurred to me, even before I became aware of the right-left brain phenomena, that there is an exact correspondence between what I call "being" and the right brain activity, and "ego" and the left brain activity. I simply note this to make you mindful of the necessity for developing both the right and left brains.

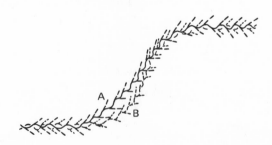

Figure 6-15. The form and design of the curves are similar to those shown in Figures 6-11 and 6-12. This graphic method of conveying an idea and its implications are discussed in the text.

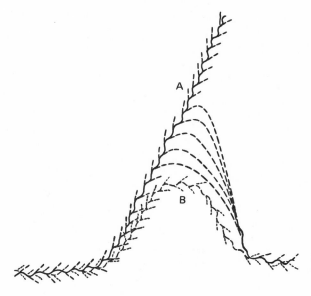

Figure 6-16.

In the past, as is suggested by Figure 6-17, the attitudes were either/or, and now, ideally, the attitude for the future must be both/and. When reference was made to Lord Snow's two cultures it was either/or. We must now dissolve that difference. In some way, we must begin to bring the two together for the wholeness that is required for the kind of human being that we would like to see emerge in the future.

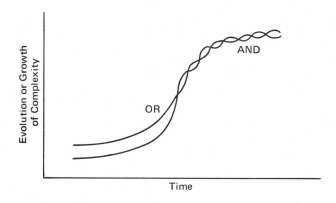

Figure 6-17.

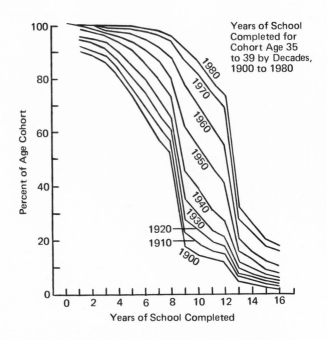

Figure 6-18. From *The Quality of Formal Instruction in the United States,* by James C. Byrnes. Published by Educational Policy Research Center, Syracuse University Research Corporation, February, 1970.

To put this discussion into cosmic perspective, I will attempt, with reference to Figure 6-20, to show what has happened in recent times in relation to man's conception of himself and his relationship to the cosmos. There was a time when the earth was thought to be flat. Then it appeared that it was round. It was then thought that the sun revolved around the earth. Then it became obvious that the earth revolved around the sun. This perception, first evident to one, eventually, became obvious to all.

In terms of man's relationship to man, we are presently at this transition, in my view, between what I call Epoch A and Epoch B on this planet. This is more evident in some parts of the planet than others. The difference now is not that we are experiencing a perceptual difference but an actual difference. Something has changed. What has changed is that we have come to the limits of the closed system and not merely in one region or other, from which people could break out by means of wars. We have come to the limits of the planet as a whole. We have succeeded and our successes have led us to the point where we have the problems that we do. We are concerned now, not with survival as was true of Epoch A, but with an epoch ahead in which our greatest concern will be that of evolution.

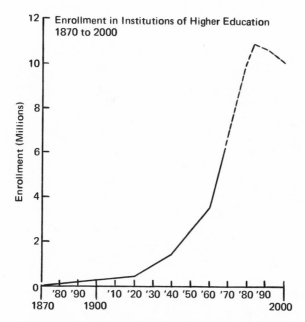

Figure 6–19. From *Quality and Equality: New Levels of Federal Responsibility for Higher Education.* **Copyright © 1968, Carnegie Foundation for the Advancement of Teaching. Used with permission of McGraw-Hill Book Company.**

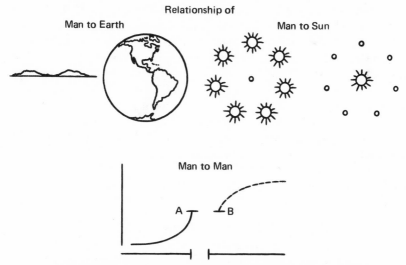

Figure 6–20. **The upper left pair of symbols refers to the change in man's concept of the earth from flat to round; the upper right set refers to man's earlier concept of the sun revolving around the sun. The lower set of curves suggests man's earlier condition, described by Curve A, and his presently developing state as suggested by the shape of Curve B.**

In dealing with the problems of evolution, the necessary strategies are the double-win, rather than the win-lose—the strategies of "if you win, I win" rather than, "if you win, I lose." This is seen in nature all the time. Suppose the genetic system and the somatic system decided to be at war with one another and one tried to dominate the other. Since they would both lose, nature found it necessary to develop double-win strategies. The same is true of life and death. If life were to win over death and death would no longer exist, neither would life exist. If death won, life would not exist. Therefore, to my mind, they both won something. Death won the individual, and life won the species. This illustrates that nature has had long experience in the use of double-win strategies for evolution. What will need to become dominant in Epoch B will be double-win rather than win-lose strategies and the use of constructive influence rather than power.

We are at a critical point between the past, the present, and the future as is illustrated in Figure 6–21. In the interval between the birth of the sun and the death of the sun, there is a long distance in time, man having made only a very recent appearance on the planet. Note when earth was born and life began. Points are indicated in millions and millions of years, and the death of the sun is presumed likely between two and five billion years from now. To those who ask whether we have enough time within which to keep from destroying ourselves, my response is that, if we do not have enough time then there is really nothing further to worry about.

I think the whole problem of education has to be examined fundamentally. I find that, by and large, people who are involved in the practical arts do things that they have speculated about or they try something simply because it seems like the right thing to do. This practical experience is transmitted from person to person and from generation to generation as in folklore. But these persons have no theoretical experience. There exists no codified theory for formal transmission.

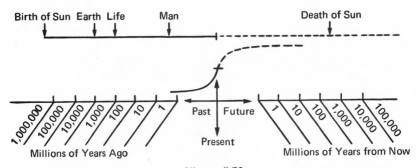

Figure 6-21.

I would like to see if we could develop a concept regarding the nature of man that would serve as a basis for a theory of education. Once such a theory has been formulated, we could then design specific experiments that would either validate the theory or cause it to be modified in some way.

There are two ways to approach the development of such a theory of education. One is that of testing questions; the other (which I have been referring to) is that of testing answers. Testing answers, as the Bronfenbrenner chapter implies, leads to more questions; whereas an answer leads simply to a "yes" or "no" and does not provide any theoretical building blocks. The scientific method would be applied to theories of education in much the same way that it is presently applied to biological and chemical theories.

The anatomy of the human mind needs to be discovered, learned, and a model formed so that it can be dealt with. Without such a model, we will continue to grope in the air, preventing ourselves from building a body of knowledge. This body of knowledge is a science that will grow out of the art—the way in which education has been carried out until now. We need to continue the art, but in the future it will be the "art of the science of education." An experienced scientific experimentalist could be of enormous value to educational research. He would know how to design a plan of inquiry, and how to break it down into subsets for the purpose of understanding.

Again, the basic problem for educators is to understand the human mind and to incorporate that understanding into our thinking and practice. This understanding is obligatory due to the change in the civilization and culture of the world from Epoch A to Epoch B. Although this process will take generations, the time to begin is right now, for with respect to the human instrument as a tool, we're still in the stage of the flint ax.

I would like to think of this transition as going through a kind of metamorphosis. This process has already evolved in varying degrees in different parts of the world. Where the change has been the greatest is where this kind of investigation should be going on. I feel that this country, for a variety of reasons, has a particular responsibility for its own development. I would like to think, therefore, of the Bicentennial year as a time—coinciding with the point of inflection on the metamorphic/growth curve (toward Epoch B), for initiating a process that will—in another two centuries—produce a progressively higher order of changes, similar to those that have been achieved in the last two centuries.

Children, being both biological and metabiological entities, must be nourished in their minds and their bodies. The basic nature of children is essentially twofold: (1) that which constitutes their genetic endowment and (2) that which constitutes all that they have experienced since their conception. Environmental influences play a very important role in their subsequent development, and the impact of all their experiences tends to bring out the best or the worst in them. Patterns of behavior, like patterns of disease, are layed down early. Yet, from childhood to adolesence and even after adulthood, changes are constantly taking place, and individuals are growing in a variety of ways. This happens not only in the body but in the mind. The purpose of education—as Fuller suggests in Chapter 5—is to provide experience, input, nourishment, and exercise for the mind so that the individual is able to live in this world, with himself and with others.

When I break down that which I call the experiential nature of man into its component parts, I find that part of what is experiential is biological, as well. After birth, a large component of the experiential component is metabiological. By metabiological I am describing a highly developed man manifested by his ability to create and to enter into relationships that are expressed by "love." Imagination and the power of transcendental experience are further manifestations of man's metabiological attributes. His intelligence and intellect (although to some extent biologically determined) is part of metabiological man by virtue of the existence of will and choice. I am still in the process of attempting to define what I mean by the metabolic realm. As I become progressively more clear about its composition, I find myself including in its definition such terms as "courage," "confidence," "responsibility," "trust," "nobility," "dignity," and other values and qualities that are sometimes said to be in the realm of good.

When I said earlier that educational experiences can either bring out the best or worst in people, it is implied that educational experiences are judged to be of greater or lesser value. That brings us to the question of *which* aspects of the mind do we want to do something about? For years we have been feeding and strengthening the cognitive aspect of the individual. More recently, we have become concerned with the so-called intuitive dimensions. Now, if in order to have a well-balanced individual, both aspects need to be exercised and strengthened, then it is clear that experiences, in the spirit advocated by Elise Boulding's essay, will have to be provided toward that end. We can and must understand what these experiences are, and we must teach them in such a way that they are learned.

How do we go about developing individuals of the highest possible quality? I think we first have to ask: "What is it that is appropriate?" What was appropriate for Epoch A is no longer appropriate in Epoch B. In the transitional period between A and B, man is the same biologically, but not metabiologically. Therefore, educational methods must change with altered concept of man. We must shake ourselves loose from thinking in outmoded terms, no matter how appropriate they were before. But we must build a new educational system upon our previous experience. In the traditional, existing pedagogy, there is heavy emphasis on the passive learning of historical events, the presumption being that knowing what others did will help the child perform as well or better. The new system will have to be more participatory than passive, more experiential than existential, because it is the experience rather than the passive process that is the major difference. The new system must lead to the development of both biological and metabiological competence. We must create possibilities for children to learn through other systems and to make use of their imagination, intuition, and of the emotional side of their lives. We must emphasize the importance of so-called noncognitive development for the full growth of the individual's capabilities. The intuitive or imaginative realm is a very important aspect of human evolution and is, in fact, perhaps the basis on which metabiologic evolution has proceeded.

I think we have to look at the educational process in stages of differentiation. Some individuals will develop particular competencies—for one reason or another (genetic or experiential)—that will tend to make them more fulfilled and productive in society while others will not. There is great diversity and variation among individuals, and this diversity, which is necessary because of our complex world, enriches the culture. Education, therefore, must provide the means (in keeping with Tyler's arguments) and the motivation that allows each individual to devlop his full potentialities. The school can serve to help facilitate the birth of these qualities. It can be looked upon as the midwife of the adult yet to be born. With this attitude, we are beginning to look at education in what I think of as the etymologic origin of the word "educare"—to draw out—as opposed to stuffing the head full of whatever seems appropriate at the time.

In the new pedagogical system (which will take a long time to evolve) we would not want to educate the child for the existing society alone, for he must be able to adapt well to an unknown future. Man *is*, already, the most adaptable of all living organisms—as evidenced by his capacity to alter his environment, to produce diverse and complex cultures, and to do all sorts of strange and curious things. I look upon these phenomena as the "metabolic" products of man's metabiologic activity.

An educational system must be contrived to make the finest human beings possible. We have to approach the problem scientifically, in the same way that we have manipulated living systems to improve health or to prevent disease. This does not mean that man should be treated like a machine. It means that we have to understand the nature of man and then treat him appropriately.

The educational system should help individuals learn to defend themselves for survival. It should teach them not only "to do," but "to be," and "to become."

commentary on salk •

Salk's basic plea is for a program of public education that will produce an informed social consciousness, as well as an emotional and intellectual commitment to a new and better social order. These aspirations are not entirely without precedent. History-minded students of educational philosophy will find in them traces of ideas that reach deeply into the theoretical past. There is, however, a new urgency to Salk's conceptions and a freshness to the framework of his arguments. It is also significant that Salk did not reach his conclusions through an examination of current educational controversy. Instead, they have been fashioned out of a probing analysis of the plight in which humankind now finds itself.

Social observers throughout the history of educational thought have periodically urged schools to teach their students about the need for a more rational society. Such recommendations have rarely been heeded; on the rare occasions when the recommendations have been acted upon, the results have usually been disastrous. The public generally seeks a school that perpetuates rather than undermines the prevailing system. It may be that while in the past the schools have been unable to contribute directly to a new social ethos, present circumstances may be different.

Several factors support this possibility. For example, our communication mechanisms have become sufficiently advanced so that it is no longer possible to hide most of the truth from our students for very long. They are as knowledgeable as most adults regarding our environmental difficulties, depleted energy resources, transnational disputes, and civil unrest. In fact, many secondary school students fault their schools for the extensive hypocrisy that they believe has been molded into the instructional program. To the extent that awareness prompts desire, the current younger generation may be a good deal more impressionable and malleable than their predecessors.

There is in our time, moreover, a clearer dissatisfaction with the existing social structure. While allusions to alienated youth have grown somewhat stale, and the protests and communal experimentation of the sixties have clearly lost their vitality, the disaffection may be more latent than dead. The rebels appear to have rejoined the mainstream but one suspects that their fury over social waste and injustice could easily be rekindled. It remains to be seen what political values the dissidents of the last decade will adopt after they enter the system and acquire a modicum of power. And the lowering of the voting age serves to make those who are recent high school graduates a more powerful force than ever before. However, of greatest significance is the fact that our own situation is strikingly different from that which prevailed in the time of Dewey, Rousseau, Spencer, and the earlier reconstructionists. It has been said that each generation tends to exaggerate the severity of its problems. Yet, it may well be that in a nuclear age the need to weave a new social fabric is greater than ever before.

For all of these reasons, a school curriculum that familiarizes students with the great dilemmas besetting the world's people—and that cultivates beliefs and values that ultimately could lead to solutions—may have more viability than has previously been the case. This point has been made at some length here because it symbolizes, in many ways, the essence of this volume. It is not Salk alone, but Boulding, Bronfenbrenner, Fuller and the other contributors as well, who stress the grave importance of a socially-conscious youth.

Salk's chapter, however, constitutes an especially powerful argument for the deliberate development of a more rational societal ethic. Its central themes are (1) that humans are blessed with great resilience and, (2) that adversity evokes the capacity to cope. The chapter's underlying rationale is derived from on analysis of the ongoing transition between two great historical epochs. Its tone is compassionate; its reasoning, tough; its conception, humanistic; its spirit, hopeful; its theory, logical; and its purpose, altruistic.

Salk's postulations suggest that we must create new kinds of schools for a new day. Convinced that humankind will need to exercise more self-expression and more self-control, he favors the teaching of aesthetics, values, world problems, and the skills of inner-discipline.

What makes Salk's arguments particularly provocative is that they cut-across a number of rationales as to the philosophical basis for instruction. There are cognitive as well as affective dimensions in his approach to curriculum. His insistence on cultivation of self-control is as conservative as his emphasis on self-knowledge is radical. The arguments are group-oriented in their accent on man's interdependence and self-oriented in their insistence on personal responsibility. Similarly, Salk is somewhat open-minded in his commitment to creative problem-solving and somewhat closed-minded in his conviction that the learning potential of individuals is diminished by the wrong kinds of education.

Salk thinks as a biologist rather than as an educator. For this reason there is a definitive eclecticism to his recommendations. Indeed some of his beliefs even seem antithetical. For example, one wonders whether a curriculum designed to stimulate self-expression and self-awareness would not in due course diminish the individual's interest in the larger social good? However, as Salk's reasoning unfolds a kind of internal consistency begins to evolve.

Some of his notions are relatively straightforward, fitting easily into contemporary theory. Others are a good deal more complex and iconoclastic. He believes children must learn to exercise responsibility from their earliest years. Such learning, furthermore, must build confidence in one's ability to manage freedom. Although there is nothing in his argument that particularly contradicts conventional doctrine, it is apparent that Salk is after something more than freedom to select colors in an art project or responsibility for keeping track of one's possessions. He seeks the painstaking maturation of adeptness in making hard choices and the gradual development of strength to assume responsibility for the consequences of decisions. He is sensitive to the paralysis induced by failure, and he wants the student to avoid defeat wherever possible and to survive when it is unavoidable.

Salk is equally clear with respect to his conviction that students must acquire a functional set of ethics. The clues to the nature of these ethics appear repeatedly in his essay: the human penchant for greed must be contained; commonality of interest must replace conflict of interest; people must achieve a sense of responsibility for others as well as themselves; human vulnerability to the temptations of excess must be contained; and the rich diversity of the species must be preserved. A few years ago Salk wrote:

> *We acknowledge the existence in each of us of different interests and desires which have to be satisfied. They may be intellectual, aesthetic, social, or personal. The exhortation to "know thyself" is based on a real need—we might call it a biological need—for an awareness of the nature of the special interests and desires which are in each of us. This awareness creates a demand for the development to the extent of our ability to develop them under the circumstances that prevail.*

It is fair to infer that Salk's conceptions of schooling are obviously humanistic and, at the same time, highly pragmatic. He is convinced that man's problems lie within himself. Nothing of worth will happen without a strong sense of purpose and a willingness to look realistically at the human predicament.

The values Salk wants schools to inculcate center on moral issues. It is important to note, however, that he would be heavily opposed to the character education of old, wherein students were taught a catechism of prescribed beliefs. Instead, he is in favor of an analytical approach to the determination of appropriate behavior, particularly in the context of current public problems. He suggests a process of goal redefinition wherein problems are explored, alternative solutions are compared and conclusions are reached as to what is, and what is not, ethical behavior. "Wisdom," he believes, "implies making judgments in advance rather than retrospectively." Yet, because of the complexity of our dilemmas, it is not merely decision-making (wherein choices are made among options) but the extension of ethical literacy (wherein the moral, amoral, and immoral aspects of a societal crisis are recognized) that should occur. Salk's hope is for a school that generates a good deal more social consciousness, particularly with respect to the critical issues of our time (population control, energy conservation, environmental preservation), and for instruction that stresses pro-social attitudes as a major objective of socialization.

The arguments have interesting curricular overtones. The work of Kohlberg, Loevenger, Combs, and others on moral growth emphasizes virtuous behavior with respect to honesty, justice, and so on. In contrast, Salk's propositions deal with the morality of social policy, thus necessitating a substantial amount of intellectual understanding and substantive fact as a preface to problem analysis. For example, judging ethical behavior with regard to energy conservation requires that the student learn something about the rate at which energy is being consumed, the possibilities for replenishing existing sources, the comparative distribution of resources internationally, and the kinds of life-styles possible under a reduced consumption rate before pursuing the question of moral choice. Therefore, to accomplish Salk's objective we need to establish a carefully articulated link between factual knowledge, conceptual understanding, moral conviction, and problem analysis.

The chapter also carries major implications for humanistic education. Aside from the specific references to phenomena rooted in the affective domain—self-expression, self-control, self-knowledge, alienation—students' concepts of ethical social policy cannot be separated from their underlying values, psychological predispositions, and personal motivations. These, self-evidently, are independent of particular subject-matter. Hence, they can be dealt with indirectly, through a variety of content or as direct ends in themselves. A significant question therefore arises: Would it be better to couple the teaching of contemporary social problems (and insights into probable future ones) with a humanistic curriculum that incorporates perceptual psychology and self-understanding, or would it be better to treat the separable elements separately, and to teach self-development and social policy analysis in disjunction. Though some educators might disagree, the advantage would seem to lie in an integrated approach. Aside from the fact that there are strong bonds between the special values relating to human affairs (and values in general) affective education is most effective when it is pursued in connection with real events.

In addition to these sweeping recommendations, Salk offers a number of specific suggestions for a future-oriented instructional program. He calls for a new mode of scientific-cultural education. He is looking for a different mix of content that is designed to (1) deepen scientific sophistication, (2) increase societal awareness, and (3) clarify the inherent relationships between these two. He is interested not only in an appropriate mental-set regarding the role of science in enriching human life, but also in corresponding anti-values—students must know, not only what they are for, but also what they are against.

Salk's notions are based on the presumption that it is possible to teach students an effective system for examining human problems. In an earlier work, Man Unfolding, *he writes*

> *The educational problem of the present—in all cultures—requires that we teach the young the greater importance of acquiring a constructive method of thinking which keeps the mind open to the discovery of new aspects of reality in a dynamic approximation of truth, than of equipping them with ideas that resist change.*[1]

He sees society as continually evolving and people as continually adapting. It is in this context that he wants students to become more receptive to change, more adept at adaptation, more willing to attack problems, more disenchanted with escapism, and more certain of their ability to build a better system.

As a researcher schooled in the evolutionary development of organisms Salk believes it is essential to provide appropriate stimulation at appropriate stages of maturation. "Not only," he says, "does failure of appropriate exposure affect the system involved, but it thereby affects the entire organism." Presumably, this means that human capacities deprived of stimulation will in time grow fallow and wasted. There is little to quarrel with in this argument. The implications for schooling are plain if we assume that humans are like other organisms in that their native potential dissipates through nonuse. Moreover, since a number of learning theorists, including Piaget, have demonstrated with reasonable conclusiveness that cognitive growth occurs in sequential stages, the merits of systematic, potential-sustaining education are difficult to refute. But, how do we determine what stimulation is appropriate at given points in the developmental continuum?

As yet, we are not able in any practical way to fix a child's maturation level and we know relatively little about providing optimum incitement at any level. It seems therefore, that Salk's conjectures should be seen, among other things, as a spur to further research. Such research will also need to deal with a number of subsidiary questions: Are alternative forms of stimulation possible at each stage of development? Can particular stimulation accelerate the developmental cycle? Does developmental rate vary with different kinds of intellectual activity? And, of greatest relevance to the present topic, what kind of instructional content would provide the best stimuli for promoting social consciousness, ethical values, constructive reasoning skills, and other objectives Salk considers crucial.

1.   Jonas Salk and Ruth N. Anshen, eds., *Man Unfolding* (New York: Harper and Row, 1972).

In what, from a curricular point of view, could be his most fertile postulation, Salk speaks of "a selection theory of learning." The structure of the theory is neatly encapsulated in a passage from an earlier writing:

> *We have referred to a "selection theory of learning," meaning that the potential for what is learned is predetermined, rather than that at the beginning there is a clean slate with unlimited potential in all individuals. The recognition that learning is a process of unfolding bears on the question of man's potential and on the possibility of educating the "more desirable" human attributes and capabilities. Whether this can be accomplished by design and plan is difficult to answer (although it would seem to be possible theoretically), but the reverse has occurred through the fault, or ignorance, or through absence of discipline, with the emergence of 'less desirable' characteristics.[2]*

There are a number of speculations inherent in this postulation. For example, there is the assumption that learning is a phenomenon in which predetermined potential is realized. Two related queries are immediately brought to mind: (1) Do children frequently, seldom, or never reach their finite limits? and (2) What signals the limit point? In addition, two further questions arise with respect to the end-goals: What should we take as the human attributes of greatest worth, and what teaching methods best facilitate their achievement?

Salk acknowledges that it is not yet clear whether these goals can be accomplished through deliberate intervention. But, he contends that since the possibilities have not yet been closed, calculated experimentation has more to offer than undisciplined guess. On this count, his logic seems impeccable: if the objectives are central to the dominant purpose of schooling, and if their viability has still to be disproved, there would be considerable benefit in further exploration. However, to truly test Salk's hypothesis much preliminary work would need to be done. A tentative, or at least representative, set of "desirable human attributes" would have to be identified, optional strategies for their attainment devised, ground rules for a legitimate experiment outlined, and criteria for estimating success or failure (in itself a task of major proportion) established. However, despite these complexities the potential profit could be sufficiently great to warrant further consideration. While, to the conventional, Salk's notions may appear far-out—and they may indeed be far-out—the fact remains that until they are tested we shall never really know.

2. Salk and Anshen, *Man Unfolding.*

The balance that Salk believes is essential to a healthy educa-tion deserves some comment. He fears that a failure to face human crisis head-on and to look for better solutions will permanently dis-able our imagined powers. He also worries about our seeming in-ability to understand our own nature, to perceive the intricacies of our interdependence, and to manage our interrelationships effec-tively. But, he is a long way from a permissive educational theology. "To free human life," he has written, "of antagonism or resistance, adversity and therefore challenge, would be to deprive it of elements akin to food, which is part of the basic process essential to its fulfillment." He feels that human talent and human spirit alike must be toughened through constructive experience. He advo-cates a curriculum that nourishes the intellect, that nurtures an optimistic spirit, reinforced by well-developed cognitive and affec-tive muscle, and that instills a firm sense of social propriety. Because the problems we confront are not easy, and because our survival depends on our ability to conquer these problems, Salk is as concerned about insufficient rigor as he is about a mindless tolerance of educational obsolescence.

He asks, therefore, for reform that will facilitate better communication between and among generations, that will counter-act the growing mood of fear and futility, that will induce an antici-pation of beneficial change, and that will convey to the young confidence in their ability to influence the coming events in their lives. One suspects it is toward these ends that Salk desperately wants to involve the younger generation as full participants in all of the endeavors through which we try to plan the human future. It may be that the young, more easily than the old, can grasp the man-dates imposed by a significant turning point in human history.

L. R.

ISSUES •

1. If, as has been suggested, people's major problems lie within them-selves, and within their human inter-relationships, what are the resulting implications for education?

2. Self-expression and self-control are widely accepted as essential in-structional objectives. What arrangements can be made for their simul-taneous cultivation, and for inhibiting one from distorting the other?

3. Some scientists have suggested that, in the education of the young, essential stimulation must be provided at appropriate stages of develop-ment. What kinds of research would clarify these developmental stages, and the corresponding stimulation necessary?

4. If general agreement could be achieved regarding desirable human attributes, could these be engendered through a particular kind of instruc-tion? .

5. In what ways might the experimental methods of the natural and physical sciences be applied to the problems of education?

6. Since our present understanding of the human mind's function is restricted, will further research on the brain have direct consequences for the operation of schools?

7. What modes of teaching best serve to enhance the human capacity for intuitive thought?

8. Could the broad objectives of education better be realized through learning activities other than those presently in use?

9. Can the student's imaginal capacities deliberately be strengthened without deleterious consequences to other educational aims?

richard s. schweiker
united states senator,
state of pennsylvania

7

PREPARING STUDENTS
FOR A WORKING FUTURE

John Gardner once observed "an excellent plumber is infinitely more admirable than an incompetent philosopher." There is, when one ponders the deeper meaning of the idea, considerable wisdom in the statement. Competence, in whatever calling, is an essential ingredient in both the individual's and the society's well being.

Gardner was reflecting the change that is slowly—too slowly perhaps—occurring in our social attitude toward the value and necessity of vocational education. We have always held the craftsman in high esteem, and the work ethic as fundamental to our value system; and yet, ironically, we have never given preparation for meaningful work the priority it deserves.

Clearly, education must train the mind, just as it must inculcate values and strengthen the individual's capacity for responsible citizenship. But it is important to recognize that vocational competence—the ability to use one's talents constructively toward productive ends—is in itself an important aspect of responsible citizenship. These beliefs, alas, seem to have fallen out of fashion. It has become commonplace to observe that skilled craftsmanship has become a thing of the past. Workers, we are told, no longer seem to take pride in their endeavors, and work itself is viewed by many as an unfortunate evil. The danger to our society, inherent in these misconceptions, is self-evident. The historical record makes it plain that no society dedicated to hedonism can long survive. It would seem, therefore, that the effort to restore the belief that meaningful work, well-done, is an essential aspect of a worthwhile life, should be made a major goal of education. In Chapter 2, Boulding argues essentially the same point.

In anticipation of tomorrow's schools, educators would do well to examine and debate the various potentials of vocational education. To resurrect a word popular during the sixties, the public desperately wants *relevant* learning. I mean to imply, by the use of the word, the concept of utility.

Utility is important for a number of reasons. First, we have become increasingly aware of the great need for vocational skill. Second, we must be concerned about the growing number of students identified by Chisholm (Chapter 3) and others, who seem apathetic both about their own personal future and the future of society. And finally, despite our present economic difficulties, and rising number of unemployed, we are puzzled as to why Ph.D.'s are driving taxicabs. We wonder, therefore, whether it is possible for the educational system to anticipate the nation's changing employment needs and facilitate a better "fit" between people and jobs.

Much of the student apathy may be attributable to the mistaken fear that there will not be an opportunity to participate in a rewarding vocation. It is important to remember, however, that a good deal more than mere income is involved in satisfying work. Of even greater significance is the intrinsic satisfaction that comes from the recognition that one's abilities are being deployed toward worthwhile ends. Few of us can find pleasure in doing something that we regard as useless. Schooling, consequently, must endeavor to fulfill three indispensable obligations. First, it must rekindle among the young a sense of the work ethic. Second, it must help students recognize that as our society continues to evolve and grow, human problems may change, but there will never be an absence of vital work to be done. Third, it must provide a foundation for vocational preparation. Fuller (Chapter 5) may be right when he observes that, in the future, education will not be particularly concerned with the earning of a living, but for the immediate future at least, vocational skills seem important.

There is a logical connection, I suspect, between general education, career education and vocational education. Through general education, the curriculum of the schools should provide children with a mastery of basic intellectual skills, a reasonable familiarity with their cultural heritage, the body of fundamental knowledge essential to active participation in the affairs of the community, and a sound set of values. Through career education, students should learn something about their own special aptitudes and capacities, the range of work specializations that will be available to them, and the requirements and rewards associated with different occupational pursuits. Finally, through vocational education, students should acquire the special competencies associated with a particular vocation.

The nature of work changes over time and some jobs in due time become obsolete. The rate of obsolescence, however, is not nearly as rapid as we are sometimes led to believe. It is little more than a mindless shibboleth, therefore, to argue because jobs change, vocational competence is an impossible goal. Aside from the fact that mastery of one vocational specialization frequently facilitates the learning of another, the person who lacks the security that comes from the sure knowledge that one's skills are marketable, can hardly be totally content.

The concept of "career education," as I understand it, means that schools will undertake to guarantee that all students on leaving school, will either be prepared for a job, or for the next step in the required training process. It also implies that students can be helped to make rational career decisions. A basic principle of public service is that institutions serving the public good must attack problems rather than avoid them. In this sense, it would be more desirable for schools to try to accomplish good vocational education and fail, than for schools to fail to try.

In a recent education bill, the Senate concluded that the youth of the nation must be able to participate fully in, and contribute significantly to, the society in which they will live and work. There was, in addition, strong emphasis on the integral relationship between success in school and later success in work. It may well be, consequently, that the entire curriculum can, directly or indirectly, contribute to the knowledge, skills and beliefs that underscore the capacity to work effectively. Tyler's references (Chapter 8) to cooperative work experiences programs, for example, are a useful illustration of what can be done.

The nation's schools have an obligation to help every student, through sound programs of vocational and career education, to grasp the part work plays in a well-rounded life, to explore personal aptitudes and employment preferences, and to acquire the general education that facilitates subsequent training and retraining. Consider, for example:

1. By 1980, 100 million Americans will be at work or in quest of work.

2. This group consists primarily of young people and represents an increase of 15 million since 1970.

3. Compared with 1968, the labor market will demand 50 percent *more* professional and technical workers and 2 percent fewer laborers.

4. Of the jobs that will become available between the present and 1980, only one in five will require a college degree.

I do not mean to argue that college offers no benefits other than those of job preparation. Rather, I mean that we may have exaggerated the importance of college with respect to work. The days when noncollege graduates were relegated to menial labor have long since passed. Many craftsmen neither wear blue collars nor earn less than their white-collar counterparts. Moreover, as technology increases, and as social injustices are corrected, new concepts of human equality are likely to be attained. The arbitrary distinc tions between so-called professional and nonprofessional will be diminished, and college will come to be seen as a liberating experience rather than as just a training means to a vocational end. More importantly, most Americans will begin to view education as a lifelong process rather than as a four-year crash course.

At present, approximately 30 percent of our students receive a vocational preparation of sufficient quality to enable them to enter the work force when they leave high school. Far more critical, however, is the fact that more than 50 percent of our young people suffer an education that neither prepares them for college nor the job market. All this means that a far stronger commitment to vocational education has become essential. In short, we seem at long last to have recognized that vocational education must be something more than shop classes for boys and homemaking experiences for girls.

If present trends are any indication, full equal opportunity for males and females will become a reality in time to come. Similarly, our notions as to what constitutes "male" work or "female" work will also alter. Traditional forms of vocational education must be replaced by other instructional arrangements that deal much more comprehensively and efficiently with the real work world.

The provision of adequate training facilities, in an increasingly sophisticated and technological society, will present serious logistical problems. Hence, we would be well-advised to initiate experiments through which the possibilities for integrating school-based and job-based vocational training are tested. We need to investigate arrangements through which students spend part of their educational time in a school and part in a real-world setting becoming familiar with tools, equipment, work styles, and—to make use of an old phrase—learning by doing.

Freedom in occupational choice is an American ideal and an educational imperative. As a result, Congress has tried to maximize individual autonomy by providing funds for the broad expansion of vocational education. Regrettably, the funds have not been steady or sufficient. Nonetheless, as our manpower requirements have changed, and our need for workers began to exceed our supply, Congress has continually acted to increase its dollar provisions for vocational education. It is ironic that persistent unemployment has plagued the labor market at a time when, until very recently, job vacancies went unfilled because of a shortage of skilled manpower.

Yet it is precisely this sort of circumstance with which education must now begin to grapple. It has, in recent times, become conventional to argue that the schools cannot overcome social problems. Perhaps so. But surely they can contribute something. Surely, we can predict in advance the kind of skilled workers the society will need and given such predictions, there does not seem to be any reason why schools cannot expose students to new work opportunities, as they occur, and initiate updated vocational training that equips them to become employable with minimum difficulty. History teaches us that most human problems do not go away by themselves. They must be recognized and attacked with creativity and intelligence. It will be through problem awareness and the use of creativity that the present ills of vocational education are most likely to be cured.

The federal-state supported program of vocational education is the largest source of formal training for occupations that do not require a college education. Established in 1917 to help increase the skills of workers, the program has been continuously modified and extended. During the 1960s, federal expenditures for vocational education increased more than six-fold—from forty-five million dollars in 1960 to three hundred million dollars in 1971. All in all, since 1963, we have spent three billion dollars.

The federal government has also begun major efforts to widen the scope of vocational education and to integrate it more effectively with general education to give young people more realistic job preparation. The Congress further demonstrated its commitment to better job training by passing the Vocational Education Act of 1963 and the amendments of 1968 that have already produced a substantial strengthening of work training programs as well as sharply increased enrollments.

The 1968 amendments authorized greater support for cooperative education programs, activities that have been among the most effective in achieving subsequent job placements for students. The odds are good that the Congress will again increase support as it undertakes this year another major review of the program. It will most likely seek further expansion of post-high-school, nonbaccalaureate, career education programs in community and junior colleges, technical colleges and area vocational colleges.

There have been a great many predictions regarding the work world of the future. While such projections are interesting, it would be unwise to assume they are much more than informed conjectures. Nothing is absolutely certain in societal evolution. We may or may not come to a thirty-two hour work week during the eighties; the balance between goods-producing industry and service-producing industry may remain constant or shift; and, the need for new kinds of vocational specialities may materialize rapidly or slowly. We cannot, therefore, regard all future projections as inevitable. Some things, however, do seem more certain than others. Employment counseling is likely to become somewhat more commonplace; efforts to minimize unemployment and to equalize employment opportunities will continue; technical skills will be increasingly essential; and virtually all employers will need to contend with rising expectations with respect to employee job satisfaction. In view of these circumstances, it is probable that the percentage of federal funds devoted to employment-related problems will increase markedly.

A number of difficulties remain. First, we find many students who could clearly profit from vocational education are not getting it. Second, there is insufficient financial support at all levels of government for vocational education. Third, job training still suffers from an unfavorable image; some students have an outright aversion to vocational education or to anything that smacks of blue collar work. Fourth, funds earmarked for specific purposes under the Vocational Act are sometimes used improperly. And fifth, we lack a satisfactory method of evaluating either the programs or their results.

It also should be noted that the General Accounting Office recently released a report that is highly critical of the nation's overall vocational education effort. Among other things, the report indicates (1) many students are being trained for jobs that no longer exist; (2) only one-third of vocationally trained students find employment in a job-skill they acquired in school; (3) many archaic programs are limited to traditional quasi-academic subjects such as Home Economics and Agriculture and high employment fields such as health and public services are ignored; and (4) there is an alarming tendency to use vocational education money to build facilities rather than to train people.

Finally, there are the alarming trends associated with negative attitudes toward work. Too many young people regard work as an unfortunate interruption in pleasure-seeking. They find it necessary to work a bit before it again becomes possible to solicit unemployment compensation. It is cynicism of this sort that the schools must zealously work to combat. A similar attitudinal problem is the scant pride workers take in their professional competence. There was a time when the desire to be regarded as a master craftsman was a high form of incentive in itself.

People work primarily to acquire income to purchase material advantages. However, meaningful work can also provide other, more intrinsic, satisfactions. Some industries and corporations, for example, reward workers who have developed a range of vocational skills while others offer incentive programs designed to reinstill an interest in quality performance. It is vital for our vocational education programs to help the student recognize that satisfying work can provide much more than a way of paying restaurant bills, car installments, and department store charges.

Even if we solve all of these problems, we will still be faced with the arduous task of improving the transition from school to work. Such improvements cannot be accomplished without major changes in our thinking about the function of schools. Scanlon's warnings (Chapter 4) about the coming crisis in school administration are equally pertinent here.

During the past decade, a good deal of speculation has gone on among professional educators about the possibilities of a more flexible educational system. The issues that have been debated include: a reorganization that makes it possible for students to intersperse their education with periodic work experiences in the outside world; the establishment of alternative instructional programs so that students of a different bent can reach their educational goals in different ways; abolishing compulsory education, say, after the age of sixteen; and the establishment of provisions that make it possible for individuals to pursue liberal education throughout the course of their lives. It would be inappropriate for a layman to express opinions on these matters, if only because they require the best judgment of our most astute educators. As a member of the Senate, however, I cannot help but observe that some of these potential refinements in our educational system would seem to offer considerable advantage. In particular, it seems clear that an educational system that made life-long learning possible—allowing people to continue their general education after they commence their work careers—would represent a considerable improvement over the present way of things.

We have, in modern times, become increasingly infatuated with the myth that every boy and girl should spend four years in college. As a consequence, all other paths to responsible adulthood are now regarded as inferior. This myth, if allowed to continue unchecked, could easily do us in.

There is a very good chance we may have greatly exaggerated the virtues of college. We are beginning to suffer from a rampant epidemic of "sheepskin psychosis." The phrase is the title of a book on the subject written by John Keats.

A number of unfortunate effects have been brought about through the irrational emphasis on "college as a must." Millions of young people, for example, endure college even though their ultimate vocational choices do not require an advanced degree. Admittedly, higher education yields a considerable number of benefits other than preparation for work, but, if these benefits can be obtained through more efficient and more economical arrangements, nothing will be lost and a very great deal will be gained. Moreover, many employers readily acknowledge that college training is not essential to the successful performance of the jobs for which they recruit. For them, the college or university diploma is a routine screening devise. Even by conservative estimates, the cost in time and money to the student, his or her parents, and the public purse—to educate individuals who enter fields that do not require college training—is staggering. Interestingly, the Supreme Court has acted on this issue by ruling unanimously in 1971 "that a company may not require education as a qualification for employment unless it can show the relevance of that education to the particular job."

An even more serious side effect of the "sheepskin psychosis" has been the downgrading of all work roles that do not require a white collar. The tragedy here, obviously, is that we have allowed artificial and meaningless status symbols to distort our values. Apart from the fact that many noncollege graduates earn more than workers with college degrees, we now have a surfeit of college-trained personnel in vocations that are already overloaded, and at the same time, there is a vast shortage of trained specialists.

There was a time in history when workers who had mastered a craft, or who had become expert in the technical skills related to a trade, were valued and esteemed. Having gone too far, we perhaps should return to an earlier scheme of values, wherein skilled specialists are honored and rewarded, irrespective of the color of their collars.

There also has been a deleterious effect on our colleges and universities. Forced to cope with large numbers of students who do not like college, and who would be happier and more productive in satisfying and productive work, institutions of higher education have been forced to distill and prostitute a good deal of their educational offerings.

It is in these connections that effective career and vocational education could make a considerable contribution. If, for example, education can help young people to understand the correct relationship between college and particular vocational endeavors, if students can be helped to recognize that large numbers of high-school graduates earn excellent livings, lead rich and fulfilling lives, and enjoy living standards exceeding those of many college graduates, and if the virtues of lifelong education—and a lasting passion for learning and personal self-development—can be instilled, a good many of our present difficulties can be eased.

The career education movement, judging by the debates that ensue at the convocations of professional educators, has become a subject of considerable controversy. Some critics have contended there really are only seven or eight different kinds of jobs, and early stress upon career selection is therefore indefensible. Others have argued the schools have inadvertently engaged in a "cooling out" process; by steering some youngsters into less-desirable vocations, and restricting entry into the more desirable ones, schools perpetuate the status quo and make a mockery of our quest for equalizing human opportunity. Yet another group of critics have suggested that attempts to eliminate the "mismatch" between workers and jobs, and to assist individuals to discover the particular vocation most suitable to their talents and interests, are hopeless because the right job can only be found through trial and error, and because young people must adjust to whatever the marketplace demands at a given point in time. It is fitting that these debates go on, since the kind of policy errors discussed by Rubin in Chapter 9 may be involved, and scholars address themselves to the identification of weaknesses in our present educational system. Only in this way can problems be understood and ameliorated. It may be, after deeper study, that some of the criticism will prove justified and some will consist largely of hyperbole. And, if it turns out, as Ivar Berg has suggested, education serves mainly to increase the life benefits of the privileged, rather than to meet the requirements of the work world, we can then deal with our inadequacies more astutely.

Until these conflicting claims are researched and clarified, however, the concept of career education remains promising and viable. So long as this is the case, educators would do well to test its ultimate potential. In this spirit, then, those involved in the career education movement might direct their endeavors toward preparing youth for the probably immediate future of the work world. Several developments, for instance, seem virtually certain.

One, the worker who is to participate successfully in the labor force will need to bring a great deal of technical knowledge to his work. Two, he will rely increasingly on technological hardware and less on manual skills. Three, people no longer can expect that a single occupation will cover a lifetime of work. We are now being told, for example, that a twenty-four-year-old man can expect to change jobs six to seven times during a workspan of forty-three years. A diversity of skills and retraining capacity will, therefore, be more of an advantage than single-skill competence. Four, more women can now expect a longer work life. In 1900, the average woman's vocational tenure was 20 percent of a man's. The percentage has risen steadily and is still growing.

This year Congress is again conducting an extensive review of the entire federal vocational education policy. It intends to evaluate what already has been achieved as well as what remains to be done. I am confident the Congress will conclude, as I have, that the federal commitment is not yet adequate.

It seems clear that we must come to grips with the relationship of vocational education to manpower training programs in general. Furthermore, vocational education must be brought more into the mainstream of the curriculum proper. Far greater attention must be given to vocational education for the disadvantaged and the handicapped. Job placement must be given greater priority, and all of our various training programs should be made more current and more job-oriented.

We would make more rapid progress if vocational educators could work cooperatively with the labor leadership and with business and industrial management in order to discover new, more effective approaches to vocational preparation. Despite the radical notions of the recent past, work is an essential aspect of our American tradition. Our typical worker enjoys a standard of living that seems unbelievable to the rest of the world. Americans have already sensed that a technological society does not need to be a bad society. Efforts to reduce human labor through the use of machines are not, in themselves, bad. I cannot help feel that labor, business, and industry would welcome an opportunity to assist young people to choose a vocational specialization, and would welcome an opportunity to collaborate with our educational institutions in their preparation.

The schools, after all, service involuntary clients. The obligation to deal with them as honestly and as favorably as possible is urgent

commentary on schweiker .

Richard Schweiker writes from the vantage point of the United States Senate. It is therefore understandable that his arguments reflect a general concern about the state of society's health and welfare. Unemployment takes a massive toll, both on the individual and on the community. Therefore, Schweiker reasons that both the citizenry and the social system will profit if education can sustain the work ethic and instill in the younger generation a permanent belief in the virtues of satisfying work. Thus he views vocational competence as an integral aspect of citizenship.

His apprehensions may be prompted by recent data indicating that jobs and work have lost their importance in the life interests of youth. Surveys conducted by Yankelovich suggest that the by-products of the counterculture movement have substantially diminished the value young people attach to vocational success.[1] *However, the exact meaning of the evidence is less than conclusive. Fully four-fifths of college students acknowledged that the careful selection of a career was a matter of considerable significance. It may well be that as the ups and downs in the belief scale settle, the most definitive changes in youth's attitudes toward work will reflect more on the quality and meaning of work than on its basic importance.*

The impressions of the young are notably temporal and fickle, primarily because of their continuous need to maintain a balance—in goals and aspirations—between the competing demands of idealism and social reality. In some instances, the views of contemporary youth are more radical than those of their counterparts of a decade ago; in other instances, they are more conservative. For example, the belief that effort should be devoted to the accomplishment of desirable social change remains relatively high, but the commitment to perpetuating such change through vocational involvement in social service (teaching, family counseling) has declined. Similarly, while the general posture of youth is somewhat more revolutionary than it was twenty-five years ago, occupational interest in affluent and prestigious professions (law, medicine and accounting) is at least as high.

Schweiker's conception of vocational competence as a facet of citizenship education is of special significance. Human desires are inseparable from human character. In large

---

1. Daniel Yankelovich, *The New Morality: A Profile of American Youth in the 70s* (New York: McGraw-Hill, 1974).

measure, what we think important, defines who and what we are. A social environment, therefore, that demands extreme flexibility in aspirations may also produce an uncertain character. In other words, as long as the ideals of young people are at odds with reality and as long as reality exerts its own inevitable pressures, the permanence of the ideals is endangered. Recognizing this, Schweiker wants the vocational aspects of education to provide a shelter against alienation, to cultivate a lasting devotion to valued ends—particularly with respect to the primacy of productive endeavor in a well-rounded existence—and to entrench, in the belief patterns of young adults, goals that not only set direction, but also give life purpose and meaning. Without these, human intent becomes random and haphazard, a sense of worthwhile achievement becomes difficult or impossible to attain, and moods of despair and futility come quickly.

Perhaps, it is for these reasons that Schweiker sees a logical connection between general education, career education, and vocational education. He uses an arbitrary set of definitions for the terms that seem as defensible as any others in common use, and he conceives of an interrelationship that is natural and organic. "Through general education," he says, "the curriculum of the schools should provide children with a mastery of basic intellectual skills, a reasonable familiarity with their cultural heritage, the body of fundamental knowledge essential to active participation in the affairs of the community, and a sound set of values." Through career education, in contrast, "Students should learn something about their own special attitudes and capacities, the range of work specializations which will be available to them, and the requirements and rewards associated with different occupational pursuits." Lastly, vocational education is directed toward "the special competencies associated with a particular vocation."

Virtually everything in the curriculum is seen as contributing either directly or indirectly to vocational adequacy. It is interesting to note, that in the report of the Panel on Youth, chaired by Coleman, a similar emphasis was placed on broad rather than narrow preparation for work. Listed first among the four objectives of self-development was the following:

Cognitive and noncognitive skills necessary for economic independence and for occupational competence. We refer here not only to verbal and mathematical skills, but also to a variety of social skills and of manual and technical skills to fit the wide range of contemporary occupations.[2]

2.   James S. Coleman, *Youth: Transition to Adulthood,* Report of the Panel on Youth, President's Science Advisory Committee, (Chicago: University of Chicago Press, 1974).

There seems to be some agreement that a comprehensive general education has utility, not only with respect to the student's overall acculturation and socialization, but also with respect to subsequent employability. Moreover, a liberal, as opposed to a parsimonious, program of occupational preparation is almost certain to elicit greater student satisfaction, if only because diversity enhances option and choice.

During the present transitionary cycle, it is difficult to judge whether the counterculture of the 1960s has reached its zenith and is past history, or whether its momentum will be sustained during the balance of the 1970s. In either case a substantial body of vestiges is likely to remain. The interest of youth will undoubtedly continue in sensory as well as didactic knowledge, in learning through personal rather than vicarious experience, and in participatory rather than spectator social involvement. Therefore, for all of these reasons, Schweiker's stress on the interrelationships among general, career and vocational education seems reasonable.

There are other elements in the changing attitudes toward work that could be a good deal more problematic. Here again, because we are in a time of flux, youths' values are not entirely clear. Nonetheless, a trend of sorts is clearly perceptible. Havighurst and Gottlieb have written:

> *There seems to be general agreement with the proposition that young people today are more concerned with intrinsic than extrinsic factors in their work. The intrinsic factors are challenge, responsibility, and achievement—the content of work. Extrinsic factors are the environment of work—pay, supervision, physical working conditions.*

The authors point out that the critical concerns of those presently entering the work force are not related to income, status and security, and they suggest that their overriding interest is concerned with:

> *finding careers and work settings that will allow the individual to do relevant things, facilitate self-growth and development, enhance the use of unique skills and ideas, encourage creativity and learning, and, of primary importance to many, enable the individual to help others and to contribute to the quality of the society.[3]*

Put plainly, the work expectations of the current generation are considerably higher than those of the previous generations. It is not merely a job that is being sought, but a job that stimulates and

---

3. Robert J. Havinghurst and David Gottlieb, "Youth and the Meaning of Work," in *Youth,* 74th Yearbook of the National Society for the Study of Education, Robert J. Havinghurst and Philip H. Dreyer, eds. (Chicago: University of Chicago Press, 1975).

satisfies in many different ways. These inclinations, are, of course, easy to understand. For many, in fact, they constitute the basic incentive for pursuing career education in the first place. Nevertheless, two difficulties do exist: (1) attractive and appealing employment cannot be made available to everyone; (2) other, less desirable work must still be performed. For example, the salary derived from an interesting and rewarding job may yield money with which to buy a good restaurant dinner. However, someone less blessed in employment must eventually collect and wash the dinner dishes. Thus we return, full circle, to the hard enigmas generated by a growing inflation in human aspiration.

Schweiker seems to be implying that an equilibrium must be maintained between those who view work as the essence of life and those who view it as distinct from recreation and play. Work is welcome routine, free of psychic tension to the former; while to the latter it is a colossal bore. Obviously, all people should find, somewhere in their lifestyle, a source of satisfaction and self-fulfillment. For many, it may not be important whether the satisfaction emanates from the pursuits of work or the pursuits of leisure, as long as it is there. Fortunately, some of us find habit and stability in our jobs preferable to excitement and unpredictability. A balanced vocational hierarchy, essential to the social system, consequently, seems possible.

Schweiker also alludes to the problems of equilibrium, and the attendant implications for career education. He places considerable emphasis on the perils of "sheepskin psychosis" and the myths regarding college degrees. He is convinced that society will survive its present difficulties and prosper. Among other things, he believes this prosperity will blur the present status distinctions between professional and nonprofessional vocations, increase the comparative affluence of blue-collar workers, and make the perquisites of the good life available to all occupational strata. He argues, therefore, that school-based career education should attempt to restore the fallen image of occupations that do not require college training. Presumably, he would not oppose college for anyone who regards higher education as a vehicle for personal growth and development, rather than as a passport to professional status.

One wonders, in this regard, whether career education might not benefit from parallel activities aimed at parent education, since, in many instances, the parent rather than the student may be the real cause. However, irrespective of whether some students enroll in college out of deference to parental wish, or out of the mistaken notion that the professions are the sine qua non of the work world, present circumstances certainly serve to reinforce Schweiker's convictions. Large numbers of college graduates, unable to enter their chosen profession because of an abundance of trained personnel, have turned to other fields and crafts. Surprisingly, many have found the work appealing and some seem to have lost interest in the pursuit for which they were originally trained.

Schweiker is open-minded regarding the controversies that surround the career education movement. He acknowledges that it may not be possible to find a suitable fit between the student's nature and an appropriate vocation. He is equally willing, until more is known, to grant the benefit of the doubt to those who insist that vocational education will work to the advantage of privileged students and further penalize deprived students; perpetuate the tendency to over-train and over-educate workers beyond the point of real need; and advertently or inadvertently aid and abet the "cooling-out" process. The reference here is to Goffman's famous statement with respect to "cooling-out the mark."[4] The maneuver is one in which individuals and groups, victimized by manipulation, are convinced that their problems are the result of their own inadequacy and gullibility. Used later by other writers, the phrase now denotes situations in which minority groups are placed into menial jobs and persuaded that such work provides the best solution to the problems caused by their circumstances. Although he does not mention the related "gatekeeping" indictment (limiting access to particular vocations through the imposition of difficult and sometimes artificial educational requirements), Schweiker seems sensitive to the dangers of exploitation, inherent in career education, suggesting that if the criticisms eventually prove valid, "we can then deal with our inadequacies more astutely."

Schweiker's objectivity on these matters is unquestionably commendable. In addition, he may be on legitimate ground when he states that we do not yet have a sufficiently adequate understanding of the potential of career education to make conclusive judgements. Still, considerable skepticism has been expressed and, at best, the movement faces a number of severe tests. Knowledgeable observers think it unlikely that career education will reap much more benefit than past vocational programs, largely because the schools cannot overcome severe difficulties that are imbedded in the social system. In an analysis of current programs, Grubb and Lazerson[5] reason that "The faith that the moral benefits of work can counteract a sense of individual aimlessness or a lack of attachment to social institutions is seriously misplaced." They are further convinced that the theory underlying career education is based on false premises, since the societal forces that create employability and unemployability are ignored. To accomplish its intended purpose, they say, career education must initiate fundamental social changes—changes that clearly are beyond its power.

4.   E. Goffman, "Cooling the Mark Out: Some Aspects of Adaption to Failure," *Psychiatry,* 1952.

5.   W. Norton Grubb, and Marvin Lazerson, "Rally Round the Workplace: Continuities and Fallacies in Career Education," *Harvard Educational Review,* Vol. 45, No. 4, November, 1975.

Fears have also been expressed about career education's potential abuse of equal opportunity principles. Entry into particular vocations often depends on the individual's ability to secure prerequisite training. Those who control access to this training—counselors, admissions officers, and others who determine entrance qualifications—therefore serve as control valves. That is, they accept (on one basis or another) some individuals for training and reject others. It is conceivable, consequently, that without the exercise of great care with respect to objectivity, career education decisions during the public school tenure could prevent some students from obtaining the required training and thus deny them the right to a vocation of their choice.

The problem is particularly acute because of the traditional biases and prejudices stemming from race and ethnicity. In commenting on a related problem Erickson says flatly: "We have found that ethnicity, race and communications style can affect the quality of counseling students receive. Because these factors are an integral part of face-to-face interaction, they probably affect other interactions in the school and therefore are important educational variables."

Yet, for all of the criticisms, the parochial wrangles among experts of different philosophies, and the inherent pitfalls, career education deserves the right to a fair and impartial trial. This, in essence, is the gist of Schweiker's narrative. It will be interesting to see what happens as career education's own career unfolds. If its protagonists can successfully anticipate and compensate for its latent defects, they will contribute significantly to an improved curriculum. And if not, perhaps something useful can be learned from the effort.

L. R.

ISSUES •

1. What balance between vocational and general education best facilitates a transition between schooling and work?

2. What particular values and beliefs enable the young to grasp the place of satisfying work in a well-rounded existence?

3. Can a system of social indicators, through which the schools can anticipate the probable needs of the work world in sufficient time to make appropriate adjustments in the curriculum, be developed?

4. Collaborative approaches to career education, involving schools, business and industry, will become increasingly important. How can the impediments to such collaboration be overcome?

5. Are new patterns of vocational education, offering greater pragmatism, possible?

6. The concept of community-centered learning is based on the assumption that substantial parts of the child's education can occur both in the school and in the work environment. What factors would permit us to determine what is best learned in the classroom, and what is best learned in the external setting?

7. As matters presently stand, vocational education and general education are viewed as separate entities. How can we acquire greater insight with respect to the common ground between the two, and the educational experiences that are contributory to both?

8. Present devices for evaluating the outcomes of vocational and career education are essentially primitive. Can we design and test better, long-range appraisal procedures?

9. Although much theoretical thought has been devoted to the *ends* of career and vocational education, considerably less experimentation has gone on with respect to the *means*. Which strategies will best allow us to compare the advantages and disadvantages of various alternatives?

10. If the concept of lifelong education is to become a reality, research must define, somewhat more clearly, the learning that must precede, accompany, and follow work experience. How should such research be organized?

ralph w. tyler
Center for Advanced
Study of Behavioral
Sciences

EDUCATION: PAST, PRESENT, AND FUTURE

It is perhaps appropriate to review, briefly, what has been accomplished by education in this country in the past 200 years. In doing so, we find that the schools of America have been more responsive to social change than the schools of any other nation.

One of the obvious illustrations of this responsiveness is the development of literacy. At the time of the Declaration of Independence, less than 15 percent of the colonial adults were literate. Except for the owners of large plantations, most Americans made their living in ways that did not require reading, writing, or much computation. The newspapers of that day were read by a small fraction of the population, and only a few families had many books. Today, it is estimated that at least 80 percent of adults in the United States are literate. Our schools are mainly responsible for this great change.

To review more comprehensively the response of the schools to changing needs and opportunities, let us look at the three fundamental educational tasks of a modern, democratic society, namely, socialization, social mobility, and individual self-realization. With regard to socialization, the task is to educate people so that they may be able to participate constructively in the economy, the policy, and the socio-civic life of the society.

 In the economic sphere, the schools, together with other educative institutions in our society, have produced a flexibile labor force that has reacted effectively, with a relatively short time lag, to a changing occupational structure. It is this flexibility with which

Schweiker is concerned in Chapter seven. The structure, it might be added, has changed more rapidly in the United States than in any other nation. The best example is the move of American labor from agriculture into industry and services. At the time of my birth, 38 percent of the U.S. labor force was engaged in agriculture, and now it is less than 5 percent. In 1900, the agricultural labor force was largely unskilled. The simple ways of producing food and fiber on the farm have now been replaced by much more complex ways of choosing seed, irrigating, and treating and fertilizing the ground. Modes of harvesting and marketing have become much more complex and are often associated with large types of producer cooperatives, like Sunkist oranges in my home state. This rapid change in agricultural production has taken place without a period of crisis, because we have people able to carry on the new technology. Contrast our experience with the great difficulty Russia has had in trying to modernize its agriculture, its labor force being largely inflexible.

Another illustration of the way in which our schools have been able to develop a flexible labor force is in the shift from one used largely to produce material goods to one in which more people are producing services. In 1900, nearly 80 percent of the labor force was engaged in producing and distributing material goods. According to the 1970 census, only 35 percent of the labor force was so engaged, while about 65 percent was available for our nonmaterial needs, especially health, education, recreation, social services, management, accounting, science, and engineering. Persons providing these services need different characteristics from those required for manufacturing. This shift is from a major need for manual strength and manual dexterity to jobs that require social and intellectual skills. This shift has also taken place without a crisis as our educational institutions have helped people develop these skills. Although we face serious problems in occupational education, we must not lose sight of the fact that over the past two centuries our schools have responded remarkably well to great changes in the occupational structure of this nation.

In the political sphere, our schools have also responded to changing conditions. We still have the government that was established 200 years ago. No other large nation has been able to maintain a stable political system over this period of time. We have not experienced the four Reichs of Germany, the three different types of government in France, the revolutions in Russia and China, nor even the kinds of changes that have taken place in the English government. Our Constitution and our way of life have been maintained in spite of the fact that we have absorbed through immigration millions of people coming from a wide variety of backgrounds.

In the socio-civic sphere, our schools have been supportive of friendly, democratic social relations. This is in contrast to the relations in a stratified society evident to some extent in England, but more so in France and Italy, where one of the problems of an effective labor force is the wide separation of classes and the apparent contempt that the upper classes have for the lower. The United States has a much less highly stratified society and the schools reflect it. I visit classes in many schools every month and I find that, by and large, children are humanely treated and there is respect for the personality and dignity of the individual. There are some exceptions, I am sure, and books like those of Holt and others speak of these exceptions. However, in general, American schools contribute greatly to the development of the kind of personal-social relationships that are central to a genuine democracy. The school does to a considerable degree exemplify, as John Dewey hoped it would, the ideals of deomocracy: respect for the individual, justice in the classroom, student participation in decisions, and personal satisfaction in tasks performed well. Our schools have responded to the changing requirements of socialization in American society.

Let us turn to social mobility. The last study of the degree of social mobility in the United States was made twenty years ago, but there have been no marked changes since then. At that time, approximately 50 percent of the American people in the probability sample studied had moved up one social class; 25 percent had moved down. The comparable estimates for Canada are 36 percent and 18 percent, and for the United Kingdom 22 percent and 11 percent. Social mobility is heavily dependent on education. A young person must learn to carry on roles different from those of his parents. Our schools have furnished opportunities for many students to gain the education required to get higher social and occupational status than their parents. This high level of social mobility is possible partly because of the changing nature of our occupational structure. There are fewer and fewer unskilled jobs and more and more opportunities for people to attain higher occupational and social positions. This is true partly because our schools have furnished the necessary education.

The contribution of our schools to individual self-realization is harder to estimate, for it is not easy to identify the persons who have been able to obtain, through schooling, the things that helped them become unique. We do know that there is an increasing number of Nobel Prize winners who have been educated in America. We have an increasing percentage of writers, artists, and musicians—persons whose accomplishments are beyond the requirements of socialization to meet the nation's needs. These talents although often useful to and appreciated by society, are not generally part of the task of socialization, nor do they necessarily contribute to social mobility. Even though we have no specific evidence as to the number, it still seems reasonable to say that the U.S. schools have contributed significantly to the self-realization of many individuals.

In reviewing the past responses of our schools to the changes in society, one is impressed by the fact that the changes in the schools have generally been gradual. The only cases I find in which almost revolutionary changes have taken place are situations in which special interest groups have developed sufficient political power to demand them. Perhaps the most dramatic illustration is the establishment of the landgrant colleges. By the mid-1800s the agricultural and mechanical classes—the small farmers and the townspeople who had shops (carpenters, black-smiths, and other kinds of "mechanics")—had become a majority and possessed considerable political power. They wanted their children to have the advantage of a college education, at that time largely limited to the children of professionals and large landowners. They were told by the Ivy League colleges of that day that their children did not have the potential for a college education. Not even knowing Latin and Greek, how could they possibly benefit from a college education? Since the existing colleges were unwilling to provide for them, their political leaders went to Congress and persuaded Senator Morrill of Vermont to introduce the Morrill Act. Passed in 1862, it provided that any state that would establish a college for the agricultural and mechanical classes would be given some of the land the Federal Government was accumulating with the westward movement into new territories. By the end of the 19th century, almost all of the states had landgrant colleges, and now every state and the Commonwealth of Puerto Rico has at least one landgrant college.

I saw the diary of one of the early professors at Michigan State, the first of the landgrant colleges. He reported how difficult it was for the faculty to identify the strengths of these new kinds of students and their interests, and to devise a curriculum appropriate for those strengths and interests, but they finally did so. By 1930 these colleges and universities were accepted not only as an important educational resource for students from the agricultural and mechanical classes, but also as good general educational institutions. Now, when we think of such universities as Ohio State, Michigan State, the University of Illinois, the University of Wisconsin, and the University of California, we do not usually remember them as "revolutionary landgrant colleges." This response to a powerful societal demand was the creation of a new type of educational institution.

A more recent illustration of a great and rapid response was the development of the junior colleges (which since 1950 have often been called community colleges). The idea of the junior college was first proposed in 1892 by William Rainey Harper, President of the University of Chicago, and he helped to establish one at Joliet, Illinois. Shortly thereafter, the idea was picked up by the leaders of the lower, middle, and working class groups in California who had migrated to that state seeking new opportunities for their children to obtain free higher learning. They were able to influence the California legislature to authorize secondary school districts to establish junior colleges, and soon a score of them were formed.

Another illustration is the rapid expansion of the American high school since 1890. The earliest American secondary schools were the Latin grammar schools. Very few of them changed into high schools. Some changed into academies, like the one founded in Philadelphia by Benjamin Franklin, to provide more practical education than that of the Latin grammar schools, but most American high schools were new institutions established to meet the demands of citizens who sought broader educational opportunities for their children.

Today it seems less likely that great educational changes will come through the creation of wholly new institutions. Our school population is not increasing and most children are already in a school. The development of the landgrant college was possible because there was a great number of young people who were not attending college and wanted a college responsive to their needs. New institutions could be formed to care for the new clientele without destroying the old ones. Now, with a near zero population growth and a sufficient number of teachers for the present requirements of the school, it is not likely that new institutions will be established in any large numbers. We do not have a new clientele, and we would have the problem of displaced teachers. Hence, when we consider reforms or great improvements in schooling to respond to new conditions and new societal demands, we must also consider the present institutions, with the present teachers, with only a modest turnover in personnel. This is an important constraint in planning "new schools." Scanlon's remarks (Chapter 4) regarding new leadership responsibilities reflect these constraints.

From the financial point of view, schools face another constraint. We are already devoting 6 percent of our gross national product to elementary and secondary education, in contrast to 3 percent prior to the Second World War. It is increasingly difficult for American schools, both public and private, to increase their financial support. It seems unlikely that funds can be obtained on a large scale to add new institutions. We cannot plan new institutions entirely apart from the present schools.

This leads to another important factor in the development of educational innovations—the reeducation of the personnel involved. The Federal Government made its first very large investment in curriculum development with a grant by the National Science Foundation to the Physical Science Study Committee for the development of a new high school physics course. Before they were through funding the course development, the Federal Government had spent about $11 million. In a study conducted by John Goodlad and reported in the book *Behind the Classroom Doors,* it was found that about 70 percent of the schools that were using the materials of this physics course were using them like the textbooks they had before—something for students to memorize and to recite—quite different from the purpose of the course: to promote student initiated inquiry and active involvement of students in learning. The efforts now underway to educate teachers for the course are estimated to require at least $100 million in order to reach a point where 50 percent of U.S. high schools will be using PSSC as intended. It seems clear that the funds needed to develop a design for a new educational program and the instructional materials required are small compared to the expenditures necessary to help teachers learn to carry out the program effectively, if it involves new ways of thinking and working.

Another illustration of the cost of significant changes in schools is the experience of Israel in developing a high school biology program—a modification in Hebrew of one of the programs constructed in the United States by the Biological Sciences Study Committee. Although there are only 3 million people in that country and, correspondingly, a relatively small number of students, the effective implementation of this program is requiring a heavy investment for Israel. They are having to spend all the money available for in-service education for twenty-one years to get that one program effectively implemented. Needed innovations in other subjects cannot be undertaken for lack of funds.

In brief, it seems likely that our society will not support a widespread comprehensive revolution in its schools. If the schools are to respond to societal demands, we need to concentrate on those critical areas where there are serious problems rather than try to mount a program requiring the complete reconstruction of the school.

The place where children are not learning the basic skills of literacy is an illustration of a possible attack upon a serious problem. The National Assessment shows that about 75 percent of the children in this country are achieving quite well, but 20 to 25 percent are not. Hence, initial efforts could be concentrated on the places where there are serious problems in acquiring the basic skills of literacy and of study. Those are largely in those schools having a concentration of children from low income homes, where the parents are not able to provide what middle or upper class families are able to provide in terms of support for the education of their children. As the points in the Bronfenbrenner and Chisholm essays (Chapters 1 and 3) show, the nation does not yet do right by those of its citizens still afflicted by poverty.

In this connection, the question should be raised about the helpfulness of individualized instruction. You may recall the study by Sidney Pressy, the originator in 1931 of the first teaching machine. He found that any kind of programmed materials were not better than the textbook and often inferior for the student who knew how to study because the textbook enabled the person to move at his own pace without the intrusion of a designed series of steps. Apparently, a considerable fraction of young people are able to find their way through instructional materials without having to have individually prescribed programs. But individualization seems helpful for the children who do not easily find their way and need assistance in learning. It seems likely that somewhere between 15 and 25 percent of elementary school children in the United States can be aided by various kinds of individualization. For the children needing it, individualized instruction provides better management of their own efforts and better feedback on how well they are doing.

However, in attacking the problem of educating disadvantaged children we should consider additional factors in effective learning. A major example is motivation. In my work with disadvantaged children, I find that many of them are not interested in the learning tasks assigned them. Motivation is not provided automatically by most of the common methods of individualization. The problem of the school is to help the youngster who seems to lack motivation to see the connection between what he is learning at school and at home or elsewhere. Often, he comes from a community and a home where the adults think the school has little to do with their problems—where they think the school is often antithetical to their own values and their own beliefs. To improve learning in this case the school must provide a way of helping the child and his parents see what the role of the school is and that it is congruent with their own hopes and aspirations.

Another thing often interfering with the learning of disadvantaged children is that they do not see clearly what they are expected to learn. A middle-class child has usually had a great deal of exposure to literature, and he understands what reading is. Hence, he sees what it is he is to learn. But many other children do not know what they are expected to learn from the exercises that they are assigned, and they are often bewildered.

A third difficulty disadvantaged children face is the lack of variety of opportunities to practice what they are learning and adequate time to practice.

A fourth condition for learning that is often absent for the disadvantaged is positive reinforcement. Although most teachers realize the constructive influence of encouraging a child in his attempts to learn, they tend to give the rewards to those who are already highly successful. The kids who really need encouragement do not get it. It is for this reason that Chisholm (Chapter 3) places such great emphasis on motivation. Furthermore, many teachers do not realize that in certain situations praise from the teacher is not viewed as a reward by the child. With some of his classmates, the kid who is praised is thought to be the teacher's pet. In such cases, the child is embarrassed rather than encouraged by praise. Teachers should understand the children and what is required to encourage them and to give reinforcement.

Evaluation and feedback are also important conditions for learning that are often lacking for disadvantaged children.

A frequently overlooked problem is how to help the child transfer what he is learning in school to the out-of-school situations in which it can be appropriately used. This is increasingly serious as the school becomes more isolated from the rest of society.

Consideration should also be given to the social influences on learning. In the early 1960s a number of publishers came out with programmed materials, since programmed instruction was being given a good deal of attention in the press. Now most programmed materials have a very minor market, largely because of the fact that kids get bored if they work alone. I have found one successful way of using programmed materials. This is to use them in a social situation in which the child identifies something he needs to learn. To use an analogy: in a game, he plays basketball, but he discovers he has difficulty in learning to dribble. He goes off for a time, gets some practice dribbling, comes back, uses it in the game and sees how valuable his practice proved. One way in which solo learning and social learning can be brought together is to alternate between solo practice and using in social situations what has been practiced. Help the child see what he needs for constructive participation in the social situation, and then give him an opportunity to work independently on it.

Another social influence is that of community attitudes. Consider, for example, the fluctuation that took place in the National Assessment results on science between 1969 and 1974. During that five-year period, the emphasis on science in the larger communities (high in 1969) dropped markedly by 1974, and more emphasis was given to other things, especially to social problems. It is interesting that the National Assessment shows that during that period there was a drop in science performance on the part of the children in the United States. There are other possible explanations for this, but I believe that children and youth are influenced by the emphasis they see in the adult society and they are likely to give greater attention to what adults consider important. When the society seems to say, as in the past few years that "science hasn't solved our problems; we have put too much faith in science" the children are affected by this.

The foregoing illustration is taken from the elementary school. Let me turn, briefly, to the secondary school. All of the plans presented here bring out ways by which the secondary school can work with the community. The most widely used means over the past thirty years has been the cooperative educational programs, in which the students work on paid jobs for half a day and go to school half a day. Unfortunately, only a small number of youth have been involved in such programs, but they have been relatively successful. In fact, a study of high school cooperative education, conducted by Systems Development Corporation showed that in the sample cases it was effective in increasing learning in the high school and in gaining employment for the graduates. Another program that relates the school to the community is one in which high school students provide community service. The Friends Service Committee organized a number of these programs in the years of the Great Depression. More recent developments furnish opportunities for high school students to take responsibility, as Boulding (Chapter 2) notes, in a wide range of community services. The National Association of Secondary School Principals recently reported that at least 1700 high schools in the United States are now offering programs of community service of various sorts. This is a way of adding to the resources for the education of young people the opportunities available in their community to render important services both for pay and without. This is one significant approach to the reform of secondary schools that can be done with a relatively small amount of investment in changing the school plant and in reeducating teachers.

We can look at finances as the resources for the employment of people in one activiey rather than another. I stated earlier that 6 percent of the gross national product of the United States is now devoted to education at the elementary and secondary level. That is another way of saying about 6 percent of the labor force of the United States is engaged in one way or the other in working for the schools. If more people were so employed, it would be at the cost of something else. The only modern industrial nations that spend a larger portion of their income on elementary and secondary schools are the Communist countries. (The Soviet Union devotes about 10 percent.) This larger expenditure seems to require a strong political control that can withhold consumer goods and assign more people to the work of education. There is no democratic country that is able to say to its people, "You must give up some of the consumer goods that you are now getting in order to spend more for education." But in the past, we were able to depend upon the home and the community to educate children for a great many things, assigning only a small part of the total educational tasks to the school. In the past, the task of socialization has been shared by the home, the community, and the school. The development of consensus on certain basic values was also a shared task involving the home, the church, and the mass media, with reinforcement by the school. Conditions have changed. The time devoted by parents to working with their children has been greatly reduced. Fifty-one percent of the mothers who have school-age children are in the labor force and are consequently unable to spend as much time with their children. A great deal of time that was formerly spent with the family is now spent with television. Surveys show that the average child between the ages of ten and fourteen spends about 1500 hours per year watching television and 1100 hours in school. The question becomes—if children cannot receive the educational services that were formerly provided without payment, can we obtain the funds, as Russia does, to support a dual teaching force? There is the teaching force in the schools of Russia from nine to three. Then there is the teaching force for the organizations of children and youth from three in the afternoon until eight in the evening. This is a serious problem. Perhaps 60 percent of the things once learned by our children were learned in informal situations no longer available. How can this constructive learning be provided in the future?

If professionals were employed to furnish the learning experiences that were previously available to children out of school, it would increase the present 6 percent of the gross national product devoted to the education of young people under eighteen years of age to at least 10 percent. It is very unlikely that public funds of this amount could be obtained for this purpose when many other public services are pressing for additional support.

To summarize my comments, our schools must continue to be responsive to the needs and demands of our changing society. It is clear that education is going to be required even more in the future than in the past. A complex society like ours could not exist without education. Our country could not continue to be productive, peaceful, and humane without educated citizens. But the changing nature of our society requires new knowledge, new skills, new attitudes and interests, and substantial commitment to social values. This places a heavy responsibility on the schools as well as on the home and the community. As society demands more of our schools, we must be more inventive in devising feasible programs—based, as Rubin indicates, on rational policies—that will meet the new conditions. I believe that a revolution in the total educational system is not possible, nor even desirable. Revolution in a complex society is destructive, particulary in its initial states, and requires tremendous redirection of human energy. What we can do is to attack serious educational problems throughtfully, systematically, and persistently, using more effectively the available resources. This is an evolutionary process like those in the past that have made our schools responsive to continuing social change.

commentary on tyler ·

The primary message of Tyler's chapter is that we must bring dispassionate judgements to bear on the critical problems confronting public education. In short, we must separate fact from fiction; distinguish what is reasonably possible from what is merely wishful thinking; establish a viable set of priorities; and test our regenerative capacities by attacking the priorities with commitment and rigor.

Tyler strives in his analysis to clarify the confusion and distortion surrounding the schools' accomplishments. Toward this end, he demonstrates that public education has made substantial societal contributions over the past two centuries. It has helped in the development of a flexible labor force; it has made a stable political system possible; through sustained socialization; it has assisted materially in the reduction of social stratification; and it has facilitated constructive social mobility. Of even greater significance, public education has served as a tireless engineer of progressively greater individual self-realization. Despite the severity and scope of its present difficulties, education has delivered major social benefits in the past and will likely continue to do so in the future.

Such clarification—in the form of ledger balancing—is important because, currently, the face of education has been disfigured, somewhat unfairly, by a punitive media. For example, it is widely assumed that the schools are in bad repair. Public opinion, shaped by a negative press, has led the citizenry to believe that the schools are rife with disease. Fearful that the attendant reaction may take a senseless and irrational course producing more harm than good, Tyler observes that while there are serious inadequacies in our educational provisions for some children (principally those described by Chisholm in Chapter 3 and Bronfenbrenner in Chapter 1), the majority are receiving a rather respectable education.

How is it that the alleged incompetence of schools has gained popularity? Since a very large percentage of the nation's students unquestionably are learning at an impressive rate—even on the barometer of standardized test scores—what prompts the presumed widespread dissatisfaction? The criticism is understandable in those instances where children are not learning to read or are below acceptable performance levels in writing, arithmetic, and so on. However, these instances are clearly in the minority. What, then, accounts for the tarnished image? The answer seems to lies in the unprecedented power of the media to mold and shape popular attitude. Newspaper reporters, magazine editors, and television commentators who sit in judgment of educational events—can, with relative ease, create a groundswell of sentiment toward any particular point of view. The spurious impression is then created that such sentiments are shared by all of society. Rarely, however, is this the case.

First, parents are far from powerless to influence the policies of the schools their children attend; second, most administrators are extremely sensitive to the pulse of their constituents' expectations; and third, comparatively few communities find it necessary to tolerate bad schools. Therefore, it is conceivable that points of view, generated primarily through the media, establish a kind of high intensity vogue that is not reflective of general belief. It was this circumstance that prompted Tyler to set the educational balance sheet in perspective, detailing both the successes and the failures.

Since the educational system must continuously adapt to a shifting society, he suggests that serious problems are more likely to stem from adaptive error than from deep-seated flaws in the system itself. It is important to think in terms of adaptation rather than replacement, Tyler contends, simply because the invention of completely new institutions is highly unlikely. Society will not tolerate a major revolution or a sharp departure from present convention. Testimony in support of this argument is apparent in the current situation where—despite rising tuitions and a declining job market for college graduates—most parents still want their children to acquire a post high school education.

If modifications must be made in order to accommodate the changing social scene, the critical question is: What kinds of alterations are most essential? The answer, from the way Tyler sees things, is not particularly mysterious. He believes, for example, that a major hurdle involves the delivery of high quality education with limited monetary resources. Similarly, more must be learned about ways to motivate learning; the amount of teacher retraining necessitated by the introduction of new instructional programs must be streamlined; and far greater provision must be made for educating underprivileged children.

Because of its overwhelming social significance, improved schooling for the disadvantaged is likely to command considerable attention as various reforms are initiated. We have accumulated an abundance of evidence demonstrating that black children in the ghettos can learn to read as well as their white counterparts, whether they are situated in segregated or integrated schools. Obviously, this is not to say that the systematic elimination of racial segregation in the schools is undesirable, or to deny that a number of socially destructive consequences may be associated with racial isolation. The fact that underprivileged children can, through appropriate methodology and adequate effort, be taught to read and write as well as other children does not disaffirm the pernicious effects of a divisive society engaged in unending internecine dispute.

Tyler's position on individualization is considerably more moderate than that of most other contemporary theorists. Indeed, the quest for greater individualization of instruction has been a prime objective in the research and development efforts of the last decade. In contrast, Tyler's contention is that the need to respect subtle learning idiosyncracies in children has been greatly exaggerated. "A considerable fraction of young people," he says, "are able to find their way through instructional materials without having to have individually prescribed programs." If, as he suggests, almost 80 percent of our students can learn effectively without specially designed materials, future experimentation on individualization should be restricted to the 20 percent of the student populaton that is genuinely atypical.

The high interest in educational alternatives and relevant curricula has given rise to a related, yet different, conception of individualization. Directed, not at optional approaches to the same educational objectives, but rather at a range of objectives that permits students to exercise personal choice, individualization has also come to symbolize alternatives in educational intent and pursuit. While Tyler does not specifically comment on this meaning of the term, it is probably fair to infer from his reasoning that once a basic mastery of fundamental skills is acquired, optional educational fare is not particularly deleterious. The lessons of the Eight-Year Study, one of his own great contributions to the field, would certainly seem to lead in this direction.

At the same time, however, Tyler's cautions regarding an austere school budget must be taken seriously. The continuance of instructional policies based on a presumed relationship between money spent on schools and students' academic achievement is unlikely. Whether or not a relationship exists, smaller enrollments and rising costs mean that a reduction in the educational budget is probable. Thus, financial considerations are likely to exert considerable influence because a program that is rich in instructional options is more costly than one restricted to bare essentials.

It is significant that Tyler sees fit to comment on the current importance of what once was referred to as cooperative education. Such activities, varying in length, duration, and organization, involve educational experiences that are cooperatively administered by schools and other community agencies. In a typical situation, the student may spend four daily hours in school and another four hours working in a post office, hospital, a tire factory, and so on. The rationale developed during earlier experimentation with such programs predates, by almost three decades, the current advocacy of community-based education.

Noting that fully 60 percent of a child's education takes place in informal rather than formal settings, Tyler believes that work experience programs provide an effective means of coordinat-

ing classroom and out of classroom learning. The present appeal of cooperative education (in contrast to the relatively modest interest of the past) is in large measure again attributable to monetary concerns. The cost of conventional education has risen to the point where tradition and custom may need to be replaced with less expensive procedures. Hence, it is not the educational benefits of work experience programs alone that account for their growing popularity, but it is also their capacity to reduce school costs. Thus, we have a dramatic illustration of the way in which a theoretical idea's timing can govern either its acceptance or its rejection.

For essentially the same reasons, one suspects, Tyler suggests that there is considerable potential in the use of "volunteer teachers." Contributions to the welfare of others are for many people a source of considerable gratification, particularly when the assistance does not necessitate undue sacrifice. For example, should economic pressures cause early retirement to become more commonplace, large numbers of people might find the unpaid teaching of children a rewarding form of altruism. Our experience with paraprofessionals has already demonstrated that professional teachers can easily coordinate the efforts of multiple teaching aides. And if (as the protagonists of community-based learning maintain) adolescents can gain useful educational experiences while providing social services through participation in community life, there is even more reason to heed Tyler's recommendations regarding the initiation of experimental programs. In the past, taxpayers have often argued that tax-supported schools should be self-sufficient and not rely on others to shoulder their load. However, the inevitable increase in necessary educational expenditures may, in the future, overshadow such sentiments.

It can also be deduced, from the tenor of Tyler's remarks, that a conservative political season is upon us, and the changes that occur are likely to reflect more caution and less daring. The humanistic trends of the past few years will be somewhat diluted by a renaissance of authoritarianism; educational activites falling outside the pale of basics and fundamentals may again be labelled frills; a more suppressed educational atmosphere, prompted by deepening public concern over antisocial behavior trends, is predictable and, in a counter-reaction to the populism of the past decade, a new wave of elitism is possible. It is presumably this entrenchment that causes Tyler to repeatedly warn us that systematic and gradual evolution, rather than bold revolution, are the order of the new day.

In this connection, it can scarcely be denied that some kind of reparative action is essential. People are less willing to assume that youthful violence, drug abuse, family disintegration, and crippled social morality will right themselves through a policy of benign neglect. The need to do something is a good deal more clear than what should be done, but mounting public concern makes it imperative that a demonstrable corrective effort be started. There is *likely to be, therefore, a return to things of the past in the areas of moral development, values, and citizenship education.*

It can also be assumed that as the accent on socialization is reactivated, the allegations of radical theorists regarding curricular subversiveness will be pushed into the background. Of course, the schools do perpetuate the political status quo and indoctrinate the young into accepted rituals and orthodox beliefs. In fact, they were created with such a mission in mind. Early in our nation's history, when communication technology was more primitive, public education was used to familiarize students with normative political culture. Schools were expected to induce an acceptance of the socie-tal creed and to teach the tenets of the political system, not as act-uality but rather as an ideal. The analysis and criticism of the system's professed virtues were delayed until the advent of college. The public schools were the principal agents of political accultura-tion; they familiarized the new generation with traditional ideology, conveyed the doctrine of good citizenship, and generally preserved the political apparatus. That the process was less than perfect was viewed as beside the point, because the transmission of accepted patterns was essential to socialization, and socialization, in turn, was essential to the conservation of the social order.

Recent criticism has protested the propriety and legitimacy of this approach, arguing that the natural consequence of delib-erate hypocracy is alienation, cynicism, disillusion, and a squand-ering of precious opportunity to open the minds of succeeding generations to something better.

Whether the criticism is justified or not, it is unlikely that it will have much effect in the immediate future. The sensed need is for a renewal of idealism. There is a growing conviction that schools cannot counteract the massive acculturation that occurs outside their walls, and, as Tyler himself notes, children are heavily influenced by events in adult society. The ancient and traditional prescripts, whether fact or myth, therefore, can be expected to again prevail, at least for a time.

L. R.

ISSUES •

1. A changing society will impose new obligat ions on the schools. These, however, will need to be met, essentially, through the same personnel, in the same physical facilities, and within the same dollar constraints. What resulting implications for planning can be derived?

2. The evidence suggests that the cost of developing new instructional programs is modest in contrast to the corresponding cost of retraing teaching personnel in their effective use. What would best facilitate the continuous upgrading of teaching staffs?

3. A major overhaul of the nation's educational system is highly unlikely. Energies, therefore, must be focused on the critical problems of greatest significance. What criteria can be used to identify the dominant priorities?

4. The limited learning success of disadvantaged children is in large measure attributable to conspicuous lack of motivation. What combination of intrinsic and extrinsic incentives is most likely to ameliorate matters?

5. Among children debilitated by the hardships of ghetto life, little connection is perceived between the events of the classroom and their own personal aspirations. Could revisions in the method and content of instruction produce salutary effects?

6. Because of the definitive lack of connection between the home and school experiences of disadvantaged children, opportunities for mutual reinforcement of learning goals are often absent. Would it be better to modify the subject-matter of teaching, enrich, in one way or another, home experiences, or pursue both potential improvements simultaneously?

7. Schools, seemingly, have given far too little attention to the social influences of learning. What kinds of research, explored under what particular conditions, might identify new tactics for developing the life skills important in adult society?

8. At present, relatively little advantage is taken of the educational benefits inherent in coordinated school-based and community-based learning programs. What particular variables might increase our sophistication in this regard?

9. There is good reason to believe that a rich supply of human teaching resources are available outside the organized teaching profession. Could systematic advantage be taken—under the supervision of professional educators—of these resources?

10. Recent findings in the social sciences suggest that, as a consequence of shifting societal patterns, aspects of the educational process once fulfilled in the home are no longer being met. What problems and benefits would be associated with a "dual educational system"—wherein children were exposed to formal education during normal school hours,—and to organized informed learning in after school programs?

11. Continuing societal evolution will require the schools to orient the young to changing attitudes, values, and beliefs. How can these required changes best be identified, discussed in public forums until reasonable concensus has been achieved, and gradually implemented in the existing educational program?

louis rubin
University of Illinois

9

THE REFORMATION OF SCHOOLING

Though it may seem pretentious to speak of school reformation in the sense that the term denotes rectification and reconstitution, it is perhaps defensible. We have reached a point where the many innovations initiated since the early sixties can be subjected to relatively objective scrutiny and assessed with regard to their comparative strengths and weaknesses. In most instances, sufficient time has elapsed for the good and the bad features to become apparent, for the achievement or nonachievement of antici- pated objectives to be judged, and for the inevitable side effects (both positive and negative) to have materialized. Therefore, an effort to reappraise matters may indicate what aspects of the innovations underway should be retained, what aspects should be modified, and what aspects should be resurrected. The peculiarities of change are such that attempted refinements often generate more harm than good and some old habits and customs—eliminated in the name of progress—must eventually be restored. Consequently, the needed reformation must involve a redistribution of old and new elements.

THE CONTINUING SEARCH

The necessity for another round of rehabilitative effort in the seemingly endless quest for an ideal program of public education is prompted by the unresolved difficulties of the past, by the infirm- ities of the present, and by the requirements of the future. There- fore, Tyler's concerns (Chapter 7) regarding our long-standing inability to produce a completely literate society, Bronfenbrenner's description (Chapter 1) of the conditions leading to family disintegration, and Salk's projections (Chapter 6) of a future that will demand both human freedom and human constraint, all contribute to the present need for a sustained period of restoration. The reformation should be in the shape of a gradual evolution that takes its direction from a variety of sources—new pieces of research evidence, the changing social environment, altering human expectations, and a multitude of ontogenetic impediments.

On the surface, the endless ebb and flow resulting from our inability to move decisively from problem-recognition to problem-solution, the interminable peregrinations between old and new theoretical ground, and repeated policy reversals seems to constitute a futile and irrational course. In the face of these recurring difficulties, it might be better to abandon our hopes and accept the inevitable. But history teaches that little in human endeavor is truly inescapable.

One might ask why the problems are so intractable; why we appear, time and time again, to misread the signs; and why so many of our efforts are counterproductive? One might also ask, why have Coleman's conclusions on the effects of segregation, Bloom's conception of mastery learning, Cronbach's theories regarding aptitude treatment interaction, and John Dewey's hallowed precepts on the educational impact of experience, all come to so little?

Having spent millions of dollars on the study of teaching, what insanity now compels us to conclude that no pedagogical method will produce guaranteed results? The answers to these questions are far from clear but an explanation of sorts may exist: education is a social enterprise, and social enterprises by their nature defy scientific accuracy, error-proof policies, and permanent solutions to problems.

It is because the disorderliness of social progress is not generally understood that the public's disenchantment with its societal institutions tends to peak during times of unusual stress. That we presently are in such a time hardly needs commentary. The mood at the moment is heavily anti-school. People have begun to question not only the worth of education, but also the prospects of human perfectability. The common presumption is that in an era of stupifying technological prowess, an effective and efficient school system should not be difficult to achieve. Nonetheless, it is probably easier to organize research leading to organ transplants in humans than to devise workable procedures for eliminating poverty, overcoming defects in the system of criminal justice, and enhancing educational achievement. In short, the unknowns of science are a good deal more tidy and precise than the enigmas of social organizations.

The disillusion has been further enlarged by the improvident bravado of some research experts. In contrast to our sweeping promises and assurances of the early sixties, for example, we are now forced to acknowledge that the intervention of the state cannot always eradicate breakdowns in family structure (Bronfenbrenner Chapter 1); that compensatory education cannot easily counterbalance social deprivation (Chisholm Chapter 3); and that we have not yet made schooling attractive for all youth (Tyler Chapter 8). Unemployment and inflation have taken their toll on the public spirit; crime and violence have maligned domestic tranquility; and corruption in high office has weakened the citizenry's confidence in its leadership. But for all of these liabilities, the ubiquitous delusion remains: sensible and rational policies could quickly produce problem-free schools, and problem-free schools would eliminate social disorder.

Because of this delusion, errors in educational policy habitually provoke resentment and retribution. For example, schools are presently being subjected to an extraordinary range of criticism. For those who viewed education as the dominant vehicle to high-status vocations and material success, schooling has diminished in importance because a declining job market has restricted vocational opportunity and because (as Schweiker observes in Chapter 7) blue-collar jobs have begun to offer salarys that rival those in many white-collar pursuits. Public education is also viewed with contempt by some radicals who see social awareness as the indispensable element in building a better society: because schools teach orthodox dogma and encourage conformity to prevailing values and beliefs, as Boulding argues (Chapter 2), youth is left with a naive understanding of the way things are and a lack of sophistication regarding the failings of the social system. And for those who are basically opposed to universal compulsory education in the first place, the schools are regarded, not only as unnecessary, but also as a major obstacle to a self-regulating societal order. From virtually all quarters, in fact, one hears complaints that the educational system's operating principles (and hence the policies from which these principles stem) are defective. Three questions therefore arise: Can the schools' credibility and respect be restored? If so, will the restoration demand an alteration in present policies? And if alterations are required, what form and substance must they take?

For the moment, let us assume that credibility can be recouped and that at least some policy changes are necessary. It would then be sensible to ask: What can be extracted from the research and theory stockpile in the way of reformation clues? It is precisely here, however, that the difficulties are compounded. For example, a return to old ways—a "back to basics" movement—may bring a return of the old benefits, but it may also resurrect the old disadvantages. Indeed, it was exactly these disadvantages that accounted for the initial interruption of earlier policies.

It is also conceivable, however, that the old ways will no longer produce the old benefits. The social scene is far from static, and with the passage of time, a shifting set of variables might yield entirely different results. Moreover, it is also conceivable that the old ways are no longer feasible or that they will, in present time, produce intolerable side effects. Finally, it is entirely possible that the reinstitution of old practices could produce results substantially better than those achieved through current methods. The critical point, however, is that we have no way of knowing *in advance* which of these contingencies will prevail. The nuances and complexities of teaching and learning are sufficiently great that we cannot, in most instances, predict precise outcomes, and must therefore rely on trial and error. If we were capable of completely accurate prediction we could do away with all of our present planning problems.

It is this phenomenon of situational unpredictability, perhaps, that most accounts for the striking lack of correspondence between research evidence and educational policy. Cohen and Garret have noted that the relationship between research-generated knowledge and educational decision making is negligible.[1] Whether educational policy is viewed as a rubric of attitudes and assumptions, as a predetermined plan for school improvement, or as a collection of organized programs aimed at a designated end, it does not seem to be influenced to any significant degree by scientific data. Policy, in the main, is based on a bit of verified fact, a bit of mythology, a bit of tradition, and a lot of wishful thinking. This is so, self-evidently, because when we do not command enough knowledge to move toward our objectives with precision, we must rely, in part, on more conjectural presumptions.

Therefore it follows that more research data—even uncontaminated data—may not be of much consequence in influencing the decisions of policymakers. The social system functions through a labyrinth of confounded variables and thus is constructed, not out of unadulterated facts alone, but rather out of facts tinctured with beliefs. Hence, while it is sensible to do research *on* educational policy in the interest of scholarly understanding, and while it may be desirable to carry on other research in the interest of reducing human ignorance, it does not make sense to perform research in the expectation that the results will necessarily alter educational policy.

1. David K. Cohen and Michael S. Garet, "Reforming Educational Policy with Applied Research," *Harvard Educational Review,* Vol. 45, No. 1, February 1975.

Nevertheless we are left with the reality that effective educational reform depends largely on devising better educational policy. The net conclusion, therefore, may be that desirable policy changes must be achieved through constructive propaganda aimed at the reshaping of public attitude rather than through the accumulation of further research data alone. While the data can be incorporated in legitmate opinion-molding activities, it cannot, in and of itself, produce corresponding policy revisions.

Policy is more flexible and less rational than research evidence because it is bound by fewer constraints. Whereas research conclusions must be restricted to inferences deduced from verified evidence, policy decisions can be based on literally anything that seems appropriate or promising. If, then, research findings and policy decisions rest on different foundations, their relationship is essentially independent rather than reciprocal. Better research evidence will not improve social policy because it has no inherent capacity for making policy decisions more rational. Thus, irrational policy must be corrected through other provisions.

Education is not alone in its policy distress. Vociferous objections are raised against programs of urban renewal, environmental conservation regulations, law enforcement tactics, placement of freeways, social security provisions, and more. The established policies are often viewed as inept, and people wonder with exasperation why the experts cannot be more expert.

REAL AND IMAGINED BARRIERS

Our limited power in formulating effective educational policy stems from a conglomerate of impediments—each of which interferes with our search for sure solutions. Considerable confusion,for example, results from the lack of consensus on educational aims. Worse, it is improbable that such consensus can ever be attained. In fact, present indications are that the future will be characterized by more, rather than less, diversity in points of view.

Consider, for example, our present quandaries with regard to the teaching of moral standards. Some people believe that moral values should be taught; others do not. But even within the ranks of those who favor some form of moral education, however, a spate of opinion differences exist: What values should be stressed? What standards in relation to these values should be established? What kinds of instructional methods are defensible? Should we defer to student autonomy in value-determination, or should we try to inculcate particular convictions? Is behavior modification an acceptable or unacceptable technique? In the absence of agreement on these and other related issues, the usual policy (where consensus seems prohibitive) is no policy.

Contradictory views on educational goals are seldom entirely evident before a large-scale test occurrs. It was not until a broad and comprehensively detailed curriculum, *Man: A Course of Study*, had been planned, researched, designed, and implemented that dispute arose concerning the desirability of teaching children about cultural norms different from their own, and concerning the propriety of government involvement in curriculum development and dissemination. In many instances, only after a program has been put into effect do the overall consequences and the policy-related fallout become apparent.

Another difficulty (illustrated by Scanlon in Chapter 4) is the sheer intricacy of the educational process. Because of the vast array of factors that affect learning, the determining of weaknesses in an instructional program is far from simple. Consider for example the invention of a new method of teaching arithmetic. It is relatively easy, after trial, to ascertain that the method does not work. Discovering specifically why it does not work, however, is considerably more complicated. The trouble may lie in the teaching method or in the way it is used. If the method is at fault, what particular element is defective? Is it better to rebuild the method in order to overcome the deficiency, or is it better to discard the method and seek a replacement? If a replacement is introduced, and the results are again disappointing, the troubleshooting analysis must begin anew.

Suppose, however, that rechecks show instead that the method is valid and has been used appropriately. In this instance, the learner's lack of achievement may stem from the absence of essential experiences in the child's background. If this is the case, is it more advantageous to provide the prerequisite experience, devise an alternative method, or abandon the objective? If we decide to institute compensatory experiences, and the method again proves ineffectual, do we then alter the compensating activities, remodel the method, test it with older learners who have reached a higher degree of acculturation, and so on?

Other impediments to effective policy (teacher personality, learner idiosyncrasies, peculiarities in school settings, length and duration of teaching exposure, and motivational factors) could, of course, also be described. It is sufficient, perhaps, to observe that the complications of teaching and learning are great enough to make the accurate detection of internal complications a formidable and treacherous enterprise, one in which the likelihood of error is exceedingly high.

Because it is easy to make mistakes and misjudgements in problem-solving, a related difficulty lies in the compounding of error. To wit, if two plus two are taken to be five, two plus two plus two are then seen as seven, and two plus two plus two plus two become nine. Unrecognized judgemental lapses at any given point in the process, will ultimately lead to more and more blunders. Yet, it is often necessary to go a considerable distance in programmatic development before an earlier error becomes apparent. In some cases, an innovation must be brought to fruition and put to practical use before its inherent weaknesses become obvious. Since problem-solving efforts typically occur in highly artificial environments (Bronfenbrenner's analysis of compensatory education efforts is illustrative), it is only after the full impact of reality has exerted its force that unsuspected softspots become known. Thus, in the teaching of reading we have shifted from a stress on phonics to an emphasis on word recognition, and we have then reversed direction to achieve a workable balance. The improbability of locating fatal flaws, coupled with an often unavoidable period of error-compounding, is chiefly responsible for the ubiquitous "pendular" effect in curriculum change. The bias during the fifties toward cognitive objectives gave way in the late sixties to a substantially greater interest in affective goals, and—judging by present trends—a reversal is again imminent.

Planning, problem-solving, and policy-setting are further hampered by multiple-causation phenomena. At present, we are preoccupied with declining scores on standardized tests. Why has student achievement dropped? Is it because less reading goes on in the home, because the young devote too much time to TV, or because the test terminology is obsolete and unclear to students? The lower scores could also be attributable to teacher inefficiency, inadequate student motivation, or a transformed curriculum wherein substantial attention is given to educational pursuits not embodied by the tests (thereby reducing the time available for instruction on those objectives that are tested). What factor, or combination of factors, is dominant? Do all of the contributing elements operate in concert, in equal or unequal degree, simultaneously or sequentially? Are the critical forces at play of parallel influence in all subject-areas, or do variations exist? The tasks of distinguishing cause from effect and of discriminating between problems and problem-symptoms, are sufficiently troublesome as to defy certainty.

Obviously, systematic knowledge is an indispensable ingredient in problem-solving. But until the necessary critical mass of understanding has been reached, the likelihood of miscalculation remains high. Moreover, since policies are rarely based on authentic evidence alone, prejudice, predisposition, and bias tend to distort policy decisions until an adequate knowledge base becomes available. In times of social dissension, when there is considerable controversy regarding the proper resolution of societal dilemmas, opposing factions are sometimes inclined to promote solutions that are partially self-serving.

In the case of shrinking test scores, for example, a great many notions have been set forth, none of which unfortunately, add up to a satisfactory explanation. As a result, the protagonists of basic education can capitalize on circumstance and argue for a greater emphasis on direct reading instruction; those who champion competency-based teacher training can explain low scores on the basis of teacher inefficiency; the aficionados of nontraditional testing can fault the methodological design of the psychometrics; and theorists advocating a curtailment of school responsibility can argue that the educational system cannot be held accountable for a lack of intellectual stimulation in the home.

It is entirely possible, of course, that none of these suggested defects are primarily responsible for reduced academic achievement, and that the major cause is yet to be discovered. Nonetheless, each potential weakness must be tested and disclaimed before attention can be directed elsewhere.

What may be the strongest inhibitor of rational policy formulation derives from our habit of relying on prosaic attitudes of mind that breed repeated problem-misconstruction. Sanity is often deceptive and all that appears reasonable may not always be so. In human events, it is not uncommon to find instances in which the seemingly irrational is really quite rational and, conversely, instances in which what is presumed logical proves, ultimately, to have been highly illogical. The systemic tribulations of New York City provide a ready illustration. One million-one hundred thousand New Yorkers are presently on welfare. The need to relieve the misery of the poor, through welfare, was unavoidable. However, it was not foreseen—in 1960—that thousands of municipal personnel would be required to maintain its welfare provisions. Between 1960 and 1974 the number of city employees increased by 69.9 percent—an expansion necessitated in substantial measure by the need to provide additional services for those on welfare. The result is that 400,000 people now work for the city. The welfare programs, in sum, have themselves become a growth industry. In short, it has become necessary to maintain large numbers of people on welfare in order to justify the employment of those who manage and operate the programs. An ostensibly logical solution to a problem was, in actuality, a form of madness.

A similar example can be found in the case of penal reform. Acting upon a rational set of constructs, criminologists once urged that prisons be made agencies of rehabilitation rather than punishment. The short sightedness of the policy is now a matter of record and we are about to embark on a remigration to old ways wherein fairly administered—but swift, certain and inescapable punishment—is seen as the principal deterrent to crime.

THE LIMITS OF RATIONALITY

Rittel and Webber have demonstrated that in many social dilemmas, the problem cannot be defined until the solution has been grasped.[2] They argue first, that it is usually impossible to describe policy problems definitively, and second, that in a pluralistic society, policies serving the overall public good are rarely feasible. They suggest that our conception of a problem, in turn, dictates the nature of the solution, just as the fabrication of a solution mirrors our definition of the problem. That is, once we formulate a conception of a problem and identify the elements to be corrected, we immediately commit ourselves to a restricted set of solutions, each of which must be aimed at the presumed difficulty. If our portrayal of the problem is erroneous, all of our attempts to solve it will also fail. As long as we stay with an incorrect definition of the problem a workable solution will elude us simply because each of our efforts takes us in the wrong direction.

Watzlawick, Weakland and Fisch, approach the same dilemma from a different context. They contend that faulty problemformation is largely responsible for our inability to solve many of our social riddles.[3] The history of theory is replete with testimony to the human capacity for preoccupation with a unitary, often misconceived, point of view. In fact, much of what we call serendipity is nothing more than the result of a sudden and unexpected escape from an obsessional fixation.

Educational policy might profit, therefore, from a calculated effort to reconceptualize the pervasive problems that have thus far appeared unsolvable. Such reconceptualization would consist of taking a fresh look at a quandary or an impasse and reconstructing its meaning. In order to avoid being seduced by the obvious, reconceptualization requires that we formulate a variety of different interpretations of the problem each of which accomodates the existing conditions and restraints. Problem fixation is prompted by emotional leanings, attitudinal predispositions, and ingrained conceptual perceptions. Once these are disengaged, and one approaches the task with an open mind, it is sometimes possible to place the

2. Horst W. J. Rittel and Melvin M. Webber, "Dilemmas in a General Theory of Planning," *Policy Sciences*, Vol. IV, No. 2, June, 1973.

3. Paul Watzlawick, John Weakland and Richard Fisch, *Change: Principles of Problem Formation and Problem Resolution*, W. W. Norton and Co. (New York: W. W. Norton and Co., 1974).

problem in a framework. When this is done, unanticipated paths often emerge and one can reason analytically about their viability. Human behavior is shaped, less by reality, than by our perception of reality and the habitual response to this perception that we call "human nature." Everything depends on the way in which we interpret a situation. To reinterpret, redefine, and reconceive, consequently, is to open our minds to a new universe of possibilities. It is these reinterpretations that are at the heart of the propositions advocated throughout the volume by Salk (Chapter 6), Fuller (Chapter 5), and Boulding (Chapter 2).

In the interest of simplicity, a common example will perhaps suffice. Many people experience difficulty in losing weight. In the conventional construction of the problem, excessive weight is seen as an imbalance between expended energy and caloric intake. The customary solution is to either reduce food consumption or expand energy output, and thus restore balance. Frequently, however, the solution does not succeed because individuals find it "impossible" to obey dietary restrictions. Hypnotism, self-deception, and similar devices may be initiated in order to reinforce self-control. The locus of difficulty is conceived of as inability to curb one's appetite. However, considerable counseling success (following previous failure) has been achieved by reconceptualizing the problem. Instead of aiming at devices for increasing self-control, attention is directed toward identifying situations that stimulate a desire to eat. Hence, the solution lies in ignoring appetite entirely, and seeking instead, to eliminate stress situations that provoke a desire for food.

The limits of rationality, too, take their toll in policy planning. Whether or not one believes in human perfectability or in the limitless possibilities for improving the social order, the fact is that human reason is not capable of resolving all human predicaments. Contrary to the conventional aphorism, not every problem has a solution. In any given impasse—for example an effective method of lessening drug abuse—many potential correctives can be generated. We could attempt to revitalize our programs of moral and ethical education; impose harsher penalties on the use of drugs in school facilities; permanently expel all "abusers" so that only nonabusers remain; liberalize our definition of drug abuse so that fewer students qualify as offenders; launch a search for drug substitutes that might satisfy student purposes; and so on. The solution possibilities are endless. As a result prudent judgment must be used in determining when the quest for cures has gone far enough, and in determining which of the potential solutions warrants trial.

It is in the exercise of such prudent judgment that the boundaries of rationality impose restraints. An accurate comparison of all alternatives, without an experimental test of some sort, is usually impossible. Also, since the optimum solution to a problem may vary from situation to situation and from school to school, any given decision may be subject to the vagaries of chance. And, to further complicate matters, experience has taught us that the solution to one problem often creates, in time, another problem. Contraceptives prevent unwanted pregnancies, but their availability may also increase promiscuity among high school students.

The implementation of a new educational policy is not simple. Massive investments in time and energy are required, the tensions created by those opposed to the policy must be endured, and, ironically, well-intentioned but misguided attempts to make something better may, in the end, make matters worse. Coleman's advice, in 1965, on school integration policy seemed sensible at the time. It may, in fact, still be sensible. The arguments were based on defensible theory, the solution to the segregation problem seemed manageable, and while resistance was of course inevitable, there was reason to believe that both the political and operational hazards could be surmounted. However, the intervening events clearly demonstrate that these forecasts were errant. Coleman himself concluded, not long ago, that the net effect of five years of court-mandated school integration has left us worse off then at the outset of court intervention.

We now hear, from critics with a special proclivity for hindsight, chidings to the effect that the resistance and the obstacles could have been predicted in advance. They could not have. Had the mood of the nation taken a different turn, had the issues not become the basis for a political crusade, had the timing not coincided with an unanticipated reactivation of pluralistic concerns, things may have been different. Although we seem at the moment to have lost ground, and although the barriers to school integration are presently more formidable than before, it is entirely conceivable that, should the social scene take another unexpected twist, Coleman's strategy could be reinstituted with reasonable success.

The limits of rationality also necessitate decisions regarding what problems are best left to expedient omission. Well-laid plans occasionally encounter unforeseeable obstacles. In such circumstances, judicious neglect is frequently provident. Moreover, since not only human judgment but also human resources are finite, the struggle to make the right choice at the right time must, at times, fail.

To note one further impediment to policy planning, it should be observed that the infirmities of evaluation also militate against routinely effective decisions. Since for any specified problem the quality of the alternative solutions is relative, comparative strengths and weaknesses are not readily deciphered. For example, in describing planned variation experiments, Elmore suggests that policy-relevant conclusions can rarely be drawn from an examination of experimental programs.[4] Correlations can be calculated and treatment effects assessed, but the evaluator's ability to set forth relevant and supportable policy recommendations is, at best, minimal. The requirements of legitimate experimental design are such that generalized inference is restricted, and variation in the ways experimental programs are implemented is so sizable that little in the way of universal insights can be claimed.

Where the qualitative differences between two contemplated policies are not great, the subtleties of discrimination soon exceed the sensitivity of our evaluative apparatus. Solutions are often neither entirely good nor entirely bad, and distinguishing between the assets of the advantage and the debits of the disadvantage further enlarges the possibility of judgmental error. For example, when two techniques for increasing teacher knowledge about individual differences in children are compared, the differences between the two may be so slight that the choice must ultimately be based on comparative costs, operational ease, time requirements, teacher preference, and other secondary considerations. As the analysis of problems becomes increasingly fine, the probability of miscalculation grows, and the resulting decision may eventually prove unworkable.

For all of these reasons, carefully reasoned policy decisions may, after the hard test of reality, fail to accomplish their intent. The obstructions are many: the vicissitudes of fate cannot be predicted in advance, human aspirations are themselves fickle, events cannot always be anticipated, and our astuteness in matters of judgemental arbitration is less than perfect.

UNCONVENTIONAL USES OF THE CONVENTIONAL

What then can be said about a suitable strategy for future educational policy? The circumstantial clues are plain enough. Education must equip the present generation of young to cope with an unusual period of rapid social readjustment. The bureaucratic structure of school organization has been rigidified to the point where procedures for implementing reform are excessively cumbersome. Many parents, particularly those of black and Chicano children, find schooling unresponsive to their educational expectations. The dropout rate remains high, student violence in schools has reached crisis proportions and, for too many, the classroom remains

4. Richard F. Elmore, *Planned Variation Experiments As Policy Analysis*, April 1974. Unpublished paper prepared for the Annual Meeting of the American Educational Research Association, Chicago, Illinois.

a place of tedious boredom. Despite the truly superb accomplishments of education (see Tyler Chapter 8) large numbers of children cannot read adequately, write clearly, grasp the fundamentals of mathematics, or reason analytically. The traditional socialization procedures still leave something to be desired; more must be done in the way of providing the groundwork for the acquisition of vocational skills; and too little attention is given to the cultivation of those inner capacities essential to a rewarding life—managing emotional hardship, distinguishing between what is truly significant and what is merely decorative, and using one's human potential to maximum advantage.

The prognosis for the immediate future of the school system is obvious. The generation born between 1946 and 1967 (an aberration in the population cycle) will soon graduate and the period of expansion, now coming to an end, will be replaced by a season of decline. Public expenditure for education, which during the same period grew from 2 percent to 8 percent of the GNP, (when college and university costs are included) will stabilize. Assuming continued inflation, schooling will have to make do with a smaller budget and be more dollar-efficient. Few new school facilities will be constructed during the remainder of the present century, and those that are built are likely to be economy-oriented glass-fiber structures. Moreover, the odds are that school buildings will be shared by other community agencies in order to increase their utility and, at the same time, constrain public expenditure.

While the number of high school students entering college may drop from the present 47 percent level, we can expect that as the inevitable leveling off occurs, half (rather than the once anticipated three-fourths) of the students will seek institution-based higher education. At the other end of the spectrum, programs of early childhood education, because of their immense popularity, are almost certain to expand.

What is now conceived of as a possible pattern of lifelong learning may become a more concrete reality. Speculation, in addition, has begun to focus on an educational system that would permit individuals to enter and leave at will. Specialization schools, devoted to specific learning pursuits, may make it possible for students to participate in short-term courses to update job skills, prepare for a career change, or indulge a personal interest in the arts or sciences. Such an arrangement, resembling the present commercial foreign language schools, could also result in the establishment of separate academies for studying reading, mathematics, literature, and even plumbing.

The present shift toward further decentralization seems likely to be sustained. Anticipating a growing disinterest in consolidation, planners foresee classrooms that are no longer totally dependent on professional teachers. An experimental program going on now in California in which large numbers of adults and high school students serve as nonsalaried tutors for primary grade children, appears to have evidenced some promise. While the approach is primitive, and the logistical problems formidable, the results to date offer a basis for optimism.

The future of the nine-month school is also open to question. Learning will be accessible on a year-round basis if present trends are sustained, and a substantially greater segment of formal education will be community-centered.

As the full force of instructional technology makes its impact, further and more definitive departures from tradition and custom are probable. The use of more prime time commercial television for educational purposes could be legislatively mandated and, inferring from present developmental currents, heavy use will be made of instructional videotapes. There is, in fact, speculation that self-instruction, through such tapes, may make it possible for students to acquire high school diplomas and college degrees without set time requirements. Individuals will engage in the necessary preparation, demonstrate proficiency on a standardized examination and receive due credit.

Machine-assisted learning undoubtedly will become a good deal more commonplace with the advent of anticipated refinements in miniaturization and computer technology. The present state of the art is less than spectacular, but there have been extensive advances, and the future is hopeful.

Against all of this—the cluttered, uncertain and sometimes contradictory panoply, created by an amalgamation of unresolved difficulties from the past, present infirmities, and future requirements—what form and substance ought to guide educational policy planning?

RESEARCH AS REFORMATION

We must embark on an era of experimental educational reform. In sharp deviation from what has gone before, we must seek to test bold new constructs that strike at the heart of our severest and most fundamental problems. As these new constructs are tried, in realistic conditions rather than in the educators' equivalent of a scientific laboratory, they must be altered and revised, bent and twisted, and progressively reshaped to fit continually changing conditions. Depending on the adequacy of their fit, they must then be retained, replicated, rejected, or reinvented. Thus through successive, small-scale approximations, we must explore one approach and then another until we reach a workable solution to each dilemma.

If we are to accomplish these missions, two departures from ordinary evaluation procedure are essential. First, we must increase our mastery of appraisal techniques that involve quasiexperimental designs, and second, we must search for new evaluation methodologies that can illuminate significant dark spots lying outside the scope of conventional scientific measurement.

Donald Campbell's insightful projections of "reforms as experiments," (which eventually led to exploratory research designs that avoided the fetters of conventional technique) constitute a promising beginning. Seeking to explain our long-standing inability to deduce significant generalizations from the evaluation of social reforms, Campbell suggests that, technical limitations aside, the research community is at a great disadvantage because of its unfortunate habit of advocating particular innovations as fail-proof solutions. Unable to bridge the gap between "promise and potential" we are viewed by our critics as either charlatans or fallen heroes.

Much could be lost if we overlook the importance of joining scientific measurement with other forms of inferential evidence. After all, humans learned from their mistakes long before the invention of regression analysis. Hunch and intuition, conjecture and speculation, perception and recognition, all provide us with ways of knowing. If, as could well be the case, our aptitude for eliminating education's flagrant difficulties is more dependent on creative insight than on sheer volume of effort, artistic discernment may be fully as important as statistical precision.

What should be avoided in such a program of unpretentious, self-correcting reform, are the dysgenic blunders that defeated so many of our earlier endeavors. The problems must be attacked in their natural environment, rather than in isolation from their context; we must resist the temptation to mount immense and corpulent programs on a national scale, if only because a usable solution in one place may be quite unusable in another; we must, as best we can, suppress the self-serving aspects of policy determination, demonstrating for our constituencies, through examples from the past, that uncooperation and obstruction in the interest of private political advantage are heavily detrimental to the common good; and we must confine our endeavors to short-term efforts that bear directly on manifestly intolerable situations.

It has, in recent times, become painfully obvious that more of the same will not do. The frontal attacks on poverty and urban renewal have produced only limited gains; the net profit, after a decade of expensive educational change is less than we hoped for; and the massive investments in compensatory education have brought, all things considered, little cause for cheer.

Finally, large reforms cannot be launched without the amassment of substantial political support. In soliciting such support, it is easy to exaggerate both the feasability and outcome of the reforms. Obligation and liability are thereby placed on the reformers; the privileges of unencumbered experimentation and calculated risk-taking are aborted; and a hard to resist incentive for overstating results is set loose. On the other hand, more modest interventions, because less is at stake, are not as subject to these dangers. Tried in the spirit of an informed, yet open ended inquiry, they permit the experimenters to respect impulse as well as deduction, to move sequentially through both planned and impromptu variations, and to progress step by step toward increasing levels of success.

There is little in the record of human action that could not have been done better. More often than not, the margin between what was achieved, and what could have been achieved, is ascribable to scant perseverance. A willingness to persist in the face of failure, particularly when immediate events give rise to a temporary mood of pessimism, is also of essence in the conduct of renewal.

Society's standards for judging the success of reform are normative and pragmatic. The needed educational experiments, consequently, must involve student as well as expert in the determination of success criteria. Few of us are content to be told what we should regard as good or bad. We prefer, not only to decide for ourselves, but also to participate in the deliberations through which our destiny is recast. What we desperately lack in this connection are legitimate approaches to educational reform in which children, parents, teachers and technical experts, together, seek solutions to problems. The nature of our time, perhaps, is such that it can be no other way.

Index

Adams-Morgan District, 69
Adolescent homicide, 25–26, 28
Administrative role, 101–106
   assess alternatives, 101–102
   assess progress, 102
   coordinate, 103
   delegate powers, 102–103
   ensure stability, 105
   initiate change, 105–106
   mobilize resources, 103–104
   promote growth, 104–105
   school reform, 104
Advisory Committee on Child
   Development, 22
Age segregation, 30, 46, 60–61
Agricultural labor force, 178
Alienation, 29–32
Almeida, Eduardo, 37–38, 42
Altruism, 71
American family, 44
Analytic skills, 59
Anti-school, 196
Apartheid, 59
Apathy in students, 160
Appraisal technique, 209
Attitudes of community, 184–185
Attitudes toward work, 164–165
Autoimmune, autoallergic
   diseases, 128

Barriers in policy making,
   199–203
Behind the Classroom Doors, 182
Being, definition of, 139, 142
Berg, Ivar, 167
Biological competence, 149
Biological deficits, 24
Biological drives, 117

Biological factors, 23–25
Biological Sciences Study
   Committee, 182
Boulding, Elise, 30, 57–81, 86,
   148, 160, 185, 197
   commentary, 75–80
Bronfenbrenner, Urie, 1–56, 61,
   84, 86, 115, 147, 183, 195,
   197, 201
   commentary, 49–55
Brunswik, E., 39
Business and administration
   problems, 99–106
Bussing, 87, 98–99

Campbell, Donald, 209
Cancer, 128
Career education, 159–168
   criticisms, 167
   development, 167–168
Change in schools, 195–210
Changing environment, 42
Changing trends in children
   20–29
Changing trends in families, 1–20
Child abuse, 24–26
Child care, 48
Child desertion, 31
Child homicide, 32
Child psychological development,
   42
Child rearing, 36–37, 41–42
Child socialization, 29–30
Children and work, 40–41, 46–47
Children changing trends, 20–29
Children returning from school,
   40, 45
Children's nature, 147–148

Chisholm, Shirley, 16, 67, 83–96,
    99, 160, 183, 184, 197
  commentary, 90–95
Citizenship, 159
Civic responsibility, 71
Clarey, T. Anne, 27
Classroom and society, 71
Cochran, Moncrieff, 36
Cognitive skills, 59
Coleman, James, 44, 196, 205
College myth, 165–166
Commentaries
  Bronfenbrenner, 49–55
  Boulding, 75–80
  Chisholm, 90–95
  Fuller, 119–125
  Salk, 151–157
  Scanlon, 107–111
  Schweiker, 169–174
  Tyler, 188–192
Community attitudes, 184–185
Community-centered school, 66,
    69
Community colleges. *See* Junior
    colleges
Community control of schools,
    85–86, 88
Community technology, 69
Competency-based learning, 64
Competency decrease, 25
Complementary dualisms,
    139–150
Conditioned reflexes, 115–116
Cook, Constance, 46
Cooperative educational
    programs, 185
"Copability", 71
Coping inability, 129
Craftsmanship, 159, 162
Craftwork, 58–59, 60, 65, 66
Criteria for research, 34–36
Cultural contrasts, 38
Cultural norms, 200
Culture integration, 88
Current Population Reports, 4, 6
Cybernetic systems, 63

Darwin, Charles, 113
Day care, 20, 31–32, 36–37,
    45–46
Dearborn, Walter Fenno, 33, 34
Decision-making, 66, 198

Dedifferentiation, 74
De-escalation procedures, 73
Destructive effect of change, 2–3
Detroit Free Press, 47
Development, definition of, 3–4
Dewey, John, 179, 196
Disadvantaged children 183–184
Divorce rate, 8, 63
DNA, 129, 139
Drug use, 28–29, 32, 40

Ecological approach, 43
Ecological experiments, 39
Ecological perspective, 43
Ecology, definition of, 3–4
Ecology of human development,
    1–56
Economic deprivation, 29
Educare, 149
Education
  definition, 196
  dropouts, 13
  flexibility, 165
  goal, 159–160
  reform, 84
Educational gadgets, 86
Educational policy, 195–210
Educational purpose, 148
Educational reform, 97
Educational relevance, 99
Educational tasks, 177–187
Ego, definition of, 139, 142
Ehrlich, Paul, 134
Employment counseling, 164
Employment, federal funds, 164
Environmental effects on
    children, 40, 45
Environmental factors, 23–25
Environmental samples, 39
Evaluation, 184
Evaluation methodologies, 209
Evolution, 146
Experiential nature of man, 148
Experiment of nature, 42
Experimental human ecology, 3,
    33
Extended families, 18

Fair Part-Time Employment
    Practices Act, 45–46, 47
Family changing trends, 1–20
Family fragmentation, 1–56

Family sharing, 62
Family support systems, 47-48
Federal funds for employment, 164
Feedback, 60, 63, 133, 184
Female-headed families, 11-12, 15
Flexibility in education, 165
Follow Through, 44
Ford Foundation's Comprehensive School Improvement Project, 98
Foundation for Child Development, 3, 34
Franklin, Benjamin, 181
Friends Service Committee, 185
Frugality, 58
Fuller, R. Buckminster, 4, 58, 113-125, 148, 160
commentary, 119-125
Futurism, 57
Futurists, 59

Galtung, Johan, 69
Gandhian ideal, 66
Gardner, John, 159
Gene, definition of, 139, 142
Genetic system, 129-130, 146
GNP, 207
Goal of education, 159-160
Goodlad, John, 182
Goslin, David A., 47
"Greening of America", 60

Harper, William Rainey, 181
Head Start, 44, 45
Health care, 22, 48
Hess, Karl, 69
High-rise housing, 40
Homicidal adolescents, 25-26, 28
Homicidal children, 32
Homicidal rates, 64
Human development, 1-56

Illegitimacy, 9, 20
Immune system, 128-129
Implications for public policy, 43-48
Implications for research, 33-43
Individualized instruction, 183
Inequality in education, 84
Infant mortality, 21-23, 137
Inflation, 197, 207

Isolation learning, 86
Isolation in society, 184
Isolation of students, 84
Issues
  Boulding, 81
  Bronfenbrenner, 55-56
  Chisholm, 95-96
  Fuller, 125
  Salk, 157-158
  Scanlon, 112
  Schweiker, 174-175
  Tyler, 192-193

Jencks, Christopher, 44
Job-related skills, 106
Junior colleges, 180-181
Juvenile delinquency, 27-29, 32, 40

Keats, John, 165

Labor-intensive activity, 58
Landgrant colleges, 180
Latch-key children, 20, 40
Learning by doing, 162
Learning by teaching, 61
Learning in isolation, 86
Leisure time, 58-59
Leontiev, A. N., 33
Literacy development, 177

Malthus, Thomas, 113
Man: A Course of Study, 200
Mandarin system, 65
Mapping social structures, 73-74
Maternal and Infant Care Projects, 23
Median income, 17
Memorization, 84, 182
Metabiological competence, 149
Metabiology, 139, 148
Metabolic support of humans, 114
Meta-dedifferentiation, 74
Metaphysics, 139
Misreading history, 65
Mondale, Walter, 83, 84
Monolithic American education, 98
Morrill Act, 180
Motivation in learning, 183-184
Moving, 42

National Assessment, 182, 184
National Association of
   Secondary School
   Principals, 185
Nature of children, 147–148
NEA Task Force on Urban
   Education, 88
Neo-village school, 66
Newton, Issac, 114
Number of adults in home, 6, 20

Occupational education, 178

Panic, 116
Parental involvement in teacher
   training, 37–38
Part-time employment, 45–46
Peace studies, 73
Peer group, 32, 40
Peer interaction, 37
Peer oriented children, 32
Penal reform, 202–203
Physical Science Study
   Committee, 182
Planning, 57
Plato, 64
Policy making, 195–210
Political stability, 178
Population
   curve, 130–138
   densities, 66
   growth, 136
   increase, 60
Population Bomb, The, 134
Post-McCluhan age, 72
Poverty level, 17–18
Poverty line, 10, 25
Premature babies, 23–24
President's White House
   Conference on Children, 30,
   31
Pressy, Sidney, 183
Pre-teenage suicide, 64
Problems in business and
   administration, 99–106
Problem-solving, 69, 72, 127, 201,
   203–205
Professional recognition, 34
Program on Ecology of Human
   Development, 3
Pseudo-mobility, 59

Psychological development of
   children, 42
Public education, 83
Purpose of education, 148

Racial difference, 15–20
"Random Falls Idea", 67–68
Reality-coping, 63
Recycling, 117
Reformation in schools, 195–210
Reinforcement in learning,
   183–184
Relevant learning, 160
Remarriage rate, 8
Research
   criteria, 34–36
   funds, 34
   problems, 39
   proposals, 36–39
   "unproposed" proposals, 39–43
Revolution in schools, 182
Rubin, Louis, 47, 167, 195–210

Salk, Jonas, 4, 23, 58, 74, 101,
   114, 127–158
   commentary, 151–157
Scanlon, Robert G., 70, 97–112,
   118, 165, 181, 200
   commentary, 107–111
Scholastic Aptitude Test, 25–27
School environment, 61, 98
School integration, 205
School reformation, 195–210
Schools and society, 60–61
Schooling obligations, 160–161
Schweiker, Richard, 64, 85,
   159–175, 178, 197
   commentary, 169–174
Segregation by age, 30, 46, 60–61
Self-instruction, 208
Self-sustaining communities, 69
Shaw, Archibald, 67, 68
"Sheepskin psychosis", 165–166
Sigmoid ("S") curve, 130–138
Single-parent families, 2, 7–8,
   11–17, 20, 24, 25, 39–40
Single parenthood, 9, 12–13
Single-parent mothers, 13
Social isolation, 184
Social mobility, 179
Social networks, 41–42

Social organization, 196
Social readjustment, 206
Social system of other cultures, 30
Societal trends, 4
Socio-biological systems, 139
Sociometabiology, 139
Soma, definition of, 139, 142
Somatic system, 146
Special Labor Force Reports, 4
Spencer, Herbert, 57
Spiritual-intuitive capacities, 59
Stimulus, 130
Student apathy, 160
Student dropouts, 206-207
Student motivation, 201
Student volunteers, 39-40
Subculturism, 60
Substitute care for children, 20
Suicidal teenagers, 64
Support system, 39-40
Support systems for families, 3, 32
Synergy, definition of, 115
Systems Development Corporation, 185

Teacher contracts, 99
Teacher inefficiency, 201
Teacher strikes, 99
Teaching competency, 71
Teaching moral standards, 199-200
Technological futurists, 57-59, 63
Teenage suicide, 64
Television watching, 186

Theory of education, 147
Trends for American society, 4
Troubleshooting, 200
Twins, 42
Tyler, Ralph, W., 29, 63, 161, 177-193, 195, 197, 207
    commentary, 188-192

Unemployment, 197
United States Senate's Select Committee on Equal Educational Opportunity, 83
Unwed mothers, 9
Urbanization, 16-17
Utility, 160

Violent crimes, 28-29, 64, 197
Visionary futurists, 57
Vital and Health Statistics, 4
Vocational education, 159-168
Vocational Education Act of 1963, 163
Vocational opportunity, 197
Vocational preparation, 162

Watts, Harold, 22
Welfare, 202
White House Conference on Children, 45, 47
Women in society, 46, 168
Work attitudes, 164-165
Working mothers, 1-2, 4-5, 10, 20, 31, 186
Work and responsibility, 46-47

Zero population growth, 181